To
Deer
at
Swim

To
Deer
at
Swim[1]

Jamison
Lee

---

1   The Early Life and O(m/p)(iss/in)ions of Benny Huckman, Deerslayer

**Lit
Fest
Press**

ISBN: 978-1-943170-30-2

Cover Art: Nevada Smith

Cover Design: Jane L. Carman

Book Design: Sarah Lyons

Lit Fest Press

Lit Fest Press
688 Knox Road 900 North
Gilson, Illinois 61436

"Persons attempting to find a [narra]tive in this narrative . . . will be [m]ani[cur]ed. . . . [M]oral . . . it . . . banished. . . . [P]lot . . . it . . . shot."[2]

—Mark Twain

---

2   Translation: Brackets, ellipses, slashes, parentheses concede the ability to transform/reveal/distort words and phrases, preventing the foreclosure of meaning, allowing us to say lots of things. And (k)no(w)( )thing(s).

Until this valise of degeneration / unhitches, I have / time to kill.
Close keystrokes / til(l) (h[e/i][r/s]) arrival, / the un(in)hip-(bi)p(t)ed
/ (n)aimless pragmatist I (h)ired—I / refuse to know which or when.[3]

• • •

Gunning down dollops of back roads, through mounds of cornfields and
wiry meadows, he thought on and off about the man in his trunk. He'd
never put a man in his trunk before and, given the shoddy restrictions
his quarry currently endured, it was apparent that nominal research had
preceded the cuffing and stuffing, the best practices of this vague preci-
sion having been of minimal interest to him. As yet, no urgent sounds
of struggle had issued from behind, but he knew the prisoner was still
alive. The transfer had been gentle enough, at least, not to kill the little
fella. And what else? A few jumping bumps in the road? Another chilly
morning? No big deal. He was alive.

Dead, however, were the sloppy strips of tan, bedraggled corn
past which they tore, as they sped through fields of Monsanto's
monocroppings: desolate-not-yet-desolate wheated plains, corned
plains, the amber web of pesticidal maize that has no weaver—for, the
shushed bees, they die.

And in the little towns through which they passed, drooping people
tapped adorable phrases into a spare variety of flip-phones—square,

---

3   Translation: Having hired someone to kill me, I plan to die relatively soon.
     Typing I am until then; an exposé seems to follow: devices of a newsless ego in
     search of an audience.

numerical T9 keyboards, remnants of a tactile species. Thank you, holy Christ and Mother, we are so fucked, is what I thought, though, as of yet, our being fucked (injured apiaries, polar bears akimbo) remained relegately framed as postulation. Major changes in our natural world. A part from which we('ve) (gr[e/o]w[n])(.) (A/a)part. Facts. Unfelt. And so(,) unfacted. Demoted to another realm—construed as sentimental— where it's been established that those who feel unfacted facts are nebbish, whey-faced, faint-of-heart. So our being fucked was h(e)arrrrr(t/d)(i)ly felt. (Worn merkins without weavers. Parallel. Concordant corn. Fucking without feeling.)

From a trunk, the day was frigid and not as flat as it really was, and fragile as the aforementioned maize that has no weaver, not, arguably, unlike the web (blah blah) or the merkin. And though I care nothing for the kind of automobile in which our driver "tore" (weaverless), you may. So, granting the respect due its lone human passenger (misanthropy be damned), here's a portrayal of the car's trunk: (Un)Felt cloth—easier on the eye than the rib—lined the floor, the smooth lobing of which belied its actual (dis)comfort. The metal interior of the trunk's ceiling had been (judging from the droplet-shaped protrusions in the finish) hurriedly painted a demure lavender—desperately ([de/]com)p(r)osed here by a frenzied purple pen—which harmonized with the (h[e]arrrrr[t/d][i]ly) felt (dark mauve) on the floor.

And consider this astonishing ambrosial anomaly: The sweet iron of vintage blood (old cars' trunks, of) joined with crushed bits of brittle oak leaves to foment a scent of fenugreek—like a rabbit cage filled halfway with oatmeal cookies—as though, coated in raw honey, one were rolling down a leafy hill in late autumn, which is basically what they were doing (without the honey or the angry/sad, dead/quiet bees) but, of course, with wheels . . . in a car, as I say.

However, the trunk's honeyish pastorality was counteracted by a lurid patch of grease, from which arose fog sufficiently putrid so as to impress upon one the rotten air of soil disturbed by a freshly excavated casket. Not wholly meretricious either, this vague olfactorily-motivated metaphor, in view of the trunk's potential for coffin-metamorphosis, which is to note (much for the benefit of no one in particular) the rapidly diminishing health of the rodent occupying the plastic humane mouse trap that rattled and careened with the sharp curves in the road, the box's little door swinging precariously with each tremor.

Conversely—conversely to the box's swinging door, that is—the trunk (now perhaps grown, in our minds, exorbitantly ornate, with its recent and dazzling sensory appeals) had latched securely and agreeably, transmitting no daylight or light of any other sort. Why it smelled like cement, I can't say, though I know your friends steadfastly abhor the word "cement," strongly preferring "concrete." (Bless them.)

Lesser a mind, however, to those and theirs (concrete), and instead with proper effort toward sustenance of this trunk description—in which, as you no doubt recall, a burgled man is presently stashed—regard the following: The trunk's well-meaning designers had evidently suffered an impoverished understanding of Feng Shui. Stuffy as it was, airflow had clearly *not* been a priority. And the Bagua had been seriously neglected.

Stiff, bulbous wheel wells bulged into the "Health, Family, and Community" (on the left) and "Children, Creativity, and Entertainment" (on the right) sections of the trunk. Consequently, in addition to the spiritual suffering of the man in the trunk were the following anatomical displacements: abdominal domain forced into the "Good Fortune" section; legs and feet pushing against "Wisdom, Self-Knowledge, and Rest"; arms fixed beside him on "Fame, Reputation, and Social Life"; while a dear noggin was slugged repeatedly by the hard floor of "Marriage, Relationships, and Partnerships." And though, by now, this foregoing slop of symbolism lies like a (sea)horse carcass on the floor(sea)boards, I aim to flog it continuously, broth to berries, satirizing carefully all we have (yet to) create/d. And so, accordingly, it should be noted that he—the man, not the imaginary (sea)horse—lay now in absolute exile from the region of "Helpful People, Spiritual Life, and [ironically] Travel."

Outside the trunk, autumn was bright and cold, almost too cold to smell the fallen leaves; if not for the warping magic of a persevering fog—processing transensual synaesthesia, i.e., crackling (sound) into slack-tart (scent)—this sentence would be much easier to read. Oared Amish girls in long white aprons stirred giant vats of pickle brine in the strange buildings obscured by hills and trees. Where maple shadows waned, frosty patches turned dewy and dribbled down sparse blades. It would have been a good morning for waking up in the woods, wet against the condensation of a grimy tent's walls.

In the gently rolling distance, deserted barns and churches jutted scantily out of the luminous turf. "Tired of being a loser? Turn to God," read the sign in the Trinity Baptist Churchyard.

There were no windmills, but there should have been because Northeastern Ohio's winds—though less notorious than some—whip across Lake Erie with consistent, cruel gusto, sufficient for to rotate turbine blades. Sufficient for to make it spin, let it here and now be noted that the hulking babble of this story comes to pass in that spunkerious territory south of the Lake Erie shoreline and north of the Ohio River, the once begrudging boundary of the Mason-Dixon Line. (Ohio, like Poland, may be sepia-toned, but southern Ohio is black. And white.) More to the north, comma-to-the-top, Kent, Ohio, to be exact, will serve mostly as the city of record. Not that the place, for us, is of very much cultural significance, homogenized as we are, inundated with (yeah yeah), overrun by, Walmarts. The idea, of course, is that you're wondering who the man in the trunk is; who the man driving with the man in his trunk is; what kind of a car it is; whether this book will pass, or even *take*, the Goddamned Bechdel Test, though now it's at least been acknowledged, which, perhaps, is of some consoling import.

In any case, there are a few ways to tell this story, and, truly, they are *roiling*! All! Equally dealing (with) m(o/y)d(i/e)fi(l)ers. Def(y/il[ing]) you. (Not really. I mean, we're dying soon, after all, so . . .)

...

The annual Perseid Meteors were meandering into the limited view afforded by a light-polluted cul-de-sac neighborhood just outside Amish country in Geauga County.

"So basically, you think any star in the sky could be Orion's penis?" she angled.

Benny (description forthcoming, full Crayola, later) was visiting Regine, who was named after Kierkegaard's ex-fiancé. Unleapable. That is to say, there's a joke here . . . about leaping and faith and failure, and it's a dark joke, but . . . it's in there. Somewhere. I think. Which is what she said. Eh?[4]

"I'm not saying that," he chuckled. "Well, maybe I am saying that. It wouldn't be Orion's *penis* for me though."

"Right. It would be the butthole." After a long moment of silence, she turned to him, implicitly accentuating the basic assumptions of conventional turn-taking, according to which, she felt, she was owed an audible response.

"Hah!" he exaggerated then continued dryly, "Yeah, I get it."

"Because of . . . you're gay, you know?"

"Right."

Lying on their backs in late summer, under separate blankets spread three feet apart, they watched interplanetary rocks fire and fade.

"I don't know," he said, "my dad told me he thinks it could work with just about any girl, if you *make* it work. But he's getting divorced."

She rolled her head toward him. "Do you agree with that?"

"Well, yeah, I think they have to. They've been pretty miserable for—"

"No, I mean that it could work with any girl."

"Oh. Maybe, I mean, to a degree, anyway."

---

4   Fair to assume by now, I think, that what this churlish narrator lacks in finesse is atoned for, if not rectified, by lavish inelegance.

"No preference then, eh, just . . ." she shrugged.

"I don't *know*," he shrugged back, "chocolate, vanilla, whatever. We're all gonna *die* anyway. At least that's what Reina says . . . used to say, I guess."

"She's not *dead*, Huck. She still says it probably. Or do you think she only said it to you?"

A sigh was audible.

"Really, though, don't any of these stars jump out at you more than the others?"

"Yeah, kind of," he focused, "but if I stare at any single one of them for very long, it gets to be all I can see. All the others get to be just like a hazy background."

"Soooo—all the more reason to, you know, choose wisely then, no?"

"Right. Yeah. I guess for me the point is that . . . or, I mean, the way I took it is that it's as much about me as it is about the girl, herself, whoever she ends up being. And I think I agree. The timing is more important than anything else. Like right now, if the perfect girl—I mean, whatever that even means—wanted to marry me or whatever, I'm not sure if I would even want to because I don't think I'm ready yet. She could be perrrrfect, and I'd just . . . keep wondering if she's perfect. I don't really trust myself enough to get married. I don't know if I could trust anyone else enough to get married either."

"Hm." Frowning slightly, she pressed her lips together.

They gazed upward for a while. Mostly, nothing happened. But sometimes, a meteor bolted by, and Benny would try to thank God for it, though that was increasingly hard to muster, even for an ironic moment; he wanted to thank someone but didn't know who to thank anymore. It was a sad realization. Like yet another breakup. Must gratitude always be so transitive?

"I don't know. Maybe I'm just not done meeting girls yet."

"So you need to sow some wild oats, then."

"Well, yeah, but for me they're just . . . oats, really."

...

Wentworth squeezed cantankerously into one of the tiny desks and began:

"'The Dancing Deer and the Foolish Hunter, *by Elisa Kleven.' Jesus Christ. Ugh. Shall I read the dedication as well? Don't care? Fine. Me neither. Who gives a shit, right? Ah, here we go. An epigraph. Yes. John Muir again. 'Whenever we try to isolate anything in the universe, we find that it's hitched up to everything else.' Well. How frothy.*

"*Oh, and of course, 'Copyright 2002 by Elisa Kleven. All rights reserved. CIP Data is available.' Just in case you need it. Aaaand 'Published in the United States 2002 by Dutton Children's Books, a division of Penguin Putnam Books for Young Readers, 345 Hudson Street, New York, New York 10014.' In addition, if you'd like to find them on the web, you sure can! at 'www.penguinputnam.com,' so that's good.*

"*'Design by Alyssa Morris. Printed in Hong Kong,' like you. 'First Edition,' ooooh. 'ISBN zero dash five two five dash four six eight three two dash three.' And some other numbers. 'One three five seven nine ten eight six four two.' Lovely.*

"*'For Thacher and . . .' Is that 'Olivia Hard'? 'Olivia Hurd'? Hm. No idea, huh? Okay. Well, let's not waste our time, shall we.*

"*Oh, okay, that must be the dancing deer. Quite contorted . . . pretty fucking sexy, actually. And this, the foolish hunter, no doubt. Also acrobatic.*

"*All right! The Dancing Deer and the Foolish Hunter. Away we go, 'Deep in a green forest down by the sea, a hunter spied a little deer dancing.' Again, you know, very firm, graceful . . . nice. 'She danced so joyfully that the birds and the trees around her danced, too. Even the sea seemed to dance.'"*

Mississippi Wood(-/)(t/D)ick(-/)Mud(-/)Deviled Egg Salad

- 1.5 cups of extra firm tofu, diced and sautéed
- Nayonaise, 2 tsp.
- Spicy brown mustard, 2 tsp.
- Smoked paprika, 1 tsp.
- Diced dill, a lot (10 sprigs)
- Diced garlic, a lot (4 cloves)
- Half a red onion, chopped
- Mustard powder, 1 tsp.
- Salt/pepper, to taste
- Mix all ingredients and serve

Please Pray for this Young Hooker (Chapter 2)

Reina (Benny's ex) preferred to cut her fingernails with scissorettas, a fact which Benny had initially found cute. Of late, however, it had grown increasingly difficult to tolerate, as took root this defensive contrivance: A fingernail was a thing to be clipped, not cut. Across the duration of their relationship, differences like this hygienic incongruity had somehow evolved from points of flirtation to cutting ruckuses, followed, often, by rattled silence.

Benny's housemates were at their respective childhood homes for the weekend. He alone was left, holding down the fort in the misty southside ghetto of Kent. The girl approached his porch while he was talking to Reina on the phone and *clipping* his fingernails. He correctly believed himself visible, and, though friends affirmed him unapproachable in social settings, she must have found him or his porch somewhat inviting, for she slowly made her skittish, sad-eyed way from the steps to the far corner of their crooked concrete porch, where she balled up, apparently trying to stay warm. The instinct of the higher animals crept in, awakening susficious pantasies in his loinses. He feared that she was trying to distract him while cohorts waited in shadows for her call to ambush. The raspy whistle of a nearby freight train intensified this paranoia.

Instead, she aborted those few moments of silence, meekly asking to use his phone.

Somewhat dumbfounded, he let her use the cordless—he wouldn't even care much if she ran off with it, as it was a suckphone—and remained on his cell with Reina. Still unsure of his safety, he held the fingernail clippers in his pocket with the pointy end of the nail file extended.

"What's going on?" Reina asked.

"Well, there's a . . ." Benny turned away and mumbled to Reina. "There's this girl. She just came up onto my porch, and uhh . . . ." He struggled to politely explain the situation as the girl dialed various numbers, finally leaving someone a message. Then she began talking to him again.

"Uh, Reina . . . yeah, hol- hold on. Can you hold on for a minute? Okay."

The girl told him she was thrown out of a nearby bar; the police had hassled her, etc. She said she was from Phoenix, had lost her ID, and had lost track of her friends, with whom she was driving cross-country in a truck. What kind of truck? Picture—if you must—angry, red-haired, mustached, cowboy-hatted, dual-gun-slung Yosemite Sam mudflaps that read "back off."

Donned fully, the costume of the diddled, she wore a sheer, beige, low-cut blouse; a short, candy-red skirt; and a brown leather jacket, which hung down to mid-thigh, almost as low as the skirt. Her boots were chunky and black, and her punk-rock olive leggings were intentionally riddled with runs and rips, one of which revealed a grubby half-attached band-aid dangling from her thigh, where one tired, white girl-colored strip of adhesive persevered. (Had one been paying much attention to the jarring disharmony of her ensemble—arguably, the blouse and the band-aid were the only two matching items—one might have speculated that the young lady suffered from colorblindness.) Her face looked fifteen, though she claimed nineteen. Her skin was still young and soft, if a little pudgy. She was almost cute and definitely paranoid, teetering manically as she babbled what must have felt like further explanation of herself and her dilemma. Eventually, Benny deciphered that she wanted a ride to the nearest truck stop. The vision, rather, of a rest area strayed into his head. This was doable, he thought, and told Reina that he'd call her back, that he needed to drive an underage hooker to a truck stop, that fingernails are to be clipped not cut, for fuck's sake.

The tattered scarlet letter on his porch continued in a frenzy to swivel her head with the snippy absorption of an air-traffic controller in the data aisle, nervously scanning all points of entry. Noting this absent/single-mindedness—along with her slurred, incoherent rambling—Benny inquired tactfully as to recent narcotic acquaintances.

"So . . . are you high?"

"No," she said defensively.

"I mean, I don't really *care*. I was just wondering."

"I'm not on *drugs*," she insisted. "I don't think."

In further celebration of caution, he asked her to let him see what was in her bag: just some cosmetics and whatnot. How about her pockets? He concentrated on the fuzzy, white innards of her jacket as she produced some gum, money and a broken cigarette; she was a peaceful non-whore.

"Would you like a cigarette?" he asked chivalrously, as he rolled one for himself.

"What's in it?"

"Pipe tobacco."

Calming just a little, she tilted her head and looked askance, both parties now sharing some healthy skepticism. After a bit of reassuring, however, she let him roll a cigarette for her, though she declined his offer to light it. For a few minutes, they stood silently on his porch, awkwardly puffing smoke into the cold mist.

Then, having noticed that she'd begun to shiver, Benny excused himself, pawed hurriedly up the stairway's brown carpet to his bedroom, and returned to the porch with a gray sweatshirt and turtleneck. Due more to the persuasion of urgent physical discomfort than any real assuagement of her suspicion, she accepted rather quickly when offered the supplemental garments.

Watching as she wiggled into the turtleneck and sweatshirt, he felt sorry for her, and so he agreed to drive her to the truck stop and asked, too, if she wanted some food before they left. She said she'd probably throw up any food that she ate, which somehow struck him as an appropriate response, or at least one he had no intention of questioning. So they smoked the last bits of their homemade cigarettes, headed for the car, and started toward the highway. She told him, clearly lying, that her name was Joni Cherry. When Benny was young he used to live on a street called Longwood, and his middle name was Oliver, so in observance of conventional porn-name construction procedures, his would have been Oliver Longwood, which complemented her fake name quite nicely. Joni Cherry stars with Oliver Longwood[5] in "Just Barely Eighteen-Wheelin'." But he lied and said his name was John.

"Why did you have a toilet on your porch?" Joni asked. Benny wondered why she hadn't asked this question twenty minutes ago when she was curled up opposite said conspicuous porcelain.

"I like peeing outside very much, so I thought this way I can try pooping outside too, you know . . . comfortably." As audible recognition of this attempt at humor was entirely lacking, he extrapolated, awkwardly reminiscing about the night that he and Uli found the toilet out in the trash. The streetlamp shone down that night on the ivory chair's mysterious film as they'd drunkenly shouldered the greasy thing into the bed of Uli's truck. "It was only about five or six houses from ours." He happily recounted the story with the hope of painting himself as more of a low-life than he was, so that she'd overestimate him with regard to some kind of ratty authenticity (or whatever it was) and be more likely to approve of and accept him—interesting to me that he sought approval from such a character as this.

---

5   Monikers for the Arthurian version(s): Lady Pillowtongue, Seaworm of the Tulip Peoples. Chickle Pea Juniper, Giver of Divine Nectar Essence to Oliver of the Girthenwood Gardens, First Dog of Hardtown, forged infamously vast of girth. All remaining fucking unto metal in the Broadwooded Holy Fuck Forests.

During their refueling detour, Benny made the crucial mistake of walking into the BP station with what remained of his homemade cigarette. Larry, the name-tagged clerk, said, "Hey! You can't bring that in here."

"Oh, okay, sorry. I'll go. I just want five dollars on pump six." He set the bill on the counter.

Brusquely, Larry repeated himself and swept up the bill, gesturing that Benny should take it back.

"Can't I just—"

"Get the hell out of here with that!" Larry interrupted, slamming his hand and Benny's money on the counter. Benny said okay and went outside to use his credit card. He pumped a couple gallons of gas into the little white car and peeked carefully around the pump at Larry.

Pulling out of the old BP and onto Route 76, Benny admired the sign for the Tally-ho-tel, which was his favorite storefront pun, besides a bar on the west side of Cleveland called "Whiskey Business." He'd always wanted to have that job, "guy who makes puns for names of businesses and stuff," and was infinitely confident in his ideas: a salon named "Mullet Over," for example, a maternity boutique called "The Pregnant Size"; "Bean and Nothingness," a coffee shop; "Kwashiorcore," a vegan music movement.

On the highway, they passed an Assembly of God church with a sign out front that read, "Is Your Life Running On Empty? Free Fillups Here Every Sunday."

At the truck stop, he found himself unexpectedly touched, struggling to deny the tearful pang that accompanied their final exchange, during which he asked permission to hug her, and she granted it. Following this, he gave her a scarf and wished her luck.

Later that night, around four in the morning, he received a call. He hadn't even slept long enough to taste his own breath upon waking—like rancid garlic juice—and had barely finished raising the phone to his ear when he heard the man's gruff voice: "Who is this?"

"Hello?" he managed.

"Who is this?!" The man sounded drunk.

"What?"

"*WHO! IS! THIS!*"

"Who's *this*?" Benny offered valiantly. He'd gotten used to phony calls like this from his jackass cousins and friends.

"Where the *fuck* is Jenny?"

"Who?" The man's words were difficult to decipher.

"You know who, *fuck*stick! You . . . dizzy little . . . maggot."

Benny's drowsiness faded entirely as he recalled his evening, and he felt distinctly alarmed by the realization that he'd yet to divulge a single part of his strange encounter to anyone other than Reina, and even she knew very little of what had actually happened. So then, who was this?

The two shared a few more moments of silence.

"If you don't tell me where the *fuck*—"

Benny hung up before the threat rounded.

Aliens and a Megalomaniacal, Self-Referential, Post-Structuralist, Post-Semitic, Post-Zen, Metabiographical Account of Benny Huckman

Certain prophetic filmgoers frenetically predict that when aliens arrive to enjoy us, it will be similar to when Christopher Columbus appeared in America—the nightmarish expansion will be solemn, slow and certain. Others feel a truer comparison is to kosher slaughterhouses, where, with merciful precision, we'll have our tracheas cut loose quickly. (What will become of our Adam's apples? Exed-pounded.) In this scenario, the most powerful person in our lot, or at least the most heroic martyr, will be s/he who displays the tenderest pathos, pulling a pinch of sympathy from the interlopers.

So shall I cry more in public.

And though I may be a twaddlous man—twaddler
i/on the (a)isle of twaddle mountain
ing twaddlesome gesture, voyage

twaddlously poised, stirring tensile ear-shunning
defiance. Resolute deregulatorily cac(kle)-cough-opus.

Motion unrestricted lion
of sight. I will give it to you
(if you let me give it to you)

as he—that knotty mummy—unravels. A piteous movement,
stenciling a life (your sympathy may be required, solicited,

no less), the low morphic oaf only knows to lunge for dignity.
A mummy's convolution, like I said, heartrending on occasion.

But lovely, too, and putative
(why not?). PUTE-uh-tiiiiiiiv
and singing when I tell it. (Sung

Won.) In fact, upon hearing my saying, in which I say "sing,"
    it says "Oh. How high, sirrrrrrrr?"

(There's a highness you can measure
if you do not mistrust music.) Even
a mummy, when unreeling, encounters a tangle:

an OCD *je ne sais pas*; a palsied kitten
raking. Quagmire of a smug rooster
and his certified humane young henny wifeman.

    The story, I mean, sometimes, at least, will be arranged according
to temporal order, with respect to the docket of passing chronology—
passovering, as some (who) have and/or will have had it have had—
following schematically horological sequences or a simple series of serial
successions, whichever firstifies—that is, *it is*, to say, *what it is*, "came"
or "went" (primarily, mind)—and attempts to portray an aboriginality;
emitting invitations. A colloquy of maximal firstitudity. But, wait, that's
. . . no, that's not actually true now that I think about it.

• • •

Unknowing any second cousin of canards, imbecilic at the lip of pre-
varication, possessing lithe innocence of cock-and-bull, and uniformly
unconversant in the tongue of fabrication, (blah) Benny, (blah) having
been our felicitous first whimsy, was a very conscientious young man,

as they say, and clearly bore an impeccable rhythm, such so as to have reaped the moniker, "rhythmpants."

As are at least a few in the rural Midwest, Benny Huckman was raised a lazy sentimentalist without proper language (yes, well, hell, what, then, friends, is a poet?). Owing to his mother's delicate conservation, he retained a heart (Ohio) soft as maple syrup and tender as the many deer magnetized to his Toyota. "Benny was a deer magnet," is what I mean to proffer. (To "kill deer" without the space, this, the wee noun, is a medium-sized plover.) He'd hit seven deer in as many years of driving, and counted twice as many near misses. (Near Misses.) "You idiot," a friend's cheerful summation.

With a deer-warning whistle newly secured to his bumper, he'd assailed the last two in broad daylight, both on the same winding road (called "Rapids"). Failing to deter the first deer were the whiskery moats cleaving smooth asphalt from the heifers' grassy hills, which typify Ohio rurale. The second mortal crossing—eleven months passing—loped over the ditch, careened after the crunch, twice clopping pliantly to pierce the glossy parcel of wet forest before Benny's car'd finished fishtailing. Burgundy hues on beige hood paint, heavy metal having met tan butts grown up from muddy hooves. (Unobserved were the grounded results of the deer's tempestuous bowels.)

These mutilations belied Benny's nature. He was, as I say, very sentimental, and he folded his clothes quite carefully. But, whether it had been through companions' happy abuses; learning the (comic) value of raging, laborious deliriums under stonemason sun; or a simpler contagious postmodern ghost; something had taught him to laugh at emptiness. At fur snarled in the car's plastic face; at dark deer blood buttering the hood, now crumpled above the dangling Toyota logo; at similar sadnesses, Benny exulted wispily (as orphaned kittens, grown to cathood, preserve the quirk to purr through trauma).

As a highly discriminable all-purpose race—like the 2-for-1 ethnically abstruse Latino-Asian mixed/multiracial persons that cell(o/)ph(o/a)ne companies parade in their commercials—he put similar purring to good use when, with the callow green gusto found in the great marinating halls of high school, he was duly curried.

"Spink," though even more audaciously incongruous than the others, had always been his favorite. Benny could have passed as a mix of any combination of countries in Europe, or the Americas, yet, of the three Easts—Near, Middle, Far—the Far (whence came the "ink" in "Spink") was, regarding Benny's features and profile, the least passable East. Hence, at least in part, the unique amusement Benny educed from "Spink," which derives from a cross between "Spic" (the mean-spirited consolidation of "Hispanic," used, less [in]discriminately in the rural Midwest, to refer to any squiggly, unrelished person with dark hair, skin) and "Chink" (the singular case of "Bamboo Coons," a dysphemistic reference which signifies that (1) "Chinese Fire Drill" remains a prominent linguistic trope in American English and (2) . . . I don't remember.[6]

Another word one might have used to describe Benny is "callipygous," as, according to the Oxford English Dictionary, "callipygous" is a derivative of "callipygian," which means, "of, pertaining to, or having well-shaped or finely developed buttocks" or, in the colloquial tradition, "an ass you could set a wine glass on," though I trust you're already well familiar. Ass unmasked or otherwise, the duty to determine what is nonetheless meant by "well-shaped" remains with the viewer; ergo, there persists a lack of specificity. As an expedient corrective measure, allow me to reveal that Benny's buttocks grew round and tight below the hip, sturdy for sprint and dimpled at smile. In fact, a nickname came soon to fruition: "Benjamin the Lion-Assed." One of our ilk suspects, understandably, an accompanying trunk full of sugar. However, no.

"I'm a nighttime rollerblader. Head down.

What happens to the raccoons when they plug the sewer holes?"

---

6   While some argue that "Spink" is an inverse derivation of "Chinxican," its loitering etymology remains fragmented. Impeding the inquisition is the fact—thank you, Reina—that we're all going to die anyway, and, it would appear, unimpressively.

It was just this sort of dimpled grin that Benny grew, spummocking into the Flock Book of Truth, or whatever, lifting the latter concern for raccoons into his blog, thereby proving once again that he existed. After he had filled full a few tissues, he'd lie sleepless and make filled unfull plans to visit his grandparents, left hand resting in his mellowed pants. But that evening his ritual was interrupted by the tepid urge to make record of the current situation. Had his spunkaperitif not been interrupted by this man-childish urge, it would have been interrupted by a phone call from Reina.

The last email to which she'd been subjected was as follows. (He'd been quite drunk and reading *The Sound and the Fury*. Isn't that nice?)

i thought about calling you, even though you said you'd be sleeping. it seems urgent. doesn't it?

tak a look at these hands.

i am thinking of the line that goes through the head of a dear mute named benji, who is chasing schoolgirls simply because they remind him of his darling caddy - real name candace. candace is his sister. she treats him kindly. benji has the mind of a three year old. benji describes candace as smelling like trees. i think of you. i don't know what to do. but, anyways, i guess. this mute retard chases the schoolgirls, as his older brother has negligently left the gate open giving benji the chance to escape. benji does not know it, but this episode causes his family to think that his hormones are raging and he is dangerous and rapey, so they castrate him.

the line that goes through benji's head (drum roll) is i was trying to say. i was trying to say.

it's a touching line. okay. i feel like a cheese person. but i feel like a benji trying to say. i don't know how it is possible that benji has no words for anything, but here it is. no words. i don't have anny words.

all we have is talking and talking isn't working. long distances screwing us. that's how it is. it wouldn't be like this if we weren't so far apart. i feel like you're saying who cares. why do i feel that way. am i the only one who cares about the rules. waving pistol.

i'm so tired of. i was trying to say. i'm so tired of.

i was talking to sean tonight about starting a devo cover band. it seems like a good idea, but then i listened to devo a little bit and realized that no one i know can really play that kind of stuff very well. or at least no one i know who lives in kent or has time. which is ironic. no? because they're basically from here. yeah? devo? you know? eh?

that's not irony. you say. oh yeah? you wanna see irony?

i wrote a poem tonight. who cares. blab blab blab lab alb alb lablab alb lab lab lab la balb ablbalb alba balbblab ablab lablab ablab lab ablablablbalblbalblbalblablablab
some of it rhymes. uhoh. im dumb.
i wish we could see each other regularly. i want to have a spasm. and pundch the desk. i haven't sufficiently let go of oyu. i haven't sufficiently let go so as to feel okay everyday. or anyday. i want to type curses. or anyday. tryingtosay.

god. i want to do anything with you. just so you're around.

i am worried. i feel sometimes like my friends are all that i have. that's how i feel. move to ny move to nyt move tony. that repeating things and misspelleeng words is really dramatic, no?

classic me. just lllllettn it fly.

sean and i though we could call the band dego, pronounced dEEgo. good huh. because were both kind of italian. it'll have to remain good in our minds. good ino ur minds good in our minds. good in iour misnd.

wait. it's spelled dago, huh. wel shit.

i do love you. i know it in my head, but the feeling is going away. just the missing now. i am losing feeling. i have no feelings. for me it's not fair. i don't operate like you do i guess. i would like more than anything to se you. i thought that i could meditatie again. i doubt that i will though. i am in no mood for spiritual nonsenses.

magic and mirrors. magic and mr ghod. who there is no.

love, i am going to have to say love love, because lvoe is becoming too ordinary of a closing. i am really reaching. i am trying to say. i feel crazy and despair. i am giving reasons excuses excuses excuses try typing that three times fast.

love loveallofher

that's it no more. i wish i could cry i want to stab pens inot my arm. i won't. the thought will give me enough excitement. it would just be a hassle. i'd have to see if i got ink poisingn. thatisit.[7]

At this time in his life, there were two certainties—among vast other certainties—which he recounted on his blog in a piercing couplet:

I've no one with whom to mate.
I've gotta turn sideways to pee straight.

This lack-mate was due to Reina's passing from state—she now attended college in New York (and received a weekly dirge, see above, from the pining Benny). They'd recently broken up, for good—this after he'd finally grown accustomed to the ambiguity of their relationship,

---

[7]   Submitted, unsolicited, is this broad, blubbering exhibition, an apt foundation on which to build a redemptive argument in favor (much for its pithiness) of the drunken text.

to excre(la)menting on the phone. He thought of her new exploits, her lunches with the young scholars in New York: people named Emile and Vittore, and most recently a guy actually named Conqueror. If Conqueror did well at war, Benny wondered, would he be "Conqueror the Conqueror"?

"Well, maybe you should make more female friends," she suggested with just enough cursory sympathy to cow from his riposte the ire he felt her comment warranted—a great manipulation, he thought, instilling the belief that one's offense is undue. What was that called?

Benny frowned, sighed, drifted into resentment. Their conversation had led steadily toward this neutered sigh. Her new detachment irreproachable.

"Okay," her voice echoed slightly from the subway tunnel, "well, my train's here."

· · ·

Benny arose with the headache he'd earned the previous evening, striving, gulping, to forget. He observed, during his groggy morning pee, a small piece of tissue caked onto the head of his penis. It occurred to him that he must have remained at least sober enough to masturbate before bed (and to attempt a bit of cleanup). Then, gently loosing the bits of flaky tissue with his thumb, he noticed on the floor a much larger aggregate of crumpled, soiled toilet paper. It was actually very near his foot.

The three of them had been all kinds of drunk that night, so, in fairness, it could have been any one of them. The following morning, only natural for a square of soiled toilet paper to lie on the bathroom's dingy fake tile, no?

Each went about their business that day without touching it. On the second day, their curiosity quickened. And by the third, Benny gallantly decided to raise the issue.

"Soooo," he said, emerging from the bathroom, accompanied by the throaty gulps of the swallowing commode, "what's going on with the ...ummm ...toilet paper," he motioned, "in the, uh, bathroom?"

"Yeah, I was wondering about that."

"Yeah."

"It wasn't me."

"I definitely didn't do that. I *fold* my toilet paper, no matter how drunk I am. I am *not* a crumpler."

They looked at each other.

"Hmm, interesting."

"Do you fold, too, Ned?"

Ned nodded shyly, aware of what this meant for Uli, the third and final suspect. The lone crumpler. Uli was not his real name, but no one seemed to know any others.

· · ·

It happened once that Reina fell asleep while Benny was lamenting some tragic fact of their long dead, long-distance romance.

"Uhhh. I know this wouldn't be happening if we could see each other's faces right now. Do you remember that night when you chased me around with orange peels?"

Then he heard the slow breathing.

"Reina? Reina?"

She never admitted to being asleep.

"Did you fall asleep?"

" . . . "

"Reina?"

". . . Uhh, you're . . . having an orange?"

"Did you fall asleep?"

"No."

"It's okay. You don't have to be defensive."

"I'm *not* defensive."

Minted Cunt-Tossed Celery Salad

- Celery
- Red pepper
- Garlic
- Olive oil
- Lemon juice
- Balsamic vinegar
- Mint
- Avocado
- Tomato

Chapter No

Alone at the hospital near Humboldt, her mourning mother named her November Amaya Koopa (*mea culpa*). "November" was simply the month she was conceived; yet to be realized was any potential relationship with the Thomas Hood poem. Nor was the coincidence likely due to any associative subconscious reverie. God, as you know, and Hope are dead.

Ms. Koopa and November's father conceived her in California, soon after riding the skunk, and almost directly following the erection of some respectable harmonies in accordance with "Doctor Wu." ("Wu," as in, "Can you hear me, Doctor Wuuuu?" Not, "Woo," as in, "No, like I said, *Woo* peed on my rug.") Thankfully, her mother's surname, Koopa, is of no litigable relation to the shell-clad villains of Nintendo's "Mario" franchise. Nor is there a family connection to the lesser known but very prolific turtle artist, Koopa the Turtle, whose paintings, though too often named "New Hope # ___," apparently hang in all fifty states, as well as several European countries and principalities.

November never met her father. He'd written her on occasion but had not explicitly invited her to California for a visit. His avoidance of invitation was at first due to her youth—she was only three when her mother first received a letter addressed specifically to November. He knew her mother wouldn't come, so the gesture of invitation was one that he held on to and delicately concealed with a hopeful denial, like carrying an injured bird to the vet but only pretending that you actually know where the vet is, or that when you get there, the vet will have enough humanity to help without charging a fee you can't afford. Or that there is even a vet at all in this town.

November's mother was a lovely woman, of Japanese and French descent, who marketed herself as trilingual, though she knew only a few basic phrases in either of her parents' respective mother tongues. She'd worked as a nanny, raising November in a suitable guest house in upstate New York before heading back home to Ohio. (They were asked to leave the Hughes' estate when it was discovered that November had been swiping the local, grass-fed meat her mom brought home from the farmers' market and bringing it into the pool house, where she'd taken in stray cats and dogs.) And, here, I seem to have lost my interest—as enthralling as this Koopa history happens to be—in the meaningless bed of dejection that Ms. Koopa had constructed for herself.

With much effort, Mama Koopa succeeded in concealing the secret of her exaggerated trilingualism, but Amaya does not mean "night rain" in Japanese, as she originally had thought. The name appears to be of Basque origin, where it means "the end."

Chapter V

The blustering frigidity of Northeastern Ohio often provoked November's shoulders to tense earward. However, during the docile summer—and its adjacent weeks of visibly hanging shoulders—November liked to walk around in the woods. She knew the names of several local wildflowers and was a proficient walker. And ambler. She could also saunter, sashay, and flounce, though she found them distasteful.

Chapter Ember

November became close with a woman named Blossie, who'd been two years ahead of her in high school, and had recently completed her B.A. in English, though, really, it was more like a degree in gender studies and Marxist theory, lenses she now applied rather frequently, though not inconveniently.

Blossie was genderfluid, and entertaining the idea of sexual reassignment. It is hard to say, but perhaps there was some irony in the juxtaposition of "being" a "woman" who hated men but also considering investing a great amount of time and resources into becoming one. (It remains to be seen how delicately a flippant white man [almost entirely unmarked, in fact, other than having contracted an assassin to suicide myself—a convenient service I requested online] can address such matters, if even briefly.)

Chapter Novenny

The first time Benny saw November was in one of the many great bastions of American freedom. "Which bar was it?" you ask. Which depressing theme? I don't know. Picture one you know, like that one with the dimly lighted patio and extremely loud music with lyrics aesthetically offensive to persons of standard cognitive function.

Rather than speaking, Benny merely peeked over at her throughout the night. When he got home, he wrote this:

I thought maybe we shared a moment when those drunken femininas came into our bar as it was closing and insisted that they should be able to use the bathroom. Upon denial, they informed all of us that they would spread word of the vile pub's utter inadequacies. Everyone laughed. But I laughed, and you laughed too, and, in our laughter, the exchange of smiling eyes, etc., I hoped we shared it. Maybe you didn't even notice, but I am a very romantic sap, and I did.

Of course, I wouldn't have to be romantic if you don't like that. I have a friend, for instance, who actually likes the lint that materializes between his toes. He feels a sort of accomplishment, not from having cleaned himself or rid himself of this lint, but from creating the lint— "That's my lint. *I* made that lint."—and I think maybe I could be that sort of person for you. While I'm unsure of my capacity for loving my own filth quite so unremittingly, I could still produce it with a reliable degree of consistency. I could be that humble, unromantic lintmaker. But would you want me to?

The second time Benny saw November, it was in this very same bar that you so vividly imagined a few moments ago. November, dealing with the encumbering funk of romantic woes, was drunker than she should have been. Bene. Benny saw her talking to a friend of his, found her ravishing, didn't realize that she was swaying with intoxication. Then, having been more or less introduced with passing small talk, the following galumphing conversation was nearly eclipsed by the shitty music in the bar.

Benny: "You look cold."

November: "What?" Her eyes fell slowly away from him.

Benny: "It's cold out here, isn't it?"

November: (Nodding.)

Benny: "Are you cold?"

November: "What?"

Benny: "Aren't you cold?"

November: "No."

Benny: "Really?"

November: Emphatic head-shaking.

Benny: "Do you want some ear plugs?"

November: . . .

Benny: "To warm your ears?"

November: . . .

Benny: "Like . . . ah . . . you know. Just kidding."

November: Slowly shaking head.

Chapter Benember

Exiting the bar, Benny's face and navy windbreaker met the unremark-able wind. He turned the corner and drummed his teeth together to the rhythm of a Stevie Wonder song, "Boogie on Reggae Woman," which had entered his subconscious on the bar's cold patio, where it served tem-porarily as an antidote to what he was now experiencing: pouting goose-bumps of disingenuous humility—what sadness sometimes poses as.

Homeward. Where the porch was so smoky that he wondered if his lenses needed cleaning. The slender deer that seemed to have been following him home, talking to itself, sounding very much like a human at times, had disappeared from view. On the dark side of the street, the church sign read, "Give Satan an inch and he'll be a ruler."

Engendered Species

Benny had enrolled in a men's studies class. Apparently, the discipline had been gaining ground, and now a portion of midwestern academia accepted men's studies, or at least, "Cultural Theory: T opics i n Masculinity," as a semi-legitimate academic pursuit. So, having some credit hours to conclude leisurely, Benny took the course. The professor was one of those people who pretended like he knew everyone so that he might abuse them frequently, but always in the gruff chic of war-buddy mockery. Benny'd never seen someone insult students so regularly, but somehow most of them seemed flattered by it. And he got away with some tawdry diatribes: "The average college student is a fucking dunce, a plebeian. He knows nothing. He's cancerous. He *has* cancer. Doesn't know enough to care. Doesn't know enough *not* to care. He thinks his government is a magnanimous institution powered by what I'll call 'Maria Law'; all others that oppose it evildoers. He believes fairy tale narratives. He's unoriginal and weak."

This fellow, Wentworth Ira Wolff, had long since dislocated the exact boundary between authenticity and farce. (Kissing distant cousins.) At first, he only confused those people to whom he spoke, as it became increasingly difficult for them to ascertain sarcasm from sincerity. Occasionally, someone would ask, however, and, entertaining an explanation, Wentworth began to recognize that he was also unsure. He did not see this as a problem, however; it was merely an observation:

He was genuine-fluid. Sincerity and sarcasm (sub/conscious semantic intentions enacted through verbal mood) waded through contextual flux, it seemed, like all other actions. Outside of their context, neither should, nor even *could* (with due scrutiny), be seen as right or wrong, proper or improper. And their murky contexts were entirely unstable— touchstones (words, signifiers, so-called "meanings") confused by the chaotic and varied trajectories of other's touchstones, an ultimately unknowable amalgamation. Like language itself. (Like Rilke. Like happy misunderstandings.) One desirous child pulling at another, multiply interwoven bunches of cacophonous realities, shovels dredging into massive mounds of clanging cowbells haphazardly tossed over shoulders. Impossible to sort such a mess. Even context, then—due to its unutterable instability—was truly inscrutable, and the ethical viability of any action depended on context, so how could any intention survive the flux of its trajectory? How could any action be judged with even a smidgen of precision? And, for fuck's sake, barring all these, in light of all this, what did it really matter: "Sincerity or sarcasm?" Because who gives a shit?

"Okay," he said, striding drowsily into class Monday afternoon, "who's got the best weekend *rape* story?" Despite similar greetings and comments throughout the first bit of the semester, a few students were taken aback, though somewhat reassured by his insouciance. Here and there a cheek scrunching, incredulous. Nobody spoke.

"Hm. Nobody? Well, no matter, I suppose. Mine are usually the best, anyhow." He flashed a giant grin at them then rolled his eyes and frowned downward at the shiny open-toed shoes of the girls in the front row. "I found this article in the 'Psychoanalytic Journal of Sex Crimes,' and I wanted to share it with you, the most forward-thinking, liberal-minded screws I know." He handed out the copies.

"I mean, seriously," he said laughing. "Are we . . . well, never mind," still laughing to, and by, himself.

His students read this:

Farcing the Issue

In recent weeks, the definition of "rape" has been hotly debated in congress. Critics of the controversial H.R.3 Bill—introduced a few weeks ago by Chris Smith (New Jersey - R)—claim the bill attempts to redefine rape in a way that is offensive and harmful to women. (The bill proposes a limit of federal aid for abortions for women who were not forcibly raped.) This has led to a public outcry against the bill, as well as a squeamish conservation of the current rape definition. (As I understand it, 'rape' is an often controversial—and, very frequently, unethical—culminating reaction to an urge that seems accurately exemplified by the sweet string of vulgarity my friend, Misha, murmurs as we pass the field of mares and fillies that he claims are teasing him.)

In this frenzy of conservatism, petitions have been cir-culated to "protect" the so-called "human rights of wom-en," while the "rapist" (male, by and large) is overlooked, treated as a beast—unacceptable, this. Due to the austere view of rape held by traditionalists, the civil rights of rape victors are persistently diminished, as reactivist perspectives on rape culture have unsurprisingly regarded the plunder with provincial gravity. Rape has been no laughing matter, traditionally, but "[l]ife does not cease to be funny when someone dies, as it does not cease to be serious when peo-ple laugh" (Shaw). And though, lamentably, the slapstick comic value of the rape is often overlooked—a calamitous omission on the part of humor theorists—I wish herein to scrutinize not the hilarity of the rape event; rather, it is my aim to illuminate certain misunderstandings regarding the exigency of society's whipping boys.

Benny looked around, bemused, disconcerted, as he neared the end of the introduction.

As an effective elder of the rather minuscule intellec-
tual community of rape scholastics, I can say with some
certainty that while most articles focus on the victim's post-
rape trauma, so-called, there remains one traumatic aspect
of the rape that seems to have been entirely overlooked: the
negative post-rape effect that such compulsory sex happen-
ings frequently have on the rapers themselves.

"Perpetrators" are regularly shunned by the common-
wealth, tried and sternly sentenced as criminals. For this
reason, it is crucial that rape studies researchers take it upon
ourselves to apprise the lay of the most essential facts re-
garding the proper treatment of citizens who make up the
group that we casually refer to as "rapists."

There are a couple common misunderstandings about
rape. First, the current opinion of rape behavior is that it
can be controlled. This is a falsehood. People who rape
mustn't be casually expected to control their actions; they
have a disease. The "raping" or "rapehood" of the raper is a
disease coined by the New Raporicists as "rapism." People
with "rapism," or "raping people," are, unsurprisingly, com-
pelled to rape. As the disease progresses, it acts upon and
possesses them, until finally they are no more capable of
controlling their raping than coprolalomaniacs their curs-
ing. The public at large has learned to pity sufferers of cop-
rolalia or Tourette's; it is in the same spirit, I argue, that we
must learn to empathize with rapers.

Benny looked up to ensure that he was not alone in his confusion.
Then he skimmed across the remainder of the page—skipping the se-
mantic discussion in which the author explained his subsequent use
of "raper" rather than the rancorously dysphemistic title "rapist"—and
flipped to the middle of the next:

Throughout 20th century European and American history, the etiquette of meat-curtain mischief has varied immensely, but there are a few enduring strategies that still set the proprietary standard. For instance, it is almost never untrue that the raper does, in fact, want to have sex, very specifically, though seldom exclusively, with the "raped." True, some rapers will coitally engage nearly any object, but these are a depraved minority. In fact, even the common raper is quite passionately discerning and highly focused, if single-minded. And there remains a noble handful—e.g., some of the more discriminating rapers of my personal acquaintance—who patently refuse to compromise their standards, who regularly decline consensual sex with beautiful women. Consider, if you will, that some of the more principled, carnivorous members of the animal kingdom refuse the nourishment of prey that is weak or already dead. Of a correspondent nature are the aforementioned men, who do not rape for the meat, but rather for sport. Their prospects are not only physically magnificent but often well-known and well-protected. And upon probing the libraries of this ilk's forceful gentleman callers, investigators have discovered clothbound dossiers strewn with rare photos of ice skaters, gymnasts, and thespians. Extensive blueprints of the women's homes, along with elaborate entry and escape routes, have been found in the dossiers. It is with this rigid breed of initiative and industry that these men have catapulted themselves into the premier ranks of this dynamic group. Such courage and perseverance situate these more refined raping gentry as paragons for the lesser rapers of the lower raping classes.

The essay's contradictions were overshadowed largely by its impropriety. Predominantly uninterested in disputing the piece's paradoxes, the students' collective reaction was characterized by awkward intervals of visible bafflement: averted stares, parted lips, eyebrows atop their holy mountains.

Wentworth scowled obliquely, taking roughneck X-rays, scraping the room with eyes that felt to the speed readers—who were now waiting painfully for the last parsing horses—like low grit sandpaper. He watched the awkward young college girls getting used to their cold sores, spilling superfluous broods of bobby pins, staring past posters advertising employment: "www.winterbreakwork.com." Winter felt distant to them. Yet near.

> The second common misconception of rape—be it gangsta rape, thug rape, or bohemian rapesody—is that it is pleasurable for the rape artist. It is not. Remember that, like homosexuals or mouth-breathers, raping people suffer from a relentless disease. Is it a choice for the obese to overeat, for the homosexual to lust after dicks, for the mouthbreather to shit itself? Of course not; these are compulsions. Analogously, the vilified proclivity suffered by the raper is tantamount with these afflictions. No one *chooses* to suffer in this way. So why should their compulsions be judged and punished as such? A man with a damaged cerebral cortex is not expected to pilot a plane. It is not his desire to crash the plane, but this is what we must expect when he is left alone with the bird, so to speak.

Benny skipped to the whacky end.

> As I have made abundantly clear, the most harmful misunderstandings of our so-called "rape culture" is that such behavior is flawed, obstinate, or wrong. Such absurd allegations have continued to cause an eerie advancement of the disease of blaming, effectively criminalizing the raper, creating a problem where there was none by falsely

manufacturing in the raper's mind a villainous self-image, and causing regrettable self-fulfilling prophecies. The real culprit here is this aforementioned accusatory behavior. On the contrary, our goal should be to provide the rape artist with a more supportive and accepting atmosphere; we should be gracious and patient, as the raper, undaunted by discriminatory mandates and trite social conventions, attempts to reintegrate into our stringent social order.[8]

For the remaining minutes of that class period, the women in the room fermented collectively in silence, exclusively communicating via grimaces, which some were careful to conceal from male pupils.

Their silence lingered throughout the following class meeting as well, as Wentworth continued to prod the students regarding gender issues, as he saw it, of culture and language: "Was it Chris Rock or Dave Chappelle who did the bit about the police responding to the black guy's call, entering his house and then assuming *he* was the robber? Eh, whatever. It doesn't matter. But you see how this term, 'robber,' is gendered and prejudiced? Robber. Picture the robber. Did anyone picture a *woman* when I said, 'robber'? Of course not. 'Robber' is gendered male. The same monstrous association has occurred with the word, 'pedophile.' When we picture a 'pedophile,' we picture a man."

After class, Benny waited to talk with Mr. Wolff and caught the end of a conversation between Wolff and one of the few students who were currently willing to talk to him. The student listened submissively as great students do, the strain of exaggerated attentiveness apparent in his carefully propped-open mouth, slightly tilted head, and quick obsequious nodding, his brow straddling some ridge between epiphany and confusion. He dared not blink until Wentworth finished, at which

---

8   Earlier drafts of the essay included additional jocular terms such as "poon plunder" and "matador de muff," but, as the author's awareness of audience became more acute, he decided some of these would detract from the piece's intended effect.

point he smiled brightly and ventured a quip: "Hahaaa. That's awesome. I want to sell that idea to an anthropology professor."

"Hah! Good luck. An anthro*pol*ogy professor couldn't sell that idea. Scholarly ideas aren't worth *money*," Wentworth laughed sarcastically, gathering the pens and books from his desk. "That currency—it's like the tokens you get at Chuck E. Cheese: they only work in*side* the building; once you leave the building, you can't *buy* anything with those tokens, not that either of us are allowed to go into a Chuck E. Cheese! We're men, so of course . . . ." And so on.

"Hey," he finally got around to Benny.

"Hey."

"What's goin' on?"

"Well, I just wanted to mention the . . . uhhh . . . email I sent."

"I've got lots of 'em, fella."

"Hmm, yeah. Ummm, this one was kind of vulgar, but it was a joke."

Benny had typed the following supplement to an assignment he'd been too depressed to complete thoroughly:

To whom it may concern:

Please find attached my writhing scrawls of soul-dead butt-licking.

Just kidding.

Yours,
Benny Huckman

Wentworth hadn't replied to the email.

"I'm pretty sure I made sure to mention that it was a joke, buuut," Benny hawed, hoping to avoid a recap.

"Hmmm," Wentworth's eyes turned downward as he frowned in thought.

"It . . . uhhh . . . I attached a late paper in the email and made a sarcastic comment about being depressed or something, and—"

"Oh! Yeaaaah! That was great. Made my night as I recall. Put yourself into it a little," he said ironically, "I don't get much of that. People are usually so full of shit I don't even read to the end . . . between you and me."

Benny followed him out of the room.

"Yeah, I got it. Don't worry," Wentworth reassured.

"Good," Benny laughed, "I—"

"Pretty hilarious, I thought. I gotta go though. Meeting of some sort. Seems important," he cawed, made a proper show of rolling his eyes.

"Oh, okay. Cool."

"Yyyyyeah," said Wentworth—nearly out of view—from the above staircase.

• • •

The meeting, as it turned out, was compulsory and more exciting than Wentworth had expected. A few "uppity femmes" had sounded the bell—the rape article catching their attention, "petting fur against the grain," as he later put it. Furthermore, it turned out that he hadn't *found* the article. He had written it, or someone had, anyway, and it had not been peer-reviewed—this discovery was, in Wentworth's view, "the best, and probably only, research those bitches have ever done at this place." Not only did the department view the article as "inappropriate material to share with students," they condemned his presentation of it as "deceitful" and added that he had "committed academic fraud," as some of the sources he'd cited seemed not to exist. Augmenting his impropriety, in the university's view, was the fact that he'd offered extra credit to students who would help him maintain any portion of the text in Wikipedia's "rape" entry (a demanding task).

Administrators were ultimately not receptive to his deflections:

"There's a tenuous line between scholarly and creative work."

"My students are conservative reactionaries."

"Yes, but the nature of 'lying,' in that case, is debatable."

What he'd wanted to say was, "It isn't rape if they like it." Then "It's only rock'n'roll, but I liiike it," went through his head, and he had a bit of trouble suppressing a gleefully malicious snort, and though he did recover for a bit, returning to the ruse of befuddled sincerity, he couldn't keep it up for long. The meeting ended when he intoned boldly, though without eye contact, that "if they wanted us to stop laughing at it," (rape) "they'd stop making it so funny." Whether there'd been any perceivable sarcasm in his voice was debatable. Regardless, if he'd intended any humor, it was lost on this audience.

To be fair, some of his earlier rejoinders were defensible: the part about "conservative reactionaries," for instance. Kent State, despite its image—having been associated with large-scale demonstrations in the early seventies, with clamorous protests demanding more humane foreign policy and an immediate end to the war in Vietnam, with the government-sponsored murder of student-protesters—had long been a more conservative institution, its business school the bastion of the university. As such, and with an eye toward maintaining student satisfaction and avoiding unwanted media attention, as well as potential lawsuits, Wentworth was shortly dismissed from the university, his assistantship terminated.

He reacted, opening a new email account and heading to the Kent Free Library for the single purpose of anonymously sending the parting poems he'd penned for certain students:

Dearest lurching slut of sluts,

Oh, you,
You are unnecessary.
I forget you.
I kick your dog.

Goodnight.

———————

Ciao, Salaam, Ms. Bortion,

(What you should have been)
Alias: yeasty rapscallion,
The reeking shitous measle
That kicks your dog.

Farewell.

—————————

You fucking fuckface fucker.

Filthy blundering
Vulgar bucket of cud-kicking
(your dog).

Salutarily yourn.

Kicking,
Your dog.

• • •

A week later, amidst further emailing catharsis, and directly after glaring down again at his unpaid gas and electric bills, he chanced upon Benny's email address. In the tame civility of the email that followed, he abandoned ribald enterprises, refraining from perfunctory notes of dog abuses to relate, rather, that he'd decided to live like a bum for a spell, "like an undergrad." He continued that he might like to "research the undergraduate lifestyle for a quasi-scholarly project" of his, despite not knowing what this might eventually entail, if anything.

Having just learned of Wentworth's infamous dismissal and subsequent emails, Benny felt somewhat flattered to be spared the malice of which some in the class had related in emphatic detail, and with more than significant suspicion. The courtesy contained a tinge of camaraderie, which Benny, speculated, probably was meant as a diversion: flattery serving to conceal, or at least distract from, the sad facts of what were likely his new financial predicaments. (In class, or anywhere, Wentworth never attempted discretion regarding the pauperly allotment the university set aside for graduate students' stipends.) This apparent cry for help drew Benny's sympathy. So he replied that it would be cool if Wentworth wanted to come be a bum at their house for a while, that it would be cool to have a professor living with them. (Technically, Wentworth had been merely a teaching assistant, and though the finer distinctions between professors and TAs were as yet unclear to Benny, he knew enough of the hierarchy to deliberately misuse the term, "professor," in an effort to assuage Wentworth.) It should be fine though, Benny thought, another roommate. Ned was never really there, and Uli could get along with anyone, pretty much. They worked out the details over a few awkward phone conversations.

The following week, Wentworth carried a lamp and a basket full of dirty clothes into their house. It didn't take long for Benny and his roommates to realize that Wentworth was as generally confounded as they. He went to work as a substitute teacher a month after moving in. Unswerving, like a dry snare drum on the twos and fours, they habitually heard him burst through the door.

"Holy fucking crap," he roared.

"And a good day to you, sir," Benny held. Was it three o'clock already?

"Yes, greetings and such and such." He stopped at the sink to wash a plastic container he'd brought in. "You can all go to hell."

"Yeah?"

"Indeed."

"I see. So . . . how's it goin'?"

"Oh, how *rude* of me," he brayed, making faces at the faucet. "Let me tell you, my good *lad*," momentarily tilting his head. "Today I was a substitute for first graders." He coughed, his mouth open just long enough for a bit of soapy water to splash in; this augmented an already caustic eye-bulge and prompted sinkward expulsion of half-washed Tupperware. "This little *bum*fuzzled *zipper*head named *Sung* drew me a *pic*ture," he coughed again, his voice rising bonnily in sneering reverie. Then a reversal of mood, as though face to face with Charlie, "fucking *cock*sucker."

"Sung?"

"Yeah," he leered upward, kicking off his shoes, "Sung Won."

"*Sung Won?*"

"Yep. I had a 'Sung Won' and a 'Dong Yon.' You believe that fucking crap?" he lamented, donning a southern accent and shaking his head. "Ain't we got laws in this country?"

"I think it's actually 'sang.' You know? Otherwise, 'have sung' is the proper—"

"Oh, here it is," pulling from his pocket the folded mystery. "Wanna see it? I can't even tell what the hell it is. There's some American fucking flags there, sticking out of a couple Viking battleships. Then there're the flags of some other country alongside them."

He handed Benny the drawing and lowered his eyes to the grubby carpet. "Probably he's Viet Cong."

Benny eyed the drawing. Hard to make out. The Dada aesthetic.

"You know what else?" he mumbled, annoyed. "I was not allowed to give blood today. Such bushwa I can't even believe."

"Umm . . . why couldn't you give blood?" Benny asked, though what was truly dazzling was that he'd even *tried* to give blood. That sort of break in character felt almost like a betrayal.

Frivolously, he explained, "Some waggery about *men*strual blood. I can't even believe I'm fooling around with these Nazis, anyway." He chewed and swallowed crossly. "Goddammit. So bloody ridiculous. No pun intended."

"None taken."

He glared coldly at Benny, who was rather pleased with himself. "Yeah, I went down to the damned gymnasium, you know? Took the time to answer all those *bull*shit questions, which are *not so simple* if you actually consider them: 'In the past year have you come into direct contact with anyone else's blood?' Um, hmmm, besides those harlots I thrashed unconscious with the tire iron in my trunk, I'm pretty sure I can—"

"I thought you were only drowning prostitutes now."

Wentworth froze, frowning, surprised at this further pollution of his monologue. He gathered himself quickly and glowered detachedly at Benny. "So I had to ask. I had to mention menstrual blood. 'Does that count, Miss Red Cross? I know in the holy biblical scrolls, it's against the law, but I haaaaave *fucked* a woman on her period, in the last year. Are *you* on your period right now, Miss Red Cross?'"

• • •

Wentworth eventually secured a regular spot on the middle school's roster of subs. And the elementary school called him occasionally, too. The high school was soon to follow. He was quite charming when motivated to such an affectation, and he quickly gained sufficient cred in the Kent City School District's substitute circuit. With all due respect, this happened easily in Portage County to willing and regularly available substitute teachers. Calls came before dawn, covering less than thirty newly-waking seconds. If consistently capable, during those crisp conversations, of avoiding curses and racial slurs, one frequently oversaw hundreds of schoolchildren.

• • •

"Jeeeeesus Christ. Ooookay. "Would you look at that!" *the hunter said, setting down his gun.* "Wowie-kazowie, a dancing deer! A deer I can sell to the circus! Great Gumballs—my fortune is made!" *With a lightning-swift swirl of*

his lasso, the hunter caught the deer . . . and led her to his house on the edge of town.'"

"Jesus. Then the hunter decided that the deer was very sexy, and so he locked her up and went downstairs to get that pan of bacon grease he'd left on the stove. After he'd thoroughly slicked himself with bacon grease, he fucked the little deer, who made noises that sounded, in turns, like a creaking door, a dog's squeeze toy, an angry cat in heat. She didn't struggle the way he'd expected, but that could have been because she was tied up so expertly.

"Then the hunter told her to get lost, and she was very sad because, though her buck–boyfriend fuckboy–friend had cheated on her the week prior, they'd worked it out and it seemed like things were gonna be different, but depending on how one looked at it, she had sort of cheated on him now, and she was really not looking forward to telling him.

"The end."

• • •

Well, like my little sister says, "Who gives a rat's pussy?" Or maybe more like, "Who. GIVES!-a-rat's-pussy?" Another question.

What's more, I have apparently hired a lazy assassin.
Whence, I blather; wherefore I ham. That is, God

dammit it's almost midnight, mid-month, and I'm still alive.
(This is why people confute welfare. What, other than laziness,

a decay of the protestant ethic, heralds homologous prattle?)
Allowed I am to blah and blah. Until violenced,

shall I, thus, redress this pagely simulation. Please come then (we say),
come now, covert Violence. Dark, dirty ([m]is)s(p)in(i)ster vicar

(poor y little y dick[less]). Violence, now! in the minster! Chew us,
closed-mouthed, our bile, obscured as you are,

or were, supposed to be (and far overdue, you lackey, sir).
And chew, as I chew, with a clothed mirth—

smack no mousy lips. (Also, remember, painless.
Name of the game here. I paid extra for this.) Aim forehead.

Save neck. Keep heart, hands. Please, donate rest.
Donate deep, dear autumn berry(,) one more cog('s/in)nate d(')earth.

Chocolate-Crusted Cat's Breath Summer Cum Cake

- 1 ⅔ cups spelt flour
- ½ teaspoon baking soda
- ⅞₆ cup cocoa
- 1 cup sugar
- ¼ cup brown sugar
- 1 ½ sticks Earth Balance, at room temperature
- 1 cat's mouth flax seed dissolved in 1.5 cat's mouths water
- 1 tablespoon non-alcoholic vanilla extract
- ¼ teaspoon peppermint extract
- 12 freshly-crushed mint leaves
- ½ cup boiling water
- ½ cup vegan chocolate chips
- ⅔ cups mint chips

Directions:
1. Preheat oven to 325.
2. Set aside boiling water, chocolate, and mint chips.
3. Blend all other ingredients. Slowly add boiling water to mixture and blend. Blend until smooth. Stir in chocolate and mint chips.
4. Place in buttered loaf pan. Bake 50-60 minutes. Let cool. Fleck with chocolate (optional).

...

The jogger looked at Benny funny. People around here always look at me with hostility just because I'm darker than average, he thought, because I'm swarthy and my hair is black and curly. When he stepped out to pump gas, he realized that it was actually because he'd left two bananas atop his car. He retrieved the fruits. And laughed at himself.

Then he left the gas station.

Then he ran over a cat.

Driving too rapidly past Blossie's house, he noticed November—shiny sweeping hair[9] swinging, shy supple hips waving dark green denim, a periwinkle t-shirt pearling over her proportion, and, over that, a faded gray hoodie—watering the potted herbs that she grew on the porch. He slowed down to protract his view of her, eyes stealing too long away from the road. And though he'd been instructed many times before, he failed to integrate the exalted two-footed break-slam technique. The downward force of his lone right foot wasn't quite enough. The doe that led was fortunate to slip across in time, but the cat that followed her was not as lucky. An ache ignited in his belly as Benny felt the car bumble over the little body.

He sat in the car and waited, feeling the slow drain of the hope that momentarily the cat would somersault into view and escape alive.

"Oh my God!" he called, exiting his car.

November pulled herself out from under the porous bark of her house-tree and gaped at the bloody fur, both hands lifted to her mouth. Benny divided tense attention between November and the body, which lay adjacent his back left tire. Her hair glimmered somewhere between amber and auburn. Sing, "She'd come down off the porch in a sweatshirt, swooning like an alder leaf on a lake." And it's

---

9   November, when she was little, thought that humans had a store of hair under their scalps, like Barbie dolls, and when that hair ran out, they went bald. The habit of keeping her hair long (never cutting much off at one time) had stuck.

the same melody as when the feller sings, "She comes out of the sun in a silk dress . . . ."

"I'm . . . so sorry!" He began to move toward her but hesitated. "Is . . . is it yours?"

"I—" she allowed interruption from a car that was slowly circum-navigating Benny's. The driver looked like a teenager, her face scrunched timidly, as if sensing the awkwardness of the accident.

November continued after the car passed: "I . . . well, I guess it doesn't really matter now. Sorry. That's not what I meant. Just, the way things come and go," and her carriage shook, as though experiencing a chill.

"I don't . . . what . . ." (all sighs). "Can I do anything?" he asked gently, hoping she wouldn't remember him from the bar. And hoping she would.

"He was my roommate's."

"Ugh, I'm so sorry," he said, relieved and wondering as to the sex of this "roommate." Then, suddenly, he was struck with the urge to flee the scene. "Oh my God. I'm late to class," he said. "Maybe we should exchange numbers?" He was shocked that this absurdity had left his mouth. "For . . . in case there's insurance or anything like that?"

November peeked over at him but did not move her head, this to maintain the ruse of staring catward. "Yeah."

With some embarrassment, he gave her one of the business cards he'd recently had printed. It felt horribly formal.

Benjamin Huckman
Music Instructor
[phone #, email, etc.]
(And there was a little graphic here—a painting of a tree.)

Back on course, in the Corolla—as he again fondled the second business card on which November had scribbled her email address—he would wonder why he felt the need to point out to her that his contact information was written below. "Hey, also the color of this card is white, and these are English characters I've chosen to signify my given and surnames." God. Moron. He looked out the window, replaying the embarrassing scene. A passing cyclist rolled his eyes at him, personally affronted by Benny's expression, which made the sensitive stranger pedal harder up the hill toward the university, where everything was complex, pointed, and yet somehow pointless.

• • •

The hinge wheezed, as the door smacked secure. Wentworth stirred on the couch, squinted up at the cup beside him.

"Hah, is that even yours?" Benny laughed, walking into the room.

"I don't know," he said, wincing and taking another gulp, "maybe."

"That's when you know you're home," Benny said from the kitchen, "when you wake up and you'll drink whatever's next to you."

"I think it's mine," Uli said, appearing suddenly. Outlined by the afternoon sun, his dark silhouette sharply contrasted with the damp yellow light in the room.

"Well then, why isn't it lying on the floor of the latrine in a heap of shitty bath tissue?" Wentworth asked dryly.

Uli looked at Benny with annoyance. Benny looked back apologetically.

"Please don't wipe your poopy little cunt on any of my cups."

"That was actually *my* cup," Uli replied, squeezing slowly past Benny out the front door.

"And do *not* sass me, young lady," Wentworth continued, turning over on the couch, mashing *Crime and Punishment* into the cushion. "I was up way too late playing choke games with a fine young lady," he mumbled into the couch's backrest before dozing off again. "She puked on my dick if I recall correctly. So . . . you know . . . I won."

...

November dragged herself back into the house: clumps of cat hair, fast food coupons, homemade cat toys and accessories, wrinkled rugs, a coffee table with specs of unwanted grass stems upon broken glass, a mug with a teabag melded to the bottom, half-toppled stacks of CDs and DVDs, burned out candles in their glass containers, a dusty piano with keys so swampy the grime came off on your fingers, kitchen towels lying on the stained fake tile of the kitchen floor, a variety of syrupy fast food cups, scissors, markers, crayons, pens, a few knit caps, and a tangled morass of video game paraphernalia, including controllers, manuals, boxes, cords for various consoles, and a video game-related electronic drum set.

She sifted through the dank closet that she now shared with Blossie—how they'd come to live together, had come to know each other as lovers, still felt murky to her. Increasingly questionable. But at least she didn't have to work at the Home Depot anymore, she thought, as, for no reason in particular, she extracted her old uniform from a pink polyester duffel bag with kelly green stitching. Looking at the crumpled thing, she remembered herself, the self from just a few months ago, as though she had been so much younger then, so full of youthful caprice. (Was that accurate?) She remembered her conversation with the sweet poultry farmer in the Home Depot parking lot, and how the chickens seemed to appear from nowhere. The slow mutual realization that they somehow were leaking from the capped bed of his truck. Why, that afternoon, did chickens dawdle in that Home Depot lot?[10]

"What the? How the?" he kept saying as she tried to corral them. This was supposed to have been a simple trip into town, precipitated by the lumber yard's big sale on treated deck posts and boards, but he now found himself divided between (1) wary lust and (2) perplexity: First,

---

10   Before the lumber yards and the last of the Mohicans, a squirrel could flicker across the state without touching ground.

she was a sight, her little bends and curves, as she repeatedly failed to grab a hen. But his enjoyment was intruded upon by confusion. Who put the damn chickens in his truck? It must have been some kind of practical joke.

November was surprised at how mangy and feisty the fat little birds were.

"He'll get 'em," Blossie had said to her, swooping in from behind, laying a bold hand on her shoulder. November jerked away, startled, but felt strangely calmed as she turned toward Blossie's motherly posture, which contrasted wildly with her voluptuous bra-less body and the eagerness that oozed from her eyes.

Blossie didn't seem to care about the poor embarrassed farmer— "Maybe one of the kids put them in there?"—or the spindly rust-on-white of wild chickens; she just stared at November, who had dressed a little goth that day: no dark lipstick or anything, just some black nail polish, boots, and dress (underneath her orange, oversized Home Depot bib).

"I need help finding some wood," Blossie said, gesturing back toward the store. November peeked back as Blossie led her toward the framing lumber and studs. The embarrassed farmer decided to just wait until everyone left the parking lot before gathering the rest of his chickens.

• • •

On the way to Towner's Woods (carting cat corpse), November stopped at Giant Eagle to buy a couple bottles of Coke. She found herself momentarily, and delightfully, surrounded by almond butter, Nutella, and orange essence prunes—these are dried plums infused with all-natural flavors from real oranges. In the adjacent aisle, she could smell the sugar through the cereal boxes.

In the meat section, "Lunchmeat Tubs" were on sale. She winced at the cottage cheese, aware of the manifold abuses suffered by the speckled bovines pooping out the cottage cheese, to say nothing of the sexual assault sponsored by all (the emperors of) ice cream.

The familiar cashier had stringy hair and glasses. She didn't seem to notice November's cloudy eyes and contorted brows. And November didn't notice that the dark circles under the cashier's eyes were darker than normal, even though she had put the cucumbers over her eyes every night that week. (Both had properly absorbed the norms of social alienation, having essentially been trained not to give a roller-skating fuck about strangers, other than perhaps to fear them.)

Towner's Woods was golden. Even the invasive garlic mustard was divine in that light. A fern, bowing with the breeze, stretched the sticky silk of a spider house. Ambling down the trail, November conceived a plan: first, walk stoically out to the little peninsula where the water had lapped away the dirt that once hid the evergreens' lakeside roots; second, toss the bag in; then, at last, calmly flee.

She felt the placid life of the forest—autumn's eve evident now, geese flapping silently above the breezy canopy. Squinting down through the root-loop on the bank of the lake into the ripple of the bright water, she brushed a leaf out of her hair, slung the bag into the water, and turned away quickly, near to a jog, as she ascended the bank.

. . .

Back at home, staring through the dusty rays of sunlight in her car, November rubbed her hand across the Coke bottle, feeling condensation through the plastic bag. She thought of Blossie. What would she say? And, briefly, she thought of Benny.

Sigh.

Achtung turning.

Blood.

With the slick bottle of Coke and a toilet scrub brush, she crept furtively down the driveway and into the street. As two cars passed, she strolled back onto the sidewalk then nonchalantly back out to the road to examine the stain. Another car interrupted her investigation, at which time she decided the blood was hardly noticeable.

•••

As the sun fell away, she sat at Blossie's laptop with a glass of Coke and ice, crying a little, listening to "Whispering Pines," and reading an animal welfare standards spreadsheet. The sadness flooded circuits, wetly reverberating, everything swirling—comforting, this murky distraction from immediate events. She parlayed sadness into other sadnesses, drifted where the anguish went: factory farms, Mom, old pets, Blossie.

Wendy, Blossie's other cat, jumped up on the computer desk and knocked over November's Coke.

•••

What did one half-lesbian say to the other?

"I want you to ravage me."

"Mmmm, yeah."

"Yeah?"

"Mhm."

Blossie had taken Hombre's disappearance[11] quite well; she was far less upset than November had expected. It was strange. Stranger than that was perhaps the fact that, for some reason, November had lied about it, claiming that she thought she'd seen an owl swoop down and

---

11   Reluctantly noted, the allusion of "Hombre" here, as again a minority character (if only by name and symbol) is the first to die.

yank Hombre up by the neck at dawn that morning, just before she'd left to visit her mom. Blossie was upset but thought maybe November had mistaken a skunk for her cat, or another cat for Hombre. She was brooding in a kind of hopeful denial. As they spooned underneath the greasy sheets, November rubbed Blossie's back and shoulder, half-heartedly trying to console her but also trying not to appear too sure about the variables in her delicate lie. All this as the snuggling caresses grew toward fondling and squeezing.

"Mmm . . . I want to taste you."

"But I want you to ravage me, too," November pouted.

"I know, baby, but . . . you know I hate wearing . . . that . . . thing," Blossie sighed.

"I know."

"And you're so . . ." she sighed again, "difficult."

"Well, it's just not quite the same. It's like . . . I just got used to . . . all that, and . . . I don't know. You wanna watch? Why don't you—" November stopped herself. "I'm sorry. I know."

In the dark silence, they held and released each breath carefully.

"Baby, let me go to California. Help me," Blossie said finally.

Workin' on mysteries without any clues. November rolled on her back and looked up at a strange spectral light that the CD on the dresser caught from the mirror that was reflecting the small bit of light that the blinds were emitting from the larger bit of diffuse light that the damp yellow street lamp buzzed forth. Workin' on our night moves. "Really?"

"Yeah! Let me do it!"

November sighed. Besides the fact that the plan was incomplete and crazy, it seemed like way too much to do on her behalf, given how unsure she'd begun to feel about their relationship. "I don't know, Blossom. It's scary for me. And you don't even have a . . . thing yet."

"Yeah, but we could get one. And you know I don't like 'Blossom.'"

"Are you sure it works that way?"

"Yes. Baby, Dick is brilliant. He—yeah, I know," she rolled her eyes. "'Dick,' dick. We need to find a dick. His name is Dick."

"That's amazing!" she laughed. "Dick?!" She allowed herself to enjoy this more than what was necessary, thick, nervous chuckles teetering at the edge of hysterical belly laughter.

"Yeah."

"But it doesn't make me feel any better about it."

"Baby, Dick told me they've already done it in China and Japan. They did it in *Italy*, for fuck's sake," Blossie said, rolling her eyes again.

"Uhh, but isn't Italy actually—"

"It's no big deal."

"Yeah, but does he know what he's doing?"

"Yes. He does. He's almost done with his internship, and he's . . ." Blossie sighed. "Dick's always been on top of everything. He's just one of those people. Always an 'A' student, always on time, always correct. I mean . . . fuck, he skipped a grade in elementary school *and* high school, graduated college *and med school* early. He's just one of those people. To be honest, I almost even *trust* him. Actually, he may be the only man I know that I almost trust, or at least that . . . I don't know," a hint of resentment in her voice.

"Isn't it expensive? I mean, health insurance wouldn't cover that, right? And you don't have health insurance anyway, do you?"

"I'm on my parents' plan, but there's no way I'd want them . . . you know. Plus, yeah, I don't think health insurance would cover it. But that's okay. He said he'd do it under the table, so to speak."

"What!?" November shouted, now fully alarmed.

"Baby, he's got the access. He's got all the stuff. It's like *rogue* research for him. He loves this shit. He *wants* to do it. I know he does. He pretends like he'd do it 'cause he's a good guy, but he's just . . . crazy to prove he can do something no one else can, or . . . I don't know. It's like a thrill for him, you know?"

"God! And you—"

"Well, not *no one*, I guess," Blossie interrupted.

November sighed. "And you *trust* him, Blossie? You really trust him? You want to submit yourself to this *thrill*?"

"Yes!" She shook her head. "He . . . I've never seen him fail. I don't even think I've ever seen him *be wrong*, literally. He's obsessed with success. He won't even *try* stuff if he thinks there's a chance he might fail or won't win or whatever. You know what I mean?"

"How does it work though? I mean, I always thought they took skin from somewhere—"

"Yeah, they used to. They still do usually, but using an actual fully-functioning organ has a lot of benefits, according to him. The only failure recorded was due to psychological rejection,[12] not physical, so . . . ."

"Where do they get the . . . penis?"

"That's the one road block. He doesn't feel comfortable . . . he said he would do it, but that part's up to me."

"What? What part?" November asked, both of them knowing she already knew, "Jesus!"

"Yeah."

"Soooooo . . . it's not gonna happen then."

"Well."

"What?"

" . . . "

"What, Blossom?"

"I had an idea."

"You had an *idea*?"

"You don't want to hear it, I don't think."

November sighed. "Yes, I do."

---

12   Truly, it's not *that* big a deal, in terms of the procedure's difficulty. Surgeons had already been attaching lab-grown penises for years, but these lab organs don't have the active nerve cells, so there's little to no feeling in them. A "real" penis has active nerve endings and can be easily attached during the reassignment procedure. At the time of their discussion, what appeared to be the most common difficulty was not logistics as much as the psychological process of acclimation to the new organ.

"You don't want me to do it," Blossie grumbled. "You know how much I need to. You, of all people. You know. Why wouldn't you want me to? It's *my* body. If things go wrong, it's *my* problem, you know."

"Yeah. Of course. I know. And, of course, I want you to be able to do it. I just worry."

"Well, I'm gonna do it. I've already talked to him about starting the hormones, and . . . I have a plan for the other part, and if you want to be with me, I think it makes sense for you to be involved," Blossie said.

"Well, yeah . . . of course."

"Really?"

"Yes."

"Okay. Well, okay, sex workers . . . God, these fucking assholes who *buy* women are fucking . . . rotten!" she fumed. "I mean, I can't even . . ." and her head shook with what came off as a self-imposed spasm.

"Yeah. Totally. It's terrible. On so many levels."

"Right. Those fucking *bas*tards are the worst fucking bourgeois ass-hole business criminals. Just because they have the money to—"

"Yeah, of course," November interrupted, heading off the familiar tirade. "Of course. I completely agree."

"It's such a gross, fucked up power play!"

"I know!" she said, placing a calming hand on Blossie's arm.

"Right. Well, did you think I was kidding? I meant it. I would kill any one of them in a minute," she said resolutely.

"I know," November said, feeling goosebumps form on her shoulders.

"Happily."

"So . . . how would . . ." November pulled the comforter over her shoulder.

"And well, I thought it would make sense for you to . . . sort of, I don't know, lure them in. That way you could, you know, try a couple and find the one you like best. I mean, that way, I mean, since you're so difficult and all . . . you know, like that . . . and if I'm going to, I mean if we're going to . . . I figured that way . . . you know?" She paused again, turning away. "That makes sense, right?"

As November filled the cavities in Blossie's plan, she began to feel the terror in her stomach. She felt sick and scared and a little bit nauseated, as though lying next to a man.

• • •

Cycling home from his seminar on southern literature, Benny, on his bicycle, flattened a cheese curl on the road. Then he beamed sideways in levitous[13] shock at a deer galloping beside and intermittently peeking down at him from the raised sidewalk. As the deer began to take the lead, Benny, feeling the surrealism of the scene, pedaled harder, as if to race, but the deer continued to pull ahead then darted down onto the road and slowed quite suddenly. Benny yanked hard on both brake levers, narrowly averting a brutal hoofing, and the deer ran off into the preserve beside the neighborhood.

On the dark side of the street, the church sign read, "Salvation ordered: allow three weeks delivery."

• • •

The next morning November stared blankly at the toaster oven, licking baba ganoush out of the container, until she realized she was licking baba ganoush out of the container. She thought about the huge flock of pigeons beside the church that she watched take off and how quiet it was; it was so quiet, so still, that she could feel the vibration of their wings against the sky with only the faint sound of people singing in the nearby church, a song she almost recognized. It had been the most

---

13   What in the bloody plaid coat of Rodney is the adjective form of "levity"? Can we all just agree on "levitous"? (I like "lief," too, a la "brevity" and "brief," even though yeah, yeah, I'm told they're not corresponding roots. Ugh.)

beautiful and surreal moment she'd experienced in a very long time. And then a man in a white truck slowed down to ogle her and yelled, "Praise the Lord!" And she ran.

The image of that man gave her goosebumps the whole night, and she couldn't help but feel as though he'd cast some eerie spell. Perhaps he'd thrown some sort of inadvertent hex, hurling the flippant praise, a mere vessel for something more sinister.

Then the very next day, at the corner of Willow and Main, a man holding plastic bags and staring at her began singing to the Lord, praising the Lord for November, and as she passed him on the crosswalk, he dropped his bags and threw up his arms in song. And, as she, once again, ran, he shouted after her to have a blessed day. She wanted to tell someone and to be comforted, but Blossie would just have a fit, holler about it all night, and then November would end up having to counsel *her*, first nursing the intervals of Blossie's booming tirades then enduring familiar, angry lectures about patriarchy: prickly monologues delivered in a tone so sharp and accusatory that a discerning viewer would assume November must have somehow disagreed with Blossie's conclusions. She didn't. Not for the most part, anyway. She just wanted a hug. She wanted wine and tenderness like at the beginning.

These realizations (even more than the creepy catcalling) pulled her into a shadowy region where she closely observed all the details of her life with a somber detachment; quotidian occurrences—down to the arrangement of water droplets on the shower wall—all gained a sorrowful, unnamable significance.

So much had changed since the Home Depot, the sweet farmer, the coincidental chickens. Blossie had satisfied November's subconscious desire for mothering, and, initially, Blossie's anger had been directed most exclusively at November's ex, whom she'd ironically vilified for suggesting a threesome with November and another girl who worked at the bookstore. These floggings—soon merely gendered rather than personalized—had been a team effort. Blossie's anger and passionate devotion to their generalized indictments of men, had felt safe and protective: faces gradually lowered onto pillows covered in cat hair; more wine offered in the warm light of maroon rooms; soft persuasions increasingly welcome, partly out of spite, partly because she wanted to accept Blossie's unequivocal views, and partly because she desperately wanted to quit her job at the Home Depot.[14] But, though she'd tried, November was not really attracted to Blossie. Never really was. And it was waning, whatever once had fueled the requisite dismissal of this fact.

Each heavy step in Blossie's apartment now drummed into a sunken pudding. The language hadn't yet broken through the fog of grief in November's bodymind, but just the suggestion that she sleep around . . . to find the right penis!? (Interrobang) Really? For the first time, she was scared of Blossie, scared that her anger was actually dangerous more than merely aloof. Not to mention, the suggestion was more insensitive than anything she'd ever heard, so emotionally vacant and bizarre, such a far-fetched almost *film noir*-esquely lurid proposition.

And what about Hombre? She'd barely even reacted to that! Sure, people grieve in different ways, but . . . shit.

November looked up out the window and saw a young couple ambling past. The girl rubbed her mouth with a small tube of lip balm. Then she kissed her lover for the purpose of sharing the balm.

November returned to composing her letter in protest of the nearby turtle racing and bare-handed decapitation-by-twisting that was scheduled to occur in a couple weeks. The whimsical first draft reflected some hostility and a bit of personal turbulence:

To the soulless whom it may concern:

I hope that your festival is rained on. And I hope the rain is acid rain. And I hope that you all melt and the turtles remain protected by their shells, the shells that you don't give a second thought to, but simply

---

14   Blossie—who had never yet paid her own rent—encouraged this, referring to such "wage slavery" as "an arbitrary wank into the skuzzpool of capitalism."

use to uuuuuse and scorn and dismiss and be the unfortunate stupid people you are.

They are better than you. The turtles. You, the people, are vile. I don't want you to feel pain. Really. Because you are stupid, and you can't seem to help it. I know. But I hope you all die in a painless accident. Before your festive hate-humping.

Sincerely,
A Concerned Party

The revisions culminated as follows:

Greetings,

I am writing to let you know that I am a concerned citizen planning to attend Snapperfest at Campshore Campground in Aurora, IN, this weekend. I am aware that countless attempts have been made to contact you to ask that you ensure no animal cruelty be permitted at this event, that turtle cruelty be forbidden, and that participants at Snapperfest be made aware that any abuse of turtles will be in violation of animal cruelty laws and will be met with punitive action. As I've written in the email below to the folks at Campshore Campgrounds, if I witness any animal abuse, I will publish an account in both print and online venues, and I assure you it will reflect poorly not only on Ohio County Commissioners, but on the County itself, as it will portray the county's awareness and sanctioning of sadistic animal and wildlife abuse. Please take action to ensure your county does not condone or celebrate cruelty to animals at Snapperfest.

Sincerely,
N. Koopa

She would not actually be attending Snapperfest. What happened in that letter was that she lied. In order to scare the local politicians. Ultimately, she felt it was a just and necessary lie, though she wondered, nonetheless, if this attempt to preserve the physical unity of several turtles necessitated in some small way, a certain abatement, a partial malingering, an evasion of the pains of being pure at heart. And while it's true that she did not consciously ponder the ethical compromise in those exact terms, and these unnatural phrases had not (yet) occurred to her, this could have been because when she looked out the window again she saw the boy who'd run over Blossie's cat. He was approaching her house. Seconds later, she heard him knock. Fuck! What was his name? "Henry" or something? Where was the card he'd given her? Should she answer? She'd felt a strange interest in him that day, and it seemed to linger silently, doing some kind of work in her that she hadn't yet identified.

And so in the awkward scene that fallowed—"Yeah. We actually met at the, uhhh, Zephyr before." "Ohhhhhh! Okay. Yeah." (And so on.)—the two again exchanged emails, both too nervy (and/or embarrassed) to acknowledge and communicate that Benny had only recently given her a business card including that sort of information.

· · ·

During the weeks that passed, they did some relatively artless and disgustingly cute emailing and Google chatting. The rehashing of old stories, the blah-ing of certain blahs, encountered by the reader in the following selections:

Docket of Google Blahs
Part the First

Noviembre: So anyway, we'd stopped for some bubble tea and christina mentioned how she sometimes gets scared she'll choke on the tapioca through her straw.

Noviembre: We had to stop for gas and we were in oregon, where they pump your gas for you--you aren't allowed to. So the attendant was this young guy, and he started talking to us about bubble tea and then said "I'm afraid i'd choke on the balls" to which i said, without missing a beat "that's what she said"

Benyeahmon: :)

Noviembre: And immediately started laughing, because i meant it as matter of factly. that's what christina had said.

Benyeahmon: right

Noviembre: about the bubble tea!

Noviembre: i couldn't stop laughing and just kept yelling "that's what she said, that's what she said" with tears. he was so straightfaced and said "are you making a sexual joke?" and i could only say "no, that's what she said."

Noviembre: maybe you had to be there.

Benyeahmon: hah. no. i love that.

Benyeahmon: and i'm just here.

SENT AT 1:18 A.M. ON SUNDAY

• • •

Log of Phone
Part the First

November: Hey!

November: Hey. Can you hang on just a minute?

Benny: Ummm, yeah? Sure.

November: I'll be right back.

Benny: Ohhhkay. Wait, where are you going?

November: If you must know, I have to go to the bathroom.

Benny: We can't talk while you're in the bathroom? You have to interrupt the conversation for that?

November: Usually I don't talk while I'm on the toilet, no.

Benny: Well . . . we can always communicate through the percussion of toilet seats, like Morse code or maybe more like binary code. Hah! Get it? Sort of?

. . .

Docket of Google Blahs
Part the Second (already in progress):

Benyeahmon: god, i'm a sap.

Noviembre: me too, secretly.
very secretly.
actually, most people don't believe me when i tell them that.
i don't like showing it. but i trust you.
i like when you smile. and when you laugh. getting you to laugh feels like winning the best kind of battle.

Benyeahmon: hah.
shidt?
weird. i feel like i laugh a lot. but i think i know what you mean.
and ditto, btw. total ditto. like TOTAL ditto. irl.

Noviembre: i'd like to see you ditto irl.

is it more of a torso move, or maybe a leg jerk?

yeah. sincere. about that.

Sent at 12:50 AM on Sunday

Benyeahmon: ummm, it's probably a . . . yes, a torso thing aaaand a temporarily dropped jaw, waiting to say, 'yeah, i know,' or something equally colloquial.

'equally colloquial' is hard to say thrice fast.

though maybe easier the third time than the second.

She sat in her dark kitchen whispering, "equally colloquial, equally colloquial . . . ."

Noviembre: i'm sitting in a dark kitchen whispering equally colloquial.

Chupacabrabor(scht/tion)

Ingredients:
- Quinoa or rice (1 cup)
- Lightly caramelized onions and garlic (2 onions, 10 cloves garlic)
- 1 can tomato sauce 20 oz.
- 1 can diced tomatoes 20 oz.
- Coconut/olive oil (¼ cup)
- 12 dried chili arboles
- Pumpkin seeds
- Oregano
- Black pepper
- Salt

Directions:
1. Roast pumpkin seeds with olive oil for five minutes.
2. Roast chili arboles with oil for only two minutes.
3. Put roasted chili arboles in food processor with a bit of the diced tomatoes. Set aside.
4. Brown the quinoa or rice with oil, fifteen minutes-ish.
5. Transfer to large pot and add water (1 cup).
6. Add caramelized onions and garlic.

7. Add pumpkin seed, arbol salsa and rest of tomato stuffs.

8. Add oregano, salt, pepper to taste.

9. Allow to cook down, simmering for half an hour, idle waves makin' devil's ponderosa pine blossom.

Serve with sweet potato home fries (long-cut potatoes, fried in lots of oil, onions, garlic, salt, pepper, and finished with parsley and cilantro). Don't worry if your hands get wet or dirty: At the college, every bathroom is outfitted with a motion-activated veal dewlap dispenser for sanitation.

...

Third Google Blah Docket:

Noviembre: how are the essays coming along? are we not speaking of them?

Benyeahmon: hah. i have been tkg care of other stuff. ugh. i will get back to them soon. sigh! novi!

Noviembre: i'm sorry!

Benyeahmon: no, no. just stressed.

Noviembre: i have to finish stuff today as well, so you can be spared one titular distraction. for a little while. :)

Benyeahmon: lqtm. a titular pun? :) sort of?

Noviembre: ha. okay, what is lqtm? i'm sorry to make you spell out extra letters...

Benyeahmon: no problem. a firend of mine seems to think she made that up ay some point, tbough i dobt really think so. it means 'laughing quietly to myself,' a nice pretentious alternative to 'lol.' and 'hah.'

Noviembre: beautiful. i was sounding it out and decided it was a native american term. probably 'idiot.'

Benyeahmon: lqtm.

...

Four Blah Goodockle:

Noviembre: i watched a movie called "timer"
where people get timers installed in their wrists
and it goes off when you meet "the one"—theirs
goes off at the same time.
the acting was horrible but the premise was very
interesting.
i think it's just a choise.
choice.

Benyeahmon: would that be better?
you have to choose to love someone and be loved
by them and you both have to be ready for it…
i think it would be better.
just to know. no doubts.

Noviembre: but that's not realistic and i'd get paired up with
some 80 year old if that's the case.
let's be honest.
today i got a mentally challenged match on ehar-
mony.

Benyeahmon: you're on eharmony?

Noviembre: have been for years. that feels so confessional.

Benyeahmon: whoa. hm. well, i'm thinking maybe… four? hail
marys

Benyeahmon: and five holy fathers. but i also don't care that
much.
the other direction i was considering was some-
thing about hail. maybe a snow/sleet mix.
you know… mary.

...

Top Secret Vaginal PentaGoog

Noviembre: Blossie told me that my vagina is a cow.

Benyeahmon: what? whoa.
what does that mean?

Noviembre: idk. it was awhile ago. she was using some astrology book.

Benyeahmon: ugh. astrology? i can't even begin to …

Noviembre: well, i have been interested in the past.
but if astrology thinks my vagina is a cow…

Benyeahmon: hah.
well, i am no astrologer. but that doesn't seem… hm. well, maybe i should not go into it. (iykwim) but something tells me that is an inaccurate vaginal metaphor.

Noviembre: as much as i dearly love cows, i hope you're right. 'iykwim'?

Benyeahmon: 'if you know what i mean'

Noviembre: oh. hah. well. hm. that's not nice, really. is it?

Benyeahmon: oh. maybe. i was trying to be respectful. trying to respect boundaries.

Noviembre: whatever.

Benyeahmon: what? really?
are you angry?

Noviembre: no. i meant whatever about boundaries. i mean, we're just talking.

Benyeahmon: oh. okay.

Noviembre: actually, i know what you mean. i would not normally say that. but i'm kind of tipsy. and honestly, i kind of like this question. i would kind of like to know what animal my vagina would be.

Benyeahmon: seems like a difficult thing to find out.

Noviembre: tell me. dummy.

Benyeahmon: hah. of course.
hmmm. well, honestly. umm. from what i know, it seems like your vagina would be at least a hundred different species of plants before it would be an animal.

Noviembre: well, that's sweet. i think.
but you're not getting out of it that easily.

Benyeahmon: hah. right. tipsy. okay.

Sent at 2:49 A.M. on Friday.

the animal your vagina would be: the big lipped sea worm. :)
a worm with 'big lips'! in the ocean!

Noviembre: i'm not sure how to take that right now.

Benyeahmon: really? look at the pictures, ffs!
okay. look. it swims more than 2 kilometers below the surface of the atlantic ocean. its scientific name is yoda purpurata! named after yoda! and the latin word for "purple," though most of its photos are decidedly pink. iykwim. :)

Noviembre: hah. "ffs"?

Benyeahmon: for fuck's sake

Noviembre: ah.

Benyeahmon: the "big-lipped damsel" is the best choice in terms of the name, but the big-lipped sea worm is much more... you, if i may.

<small>SENT AT 2:51 A.M. ON FRIDAY.</small>

Benyeahmon: no?

Noviembre: well. it's at least better than a cow. i guess.

Benyeahmon: you 'guess'?! sheesh. it's waaaaay better than a cow. i mean, for the metaphor.

Noviembre: yeah yeah. okay. thanks.
:)

Benyeahmon: man. so hard to please.

Noviembre: no. hah. sorry. i mean it. i love it. i was just kidding. being difficult.

Benyeahmon: i also considered the star-nosed mole, but i didn't think it was nearly sultry enough.

<small>SENT AT 2:53 A.M. ON FRIDAY.</small>

Benyeahmon: and if i were making a joke, i would have chosen the blobfish. :)

Noviembre: that is a very convenient 'if.'
good thing you're not a comedian.

• • •

These sorts of electronic flirtations led to facetime. A walk. A date. A fig. (No aplomb.) A leaf falling away slowly. Soon exposing. Flittering from drowsy trees, wafting into yards of manicured suburban grass. The

smell of autumn, cold and thick, in the air. Dryer sheets and fabric soft-
ener huffing out of vents, imploding fresh piles of brittle maple leaves.
Small animals in Benny's vicinity gathered to watch him pass. Magne-
tized, each gawked from a safe distance, moved their bowels distressed-
ly, sweetly sullying the grasses.

Benny was a demon in the animal world, but a curious one, inter-
ested in the mourning practices of rabbits: Driving home late one night,
he saw what looked like a rabbit lying in the road—and what looked
like another rabbit standing next to it. He turned the car around. It
wasn't easy to find a spot to turn around because this part of Route 43
wound through large, unshorn, grassy fields cut sharply by deep ditches.
As he approached once again, passing in the opposite lane, he saw the
live rabbit stationed next to the dead one. He turned the car around
once more, as was his wont, and accelerated slowly toward the maimed
body to run it over properly and make sure it was indeed dead. But even
as he inched toward the fallen bunny, the other did not move. Instead, it
stared at him, refusing to give ground. Benny stopped, put on his flash-
ers, got out of the car, and approached the prostrate rabbit, consoling it,
asking it if it was dead (all this use of "it" irks me: gender-neutral third
person pronoun needed, as you can see).[15] Only when he was within a
few steps from rén did the yet mobile rabbit finally move away from rén,
whom, it seemed clear, had been run over by a motorist. Benny made
noises, trying to signal that he was friendly, irrationally hoping for a
short second that the mourning rabbit would come back over. For what
purpose he didn't know.

Instead, from only a few feet behind the guardrail, the live rabbit
watched him talk to the dead rabbit, as he poked rén with his foot to see
if rén was already dead, which, as I'm considering now, was potentially
unsanitary since Benny was wearing those same shoes on his walk with

---

15   In Chinese—Mandarin? Cantonese? Which one, fuckhead?—the character tā is
      formed with the ungendered character for person rén. Process by which I have
      forged a gender-neutral third person pronoun: Tā rén. Da rén. Daaaaa rén. The
      rén. Rén.

November, and rather pointless since, realistically, he wasn't going to take rén to the vet anyway because he didn't have any money, and who knows if the vet would care enough to actually do anything. He was going to finish rén off either way. After all, that was the main point of turning around, though tonight the point was also to check and see if there was some kind of kinship between an animal who sticks by the scene of a slaughter. There unquestionably was. The rabbit he encountered was uncharacteristically brave and protective of the corpse on the road. Benny kept trying to console rén/himself, telling someone that it would be okay. (Because he was "alone," this was acceptable and did not compromise his masculinity.) From behind the guardrail, the live rabbit looked at him sideways with one eye, the way rabbits do. He trudged back to the car, got in, and sped forward, hoping to run over rén with both tires.

To him, it was a mercy killing.[16] To them, it was ritual corpse defamation, at best: a misunderstanding, naturally, within the animal kingdom, as Benny's goals were clearly humanitarian, only taking those who were ready and needed to go. A curious demon, taking interest in the mourning habits of rabbits. Mourning rabbits' habits.

So you see, not only was he unofficially monikered "Benny Huckman, Deerslayer," but he'd made a habit of repeatedly running over roadkill—the glib euphemism—to make sure the animals were dead. The humane intentions underlying these maneuvers were mistaken as sadistic by nearby wildlife. And, from this, the rumors grew. He was like a freak show; animals came to observe the miscreant. They couldn't help themselves. Feeling the pull, even from miles away, they had to view him at least once, at which point they almost inevitably shit themselves.

"When I was in high school," November was saying, "I was leaving play practice. Hah. Theater. Ohhh boy . . . and there was this moth on

---

16   It is interesting how I have implied a waiting to be killed, a waiting for a silly person killer who is funnin with me. Interesting, among other reasons, because Benny is (mis)perceived as a killer of animals. But you wouldn't think of me as an animal. (Give it time.)

the ground. The lights in the parking lot were shining on it in a very particular way. I stooped down to look at it. It didn't move for some reason. Its wings were moving really slowly and oddly, like it was drunk or something. I tried to get it to fly away so that it wouldn't get run over. I blew on it gently, but it just sort of flopped over and barely even tried to get back up."

Benny looked over at her without picking up his head. (Neither had noted the language's failure to provide a suitable pronoun for the ungendered moth of her story.) November was, with one hand, sort of holding her hair, fondling the ends of it. He could feel a silly light in his smile, shining with inappropriate candor. And he didn't quite trust it. He didn't quite trust anything.

"I picked it up as gently as I could and started encouraging it. Maybe I felt responsible at that point. I don't know what I was thinking. As though if I spoke to it the right way or if I did the right thing with my voice, it would fly away."

Two bickering squirrels ceased their quarrel (much in sync) to fix their little eyes anxiously on Benny, as he and November strolled past.

"But it just kept sitting there. Wouldn't move. I had to set it down eventually. I *thought* about bringing it home with me, I'm not sure what for. But I ended up setting it in a bush, where it was kind of hidden from view. I don't know why I just thought of that."

An old man in a Cleveland Browns jersey and a wheel chair rolled past whistling Bobby Darin: "Somewhere . . . beyond the sea . . . ."

"When I got home, I googled moths and found out that right after they procreate, they die. Maybe . . . well, you know."

Benny smiled at her again. He wanted to say, "I like the things you keep in your mind. I like hearing you say them. It's like remembering things I didn't know I needed to remember." But he would just end up saying something corny about life. Something that it *is*. It *is* this. That. Determined. Antecedent. Without rhythm.

Life. a word. a part. of. speech. Rrrrrrén. a drop of golden suuuuuuuun.

He'd yet to learn how words dull aromas, foreclose meaning, lessen awe.

"Oh!" he spouted. "Umm, I'm supposed to walk on *this* side." He stepped behind her and presumed to gently guide her body to the inside of the sidewalk so that he was now between her and the street.

"Oh. Yeah. Thanks, but I should probably be on *that* side, actually. I don't really hear out of this ear," she explained, answering the implicit query of Benny's bending eyebrows.

"Oh, wow. Really?"

"Yeah."

Benny remembered the cold night they'd first met at the bar. The drunkenness. The ear plug jokes. Shit.

They stopped simultaneously and strained up at the floppy trumpet melody issuing from the butt of an air conditioner lodged in a second-floor window frame. November's eyes seemed to follow the languid notes that fell below into the giant wavering sunflower swaying lazily against the wooden siding.

When the song ended, they applauded shyly.

"You know, about your moth story, I actually remember something similar happening with me and a cat. I was walking home from class, down Oak Street," he pointed behind them, "and there was a cat sitting, or . . . lying, really, in the sidewalk. As I approached, it didn't move at all. I stepped away and pretended to charge at it. Well," he responded to her disapproving look, "I just wanted it to leave the sidewalk so it wouldn't get hurt. But, anyway, it didn't move. Which was weird to me. But then, once I bent down and began to pet it, it stood up."

She looked at him quickly through the corner of her eye. He sighed deeply.

Neither party possessed similar stories full of pathos for the lives of plants. If the progression from Descartes to your local ragtag Humane Society is any indication, it would be another thousand years before that sort of consciousness permeated our grand little narratives.

"Was that high school, too?" she asked.

"Ummmm, no, it was recently. Hah. God. High school."

"I remember this one day at school I was *so* depressed—I don't know, I think my mom was having some kind of breakdown or whatever . . . that would be a safe assumption for my high school years—but this one day I somehow got poop on my underwear."

Benny laughed deeply, his head tilting back a bit.

"And it was on the *tag*. It was on the tag, and, and I . . . peed . . . I mean, I *only* peed, so it wasn't even *mine*."

"Hohohoh my God!" he giggled.

"Yeah. And my mom was having a nervous breakdown already, so . . . ."

"Holy shit! God, what did you do?"

"Nothing. That's the thing! I was *so* . . . overwrought I just . . . I wiped it off and went back to class."

"It must have still stunk though, right?"

"Yep. It did . . . I even wore it to work."

"Ah, at the cleaners?"

"Yep."

"Man. The irony."

"Yeah, the *iron*-y!" she annunciated slowly then looked at him somberly.

That pun, that look, that moment assured Benny that he was into something good.

• • •

Upon his uncharacteristically cheery return, Benny noted an unfamiliar smell and heard agitation issuing from the kitchen: "Aaaaaah! Flip!"

He turned the corner to find Uli peeking out from the stairwell at Wentworth, positioned in front of the stove.

"Flip. *Flip*, youuu *niggerrrrrr*!"

He was making an omelet.

Uli turned wide-eyed to Benny, who answered with an expression indicating "yeah-I-heard-it-too-I-know-holy-shit!"

"Ffffuck!" He pelted a clipped staccato, angling the pan, his head with it, as he again insulted the omelet. "You *nigger!*" Then he noticed Benny, who had by now rounded the corner entirely and was staring cautiously, rather appalled.

"What?" Wentworth expelled, glancing up from the pan and then back down and then back up to return their stares. "It's barbaric to say 'Jew' after World War Two."

Benny sensed the implied humor, tried to force a smile, but some discriminating urge in him wouldn't allow it.

"That's a joke, son."

He looked at Wentworth's pan. Was that bleu cheese in the eggs?

"Okay." Wentworth jiggled the pan cacophonously. "Run along now."

Having a sense of the upper hand—despite his inability to answer, he *had* witnessed the spilling of the N-word, and in absolutely unnecessary excess (if it could occur in any other way)—Benny curled a smug brow, turned slowly toward Uli, and started up the steps.

The accoutrements of the house were dreary. Somehow, no matter what color anything was, it looked like the paint had been mixed to match the hues of frozen dinners: white cheddar mac and cheese walls; a sandy yellow french fry desk; and a furry, red pepperoni bulls-eye in the center of the dingy dart board. For whatever reason, a nearly full container of actual cottage cheese rested atop the bookshelf in the dining room.

"Dude, that guy is fucked up," Uli whispered, closely trailing Benny.

"You should have seen him in class," Benny chuckled.

"Uuuuuuuugh!" Wentworth's grisly crescendo followed them into the stairwell.

"No. That's not what I mean. I mean, I wasn't in your class, but I'm not talking about in a funny way. I think something is very fucked up with him. And . . . fuck, a racial slur, sure, whatever. That's not what I mean. I mean, I think something *really . . . real.*"

"Really?" Benny answered absently and dropped his backpack next to his bureau.

Angry, vulgar clattering rose from the kitchen.

"How long is he gonna be here?" Uli asked, gingerly closing Benny's door.

"Well, we never really talked about that. I don't know. He seemed cool, and we needed a roommate," Benny responded, surprised that he found the need to explain himself. Uli had never been this direct with him before.

On the dark side of the street, the church sign read, "God is a little bit like hallmark cards - he cared enough to send his very best."

•••

Further Google Blahs

Benyeahmon: bonjour!

Noviembre: hola!

Noviembre: hah. that actually reminds me . . . there was this quote . . . i can't remember now. it was someting like: 'ii speak spanish to god, italian to women, french to men and german to my horse.

Noviembre: '

Benyeahmon: hah, perfect… what if your lover is a horse? and you're not sure the sex.

Noviembre: good lord, what kind of lover is that?

Benyeahmon: i mean… idk. but you're answering a question with a question.

Noviembre: :) hmmmmm. german, i guess.

Noviembre: a horse is a horse.

. . .

Autumn is perhaps the only good reason to live at that latitude—the one we've been talking about. Even in the thinning roadside woods, the colors make you tipsy: muddy, coughing brown and pale green, like a dog's dead tennis ball. You know how the sun shines through rust-colored newly-yellowed trees? And then, deeper in the background, they're bright orange and red? This is an autumn day dying in Towner's Woods.

"She's really smart, but . . . I don't know. I don't usually care to . . . talk about things with her. She makes me feel like I'm not smart enough, I guess, to put together her puzzles of . . . pictures that are not attractive enough for me to really care about."

"Wait. A woman?" he said, confusedly gesticulating. "So you'rrrrrre . . .?"

"Traditionally, no, but . . . I don't know. We're . . . we're close, yeah."

"Hm."

They walked on. He heard her sigh as he puzzled silently over this new information. She stopped abruptly and bent over to support flappy leaves. "Aren't these beautiful?"

A certain week in autumn is a good time for people who walk with their heads down.

"Yes," he said, still a bit dazed. "They're nice."

"They're Mayapples."

"Hm. I kind of like that name. I might even remember it."

"Really?" She returned his smile, minus the wryness, and traced the veins of the plant then stood and moved ahead.

"Yeah." He followed her undulation, the cliché movement of two indigo crescents, "I like them."

She stopped and looked off through the trees at the lake where Hombre was entombed. She wondered if he'd floated at all. "I'm glad," she said, turning to him.

He half-tried to hide his excitement, as the familiar rumble of a train approaching unraveled from a distance. "Me too."

Slowly she turned to face him and, gesturing unconsciously with her eyes and body, placed a gossamer kiss on his cheek. He felt his heart slamming against his chest, as she stood with uncommonly poor posture, her head oblique, eyes dancing on and off him. Falling forward and pulling her close, he made the boasting decision to share his excitement with her. As the train tore past, they kissed and lurched and squeezed, stopping now and again to reassure themselves of their solitude . . . and laugh. And something in them knew not to speak.

Beyond the train tracks and the filthy taupe lake, the clouds hovered over a breadth of green and pillared brown. Darkness fell nadirless (nadir-will nadir-will) where it did, imperially lazy, turning sepia the deciduous hues. It smelled like when you hit lightning bugs with your car and splatter their guts all over the windshield, a murderous rumpus of lightning bugs.[17] Bright corpses and howling train-breath warning, crying, "Catty Whompus."

• • •

"You out with that girl again?" Uli asked with a dull smirk.

"Yeah," Benny answered, shoving the front door halfway shut, "November."

"It's a memorable name, though I can't actually remember it for some reason. Is it her real name?"

---

17   Do you cringe and feel uncomfortable about this flippant treatment of lightning bug death? Perhaps not. This is called "speciesism," (first seen in 1975 in R. D. Ryder's "Victims of Science"). How similar must a body be to yours? How much entwined must a life be with yours before you disapprove of its annihilation? Or is a concern for suffering superlative? You might kill a fly, but would you knowingly torture it? Would you comply, for the sake of convenience, with rén's torture?

"Yeah, apparently."

"You gettin' some pussy?" Wentworth hurled from the bathroom.

"Ummm, what?" Benny laughed and looked at Uli. Uli looked at the bathroom door dryly. (Interaction with toilet: Pee, lustrous yellow, bothered the toilet paper that held a spider's corpse, its body rupturing against the falling urine.) The toilet flushed.

Wentworth continued from the bathroom, "You know what I did today? I passed a church whose sign informed me I was traveling at 144 abortions per hour. I almost crashed from laughing. I don't think that's the response they intended when they stuck 144 tiny, white crosses in the ground. Ha haaaaaaaaa. If I were a woman, I would stay pregnant, always, just so I could film my many abortions."

"What?"

"I said, 'Are you getting some pussy?' my dear lad," Wentworth repeated, swinging open the bathroom door.

"Funny you should ask."

"Oh?"

"Hah, yeah, there was this little black kid at the park who rode by on his bike and said the same thing."

Uli laughed.

"These little kids, like nine years old, rode by, and one of them was like, 'Gettin' 'at puuuuussaaaaaayyyyyyy?'"

"Vulgar little animals," Wentworth mumbled.

"Oh, man!" Benny laughed. "And side saddle! He rode by on this little dirt bike thing, and he was riding it side saddle! It was so iconic! He was like a caricature of himself."

"Like a superhero," Uli said.

"Yeah or . . . a gamepiece. A little 'Afronopoly' gamepiece."

Benny laughed agreeably. "Someone needs to make this game."

"The other gamepieces would be, like . . . a doo-rag and the Kool-Aid man."

"And chicken. A wing, a thigh."

"A piece of cornbread. Maybe a watermelon."

"All the trains, like the B&R Railroad or whatever would all be Greyhounds."

"The other properties would be Popeye's and barber shops and basketball courts."

"And liquor stores or convenience stores."

"Oh, and Harlem. Harlem would be like Park Place."

"And half the squares on the gameboard would be jail. You would actually *start* in jail."

"Indeed. Sooo . . . *this*, what we're doing right here, is okay, but I can't say 'nigger'?" Wentworth queried.

"Uhhh, well that seemed kind of different. You were . . . really angry and . . ." Benny faltered.

"Yeah, we're just sort of joking in good humor about it. And even so, I actually feel a little guilty anyway," said Uli.

"I don't," Wentworth held.

"Yyyeah. I don't know."

"No one heard me say it. Well, no *black* people heard me say it, anyway. I'm not racist. I mean, I am probably classist or something, but I'm not racist. People who are loud and dirty are repellent to me. I can usually pity them from a distance, but I don't want them around. Whatever color they are. I don't care."

"But if black people are more often like what you're describing, then isn't that racist?"

"Doesn't *that* actually sound more racist? 'If black people are that way more often'?"

"I just mean that it could be seen as racism, if—"

"Every Goddamned thing we do is racist or sexist or classist or what-the-fuck-ever. We're constantly on guard for this trite bullshit. There's no point in any of it. It's a prissy, censorious approach to language. The lexicon is there for us. Our thoughts are capricious, and contexts are big. It's stupid to limit ourselves, especially when in the company of friends."

"I'm not sure I feel very friendly around people who use the word 'nigger,'" said Uli.

"What! But you're cool with a sambo-themed board game? C'mon. Why should we never be allowed to use the word, 'nigger' again? Is there no such thing as a 'nigger'?"

"I don't know. I guess that depends. I mean, is there such a thing as a 'retard'? I guess there is, but we don't use it to refer to retarded people."

"Hah. God. Well our phenomenological . . . I mean, do retarded people think that 'retard' is their word?" Wentworth rolled his eyes. "Do they *claim* it?"

"Not that I am aware of," Uli answered, beginning to tongue the underside of his maxillary molars.

"Maybe that's not a one-to-one comparison, but what does it really matter if we laugh about a retard, and she never finds out about it? I'm babysitting one everyday lately, and believe me, it's not gonna hurt her."

"Yeah. Well, I'm offended by it. And . . . it might not exactly hurt someone else directly, but it might hurt you or your . . . you know . . . *soul*," Uli said, arising from the couch and heading toward the kitchen.

"'Souuuul'?" Wentworth bellowed.

"Whatever you wanna call it."

"Well, I want to call it a '*nigger*.' And since no such thing exists, that should be no problem, right?"

"Sure."

"Sire!" Wentworth turned toward, Uli, who was walking away now, "Your immortal 'souuuul' is a *nigger*."

"Yeah. That's fine with me, actually." Uli exited, closing the back door with constrained, though due, force.

Wentworth rolled his eyes disdainfully and turned away from the door.

"Hey, umm," Benny began bashfully, "Uli was raised Christian, and he's sort of—"

"Oh, *Jesus*. What about the other one?"

"Ned? No, not really. Well, he was, too, but he doesn't really, I mean he's never seemed to care about it."

Wentworth pretended to breathe a sigh of relief. "So you really *are* gettin' some pussy, eh?"

"I'm not sure I would put it like that. But . . . sure."

"Ugh. God. That's how *I* would put it."

"Are you seeing anyone?"

"Hah. '*Seeing anyone*'? Well, I'm not sure I would put it like that. Maybe not indeed like that. But sure. I see much . . . and many *ones*."

• • •

There's this thing that happens. It's what's supposed to mean meaning. And it's what's supposed to be discovered in and during and after. And no one else's departure will start or stop it. And we're not really discovering. But maybe learning to remember.

Benny and November. Drank wine and. Making out noises and. On the loveseat in Benny's room, where neither was entirely comfortable yet. With sleeping together and. So they decided to have a slumber party in his room, November, on the loveseat and Benny in the bed. And then later, when settled, they started joking about masturbating, gently making fun of each other.

"I knew this kid, my little brother's friend." Benny laughed at the silliness he was about to relate—and reveled subconsciously that he and November had achieved the warm familiarity necessary to relate something so silly. He told the story of Gerald Bates, boy of the world of rural entitlement, Gerald Bates, who slapped a Burger King cashier with a twenty-dollar bill. Gerald Bates. It was never clear from one day to the next whether the various fast-food cashiers would be spared or harassed, and, if so, in what way, precisely. Beckoned, on occasion, was a tenderer and more intimate denigration, in which a Gerald Bates, nonchalant, might lean over the countertop, gaze up at the menu, and placidly make inquiry into the issue of the coffee beans' country of origin, as he caressed the cashier's young hand.

"If he ever had a butler," Benny cawed, laughing almost too hard to finish, "he'd be 'Master Bates.' 'Master Bates!' That really works for me . . . get it?"

"If he were a kid, he would be 'Young Master Bates.'"

"And his dad would be 'Master Bates, the Elder.'"

. . .

Please enjoy this snippet from Benny's dream that night: He and old friends from high school are throwing a baseball back and forth beside a parking lot. Benny throws it way too far, and it skips across the pond into the woods. They go in to get it and stumble upon a small bear. Benny runs back to the house to get the shotgun. When he returns, the bear is just a baby bear, and the baseball is just a wiffle ball. Then the mother appears, and the mother can talk. She's sort of mean and abusive, and has slapped the cub and made it blind in one eye because she's slapping it too much. Benny shoots the mother bear, and she gets upset and says that she's gonna call the police. He shoots her again, and he's beginning to wonder what they're gonna do with the cub after he shoots the mother bear again. He shoots her a third time, and now they're wondering how they're gonna deal with the police and/or how they're gonna keep this baby bear from telling on them, and they try to convince the cub that the mom was abusive and bad, which she did seem to be.

. . .

During the week following their slumber party, Benny often pressed to his nose the pillows on the loveseat. Such behavior borders on the "Snarf(f)ish," according to Vonnegut's conception of the "Snarf."

...

Hoping to bypass the miserable banter that precedes such things, November jumped right in:

"I have to go."

"Oh. Where are you going?"

"I mean . . . I'm moving out."

"What?" She looked up from the tuna wrap on her plate and set down the tahini sauce. "Where are you gonna go?"

"I met someone."

Blossie paused and gathered herself, pulling her eyes up from the carpet to stare maliciously at November. "Who?"

"I don't want to talk about it, Blossie," she said, carrying her mug into the kitchen. This was a more inconvenient question than "Why?"

"No? Of course not. Fine." She moved her plate to the coffee table and followed November to the kitchen, filling the doorway, leering at November. "That's fitting. What *do* you wanna do then?"

"Nothing."

"Yeah, that seems about right."

"Oh yeah?"

"Don't you think?"

"Hm. You know what's really weird," November said spiritedly turning on the water in the sink, "I don't care. I'm sick of . . . not just . . . talking. I miss saying things for no reason and not worrying about . . . what they mean in ten different ways"—here, she mumbled some—"or how they *sub*jugate *wo*men." She put her mug in the cupboard and her hand on her hip and tried to fling something hurtful: "I miss being the *enemy* or whatever: flippant, silly . . . straight."

"Pfff, it's a man? Hah. Yeah. You fell in love with one of your new *pimps?*"

"That's ironic. I thought that was *your* job," she mumbled, squeezing past Blossie into the living room.

"What?" Blossie gasped, a glottal sigh imploding, "What did you say?"

"You know what I said. Never mind."

"Well, I miss eating meat, you know! But . . . I don't *do* it, you know, because of all your crap with your childhood and all that, because you'll freak out."

"You're eating meat right now."

"Fish."

"Yeah."

"That's not—Whatever, people *need* meat to be healthy, you know. Yeah. It's so sad and all, but that's how we are. Carnivores. Or what*ever* . . . fucking *omni*vores, at least!"

"Right, tell yourself whatever you want. Ignore everything else. You always do."

"I was healthy before you came along. Now I'm sick all the time."

"Oh? Before me you were stabbing at chicken nuggets with a broken pencil because none of your forks were clean. God, I thought we'd been through this, but you don't—it doesn't matter. This is not the point. This is . . . it's not," she choked, pulling her cheeks in and her eyebrows down. "It's not right. It's not true." She lowered her forehead onto her palm and began to cry. "I don't think it ever was."

"Not *true*?" Enduring this bit of emotional annoyance, Blossie looked down at the carpet and generously allowed November to occupy her periphery. November's crying used to be more manageable. One might simply remind her of the gender inequities influencing her present experience, and console her with corollary feminine empathy. But recently she'd been more difficult.

"I assume you'll be moving in with your new fella then?"

"I don't want to talk about it, Blossie."

"Yeah, you said that . . . okay. Well, I would like you to give me your key."

November raised her head searchingly, "Right now?"

"Uh, yeah. *Right now.* You can't just come back and forth, in and out whenever you want, if you're not with me anymore. We're not roommates. You *sleep* in my *bed*! Used to, I mean. So . . . yeah. *Right now*."

Perhaps she was aware that power cannot be given, only taken, demonstrated in the taking. The process of taking is empowerment, whereas love seems the opposite. Though both perhaps require active demonstrations, love is giving, whereas power—and its bedfellow, a shit—is taking. Consider what, colloquially, one "takes" and "gives," and the subtexts read by our collective idiomatic subconscious author.

November arose silently, and sullenly wrangled the key into submissive separation.

• • •

They met at Smith Park.

"I didn't want to see you tonight," he said, brooding and averting his eyes, gazing carefully at a smoothly graded covering of mulch.

"You didn't?"

"Well, I'm really high, and when that happens and I end up around people, I just want to watch things and focus on them and let them tell me what's going on and try to listen. But when you're around, I'm always wanting to say something really smart. And I don't think that will happen tonight."

"Oh, Benny. Don't say that. You don't have to say any certain thing."

He sighed.

"I broke up with Blossie, so if you feel like listening, that's even better. Plus, I think you're a good listener." She pulled her eyes upward at him for a moment and quickly hid them again, her head hanging over onto her knee.

"You broke up with Blossie?"

Upon hearing that she'd been kicked out, Benny, naturally, invited her to stay with him, and, naturally, she accepted.

On the dark side of the street, the church sign read, "I kissed a girl, and I liked it. Then I went to Hell."

• • •

If I could address Bobo the worthless assassin clown, I would speak suchly to him: "Hey, Bobo, you should . . . be better at your job, Bobo. Because this is annoying. As anyone can tell, I'm still alive, and like I said, it's really annoying. What are you, on food stamps?

"Me too, pretty much."

• • •

Under a wide frayed mushroom, willow sighs, and airplanes, a mole made a knot with itself and the grass. Rén was a weed-whacking body but lacked the yellow plastic fronds to lacerate plants, fortunate for them perhaps, but who has any clue—Swiss researchers revealed a sentience in plants. Should the Swiss have to choose between the Mayapple and mole . . . well, actually, they weren't Mayapples. Beauty, on occasion, just won't conform to truth, and on this occasion, they could not have been Mayapples. That wouldn't be logical because I'm pretty sure Mayapples are too tall and broadly spaced to really gnarl a mole. It yet eludes Google: Can a mole get tangled in Mayapples? (B[o]o/ar[n]eded no fruit.)

Benny's loyal faffling lay with the mole. Allegiance, oscillation, less like a pirouette, more like Drano. This mole may have been happy to spin.

Later that night, one of Wentworth's recent conquests trampled in the door, jangling her keys, like the chain of a German Shepherd. "Um," she smacked her lips and rolled her eyes upward, standing in the doorway, mouth ajar. Ding. Ding. Ding. Mouth ajar. O, Anticipation. We shall dialogue now, yes? "A few houses dowwwnnn?" her voice rising to a question with each phrase, "I was just walkiiinnng?" another question, "and," a breath here, "there was a *possum*." Noting Benny's lack of excitement, an embellishment, "like . . . *this* big."

"Hm."

"I know, right! I was afraid of it, kinda." The cadence of her accent (Latina) somehow resembled a Minnesotan rhythm, don'tcha know.

"Yyyyeah . . . I wouldn't worry yourself. I've never heard of a possum attack."

In Ohio, they were called "grinners." I think that had something to do with the way they looked either before or after they became roadkill. If you Google "possum," you may find a middle-aged woman with large breasts pumping out of a button-down, blue and white pin-stripe shirt. By its tail, she'll be holding up a distraught possum. Her hand could cover your whole receding face.

This woman is presumably Katherine Harris, one of the stars of the article, "The Politicians and the Possums." Crudely text-wrapped around her and the possum, the article notes that Florida is subdeveloping its rural areas as quickly as possible, but there are still parts of the state that require a certain touch to gain the voters' trust. As such, Floridian political candidates must visit these areas (for the Wausau Possum Festival, in this case) and "prove they are good country folk by mistreating a possum." They must first bid on a possum and then—if they win the bid—take it out of its cage and shake the shit out of it so that it is terrified "into going limp so it won't claw them." Katherine Harris, who bid $400 for her possum is, according to the auctioneer's drawl, a "gal" who "knows how to shake a possum." According to the article (available from workbench.cadenhead.org), Tom Gallagher paid $475 for his possum, and Rod Smith paid $250 for his. They then used their possums at their campaign sites, Smith keeping his visible (limp and shivering), while Gallagher indicted his rival, GOP candidate Charlie Crist, whom he apparently outbid for his possum, taunting him like so: "He didn't look like he wanted to touch it."

The auctioneer's alternate, denied a proper mic and stage, shouted anyway, "Boy howdy, if the torturer's horse could see us now!"

...

Wentworth[18]—subbing for the accelerated sixth grade reading class, running dystopic experiments—strolled expansively between the rows of desks, eating the old pizza he'd had delivered there the previous day. The room smelled of it, as, somehow overlooked by the custodian, it had remained overnight, resting on the teacher's desk in its damp box. The kids were working through *To Kill a Mockingbird*. "That's *tripe!*" he managed, having just stuffed a large bite of pizza into his sour, cavernous face; imitation cheese rubbed the roof of his mouth, as the greasy and corn starchy crust met the back of his tongue. He mushed his jaw through the thing, yellow tallow filling his cheeks. "You little God-damned peanut. You don't know Cal*pur*nia," he chewed. This banter had begun in the spirit of unsanctioned empirical research. He was, presumably, creating a control group to study the effects of abusive misnomers on female preteens. "Don't tell me about Cal*pur*nia, you little faggot. I'll slap your face with this pizza . . . you little faggot." (Only loosely had he construed the research terms as bearing gendered weight.)

One of the boys said that he didn't need to because the girl already had a pepperoni face. A few other boys laughed. The girl slumped forward, forehead on forearms on cold desktop laminate. Wentworth glibly poked her cheek with imitation cheese as he strode past. Then he re-perched ceremoniously atop the teacher's desk and craned his neck a bit, reaching his lips toward his elbow pit to suck a flake of errant dough.

...

---

18   Contains one or more of the following: lard, hydrogenated lard, partially hydrogenated lard.

"Really? You wanna read this shit again? What in the piddling fuck is wrong with you? Yeah. Never mind. Okay, but fuck that John Muir epigraph. Yeah? Okay then.

"Deep in a green forest down by the sea, a hunter spied a little deer dancing,' so he went closer to watch the lusty movements but found, as he neared, that the deer was pregnant and was dancing a sultry dance of sadness because her best friend, a fat, stupid cat had just been killed, and her boyfriend had just cheated on her again, and left her, and she was pregnant and all alone.

"Then he remembered how, just a couple months prior, he had tied her up, covered his cock in bacon grease, and really juggle-fucked her, the young beasty. And this made him wonder whether the fawn might be his, but then he remembered that the deer was a whore—sorry, I mean 'hussy'—so it could have been anyone's, and he got the fuck out of there before she could start making hysterical accusations.

"The end."

· · ·

Excitedly carrying home another bottle of wine in his backpack, Benny cycled through town, where drunkards yelled "Lance Armstrong" at him. Usually, the shouting waned at this time of year, as the increasingly frosty nights throttled the students' raillery, but the race is not always to the swift, as the jeering is not always to the . . . warm. He rode happily past the riff-raff and scolded two squirrels for fighting and scrambling about in the street, as if they were children caught in a mindless fracas.

It had been one month since November moved in, but she still insisted on confining their relationship to the house. This was because she did not want to parade her new partnership around town, for fear of a chance meeting with Blossie. She'd heard that Blossie'd been seen in her old front yard at night with a shotgun pointed up at a tree. (No one, including November, could have guessed that Blossie had been vengefully hunting for the owl that she thought killed Hombre.) But even before this news, she'd feared Blossie's reaction might turn violent if Blossie saw her with Benny. Only once, and never since, had they even gone out to get coffee together. Here's what that was like:

He'd hardly taken his laptop out of his bag, and her anxiety was already evident. She fidgeted continuously, as her eyes flickered across the sparse café.

"Look at that guy in the corner," he said, trying to lighten the mood.

"He's been doing that for a while," she replied, calming slightly as she focused on the strange man.

"Really?"

"Yeah. I'm trying not to look too much though."

"God, it's awesome."

"I know," she smiled.

"Maybe he's a choreographer," he said, coolly pulling her mug to him.

"Maybe he's on drugs."

"Hah. True," he muttered, and forcefully inhaled through his mouth, having just burnt his tongue on the green tea in her mug. "Wow. Am *I* actually the one giving a hopeful assessment here?"

"Depends on the drug, I guess."

He smiled, imagining that he'd pacified her. "Still though. C'mon. Choreographer? Druggie?" He cupped both hands, simulating a scale. "Positivity!" He raised his fist for an ironic fist bump. Ignoring this, she peeked over again toward the undulating man at the corner table. He was gaping at his computer and swaying, his arms worming slowly through the stale, caffeinated air.

"He's not a choreographer," she sighed. "I wish he were."

• • •

Benny grabbed the corkscrew and excitedly climbed the steps to his room, which, he reviewed with momentary concern, was now basically *their* room. November had just returned from dropping off a prim letter at the neighbors' house; Benny read the copy on her computer.

Dear Neighbors,

My name is November Koopa. I have recently moved here and will be a part time student at KSU next semester. I have ridden my bicycle to and from the university many times during the past couple weeks, and I've found it necessary to clothe myself ever more thickly as the temperature has begun to drop fiercely, sometimes below freezing.

Each day when I arrive home I hear the desperate crying of your dog, and it saddens me. In the first couple weeks I was here, I inquired around the neighborhood, as there was no answer at your door, to try to discover whether the dog had been abandoned—I know that is more common during the tough recession in which we find ourselves. However, I was told that the house is indeed still occupied by the owners of the dog, and I believe it must be so, as the dog does seem to go inside at some point during the night; in any case, his/her steady bawling dissipates before bedtime, which I appreciate.

However, during these freezing cold days (and, sometimes, evenings) the dog rarely stops crying for more than a minute or so. I do hope you have a plan for the dog's well-being as the winter approaches. I certainly understand how busy things can get, and I would like to volunteer to help with the care of the dog if you need it, whether that means letting the dog out to make sure that he/she does not soil your floors, etc. I would hate to witness the dog being left in these freezing temperatures, as I don't think he/she is bred for them.

Thank you for reading my letter, and please understand that I have no malicious feelings toward you or the dog; the sounds of the barking do not bother me except to make me feel sad and concerned (I hear them even inside my home), and I would certainly like to help you with this or any other occasion that might require neighborly assistance.

Sincerely,

November Koopa

"So?" he pressed, holding up the printer cable that was now attached to her laptop, searching her face for confirmation. (She'd been talking about this for a while now.)

She poorly feigned guilt through the pride evident in her face.

"Oh, man, I really wish you would have told me about this."

"Do you pick up my computer and just start reading often? Is that what you do?"

He looked up at her sternly and sighed.

"Why? It'll be okay. I was very cordial. Plus, that dog is gonna freeze. He's clearly not happy out there . . . or *she*."

Benny sighed again, felt his mental position weaken and his body strengthen at the shape of her rationalizing posture: one hand on the dresser she was leaning against, one hand on her hip. She noticed his attention and smiled coyly, holding her ground, knowing now she needn't move.

Benny arose from the loveseat, looked down at his jeans, returned her coy smile, and put his arms around her waist. She allowed herself to fall cozily against him, balancing her body to appear dependent, submissive.

They pushed and pulled each other onto the bed. November wiggled slowly out of her jeans, socks pulling halfway off in tow. Scaling. Windmills. Playing. Overwhelmed. No mind. Colorless. Us. A name she called herself. Benny threw her bra behind; it landed in the waste basket.

"I want you inside me now," she huffed through soft wheat hair.

· · ·

For November, sex had always been a chore and a pleasure, like sifting through the bottom of the bag for the last reasonably-sized chips she happened to be craving. But it was different with Benny; he seemed trustworthy. He made her feel safe, as though remembering some sort of hopeful naivete. It felt good to share herself openly. Trusting someone so fully and vulnerably revitalized her, such that she felt free and secure, invigorated by the renewal of a generalized faith.

"Mmmm, I'm tired," she cooed. "That was so good."

Benny realized at that moment what it meant, why she had fallen for him: She had *allowed* herself to be possessed, to be led, to be reliant, in a certain sense. And whether he knew it or not, he had encouraged it. Subconsciously, he knew the sex would be better this way because if she would surrender emotionally, her body would follow. But what was she surrendering to? What had it meant for her to surrender? What did it entail? Was it a simple matter of trust?

Maybe that was why *he* could never seem to fall in love? Because he refused to allow himself to trust? Refused to be made truly vulnerable?

• • •

Sitting in another open window of her computer was this Google Chat conversation, which they'd had earlier in the day:

Benyeahmon: i'm going super nostalgic tonight.

Noviembre: nice. that's in order sometimes. maybe more than not. maybe not more than.

Benyeahmon: perhaps more than you're not moring.

Noviembre: if not more. perhaps.
peanut butter noodles: http://allrecipes.com/recipe/
peanut-butter-noodles/

Benyeahmon: that looks like a good one. and easy. (i'll exact a fistbump from you later.) all the thyme is gone though. died. sooooooo gay.

Noviembre: that is overwhelmingly gay.

Benyeahmon: it's a triple assgay fag[19] score.

Noviembre: it has three q's and a z. if you know what i mean.

November remained ill at ease with the reverberant bigotry of Benny's "gay," but felt somehow rebellious and vindicated every time she used the word, particularly as Blossie's vaguely threatening presence continued to loom in her mind. This lingering fear helped her justify their usage of the word, and convinced her it was benign.

· · ·

Killing a deadening gusto for duty. Wafting in . . . out of the grip of that sort of duty. (One of the limits of this medium is that right now I cannot—with real precision—represent animal or fart noises. Because, hold the phone, I would jettison any cosmopolitan pretense just to make a fart noise here, but for . . . well, the silence of our endeavor—overkill, ugh, overkill to call it an "endeavor.")

B: Did u wanna get in here?

N: Yeah.

B: Because you wanna pee?

N: . . .

B: 'cause you're suppose to pee after, you know.

---

19   Such impropriety remains well-rooted in the common tongue of the slithy Midwesterner.

N: Uh, yeah, I know. I would like to do that. Yes.

B: Yeah. You're supposed to. I probably should, too.

N: Mhm. You should do that, too.

B: You can go first.

N: Okay.

B: Okay.

N: I was just waiting. You know.

B: Yeah. What for?

N: Well . . . (She winced slightly.)

B: You don't want me in here for that?

N: Well, I guess, you know, yeah, you could leave.

B: Really?

N: Yep.

B: I'll stay. We can make an 'X'!

N: Uhuh. Maybe next time?

•••

And now the thing happening, while you are being filled with color words and words of animal foam, is that Benny and November are back in bed and deciding to arise again to brush their teeth together. Spumously. As a pair.

"Toothbrush," he pointed his finger to her forehead and looked at the pleat of her shirt which had exposed an extra portion of her breast.

"Yeah," she sighed, exhausted. "My breath is bad."

"So's mine."

"We should combine them and make something awful."

"Like some kind of a cleaning agent for chemical waste?"

"Or bombs."

They ambled toward the bathroom and spread the vastly inactive paste onto their toothbrushes then began the delirious talk of post-sex, pre-bed.

B: This is the messiest I've ever been with a tube of toothpaste.

N: Yeah, me too.

B: I think it's the tube.

N: Yeah, the way it comes out.
    (Brushes agitating mouths' huddled toothpasty masses, pro-
    nunciation progressively muddling.)

B: Uh-huh. Wait, you mean the paste?

N: Yeah.

B: I mean the tube.

N: It's thinner or something.

B: The tube?

N: Yeah, it oozes out and, like, sticks in the cap.

B: Oh, yeah! It does. But that's the paste. I'm talking about the
    tube.

N: The tube?

B: Yeah, it's a different material.

N: (incredulous, scrunchy face)

B: There's no suction.

N: (same face)

B: There's a suction on the other ones. There's no suction on
    this one.

N: There's never suction.

B: What! There's a suction sometimes!

N: No.

B: What! You're fucked.

N: You just wish there was suction.

Then she conceded a fistbump, and spat foam into the sink, rinsed her mouth, and folded the toothpaste tube—like a worming whale's tail exposed above water—to fit in the short row of the medicine chest.

It was not long after this that a back massage turned into an intimate pimple-popping session. And that was the night Benny learned November would give him back massages as long as he allowed her the apparent catharsis of exploding blemishes on his skin. She was clearly embarrassed by her preoccupation but also had become quite comfortable with him, enough to gleefully pop a pimple on his back and admit to a scab-picking fetish.

And that's how it happens.

• • •

Lying next to her in the early hours just before sunrise, Benny rolled over and felt his long hair push against her hand. November rubbed her fingertips along Benny's scalp, grabbed and pulled the hair, dreaming that she was pulling Blossie's thick pubic hair in that deferential way Blossie used to love—and November used to hate. And she hated it now, too; it added a sensation of rust and screeching and scraping to the sexual nightmare she was having, and it seemed to emanate from the woodwork and permeate the soundfloor of the bedroom, as Benny felt for a moment that he heard muted yelling but groggily concluded that it was a part of the searing intermittent throb he was abiding on/in his scalp and head. He could only blame himself though, for he had let it go on, November pulling his hair gently at first, but with a gradually increasing ferocity that became painful. Equally curious and considerate, he let it continue so as not to wake her.

In their respective realities, they each heard muffled screams and thumping sounds, which slashed through the night in a brief high fidelity, before being rubbed out by a dull, bassy thud.

On the dark side of the street, the church sign read, "You can't enter Heaven unless Jesus enters you."

· · ·

"How are things goin' down here?" She began to fondle him as the early sun rushed into the room.

"Oh, yeah, you haven't had a report in a few hours," he said sleepily, turning to her. And they laughed sweetly, annoyingly. "I'm imagining a little, tiny guy who walks out to the tip of my penis and salutes you then reads from his clipboard."

"But then he turns on you and pulls out his gun, a pump gun, a pumpernickel bread gun. That shoots jalapenos. Remotely. From your urethra."

"Oh, shit! This was kind of hot before that part. That sounds terrible. Passing a jalapeno pepper?"

"Don't be dramatic. Life is not a Disney movie. It's not even a Vonnegut novel. Everything is *not* beautiful. And some things *hurt*." She poked his belly.

"Umm . . . that was disturbing. Hmmm. Speaking of 'not beautiful,' would you rather . . ." (she rolled her eyes and groaned in protest) "use Walt Disney's head as a pillow or get a Dutch oven from Roseanne?" Benny inquired lazily, as he repositioned himself in bed.

"What's 'Dutch oven'?"

"A 'Dutch oven' is when someone forces your head under the covers and then farts, holding your head, you know, beneath the . . . fumey covers."

"Is Roseanne a famous lesbian?" she said, looking down at Benny's penis, which he'd begun slapping against his thigh.

"No, there is a Rosie O'Donnell, though. Roseanne's that sassy broad who had the show, *Roseanne*. Also, she sang the national anthem somewhere and grabbed her crotch. I think that's what she's most recently famous for. It was a big deal in the '90s, that crotch-grabbing. Folks didn't cotton to it. Found it disrespectful. She could be a lesbian, too, I guess. I don't know," he shrugged.

"Well," she rejoined, after some consideration, "probably the Dutch oven."

"Totally the Dutch oven! Agreed. It would have to be a hundred Dutch ovens, at least, for me to even consider the Disney. And even then, I'd still have to go with the Dutch ovens. I really don't think I'd get any sleep with the head. Someone told me his head is frozen. That does not sound restful."

"His whole body, I think. They froze his whole body."

"They froze his whole body. God. Disney. What a dildo."

"What a Dutch dildo."

"What a . . . dildo . . . oven."

"I wonder if he's dildo-ready?" she pondered. Disquieting this, the sound of one wang slapping.

"Who? Disney? What?"

"Yeah. I wonder what . . . state that's in. I wonder if anyone has checked it out."

"Probably a few people."

"I mean, in his life, yeah, but now?"

"Well, yeah. You know, like the coroner, aaand . . ."

"I am thinking a lot about Walt Disney's penis right now," she said, arising to search for her clothes.

". . . probably the mortician."

Finally locating her bra, November pulled it out of the waste basket.

"The bra smells good this morning; there must be some some incense or something in this trash can, you hippy fruit."

"Oh, I think it was those black bamboo fronds, whatever they are . . . to conduct essential oils . . . I replaced them last night."

"Oh, man. I really need to wash my hair . . . tomorrow."

"Me too."

"Actually, I need to *shower* . . . tomorrow. I haven't for three days. I've just been spot-cleaning my vagina after we have sex. Yyyep. That's what I'm working with over here."

"Well . . . Rome wasn't built in a day. I mean . . . you can't make a silk purse out of a sow's ear."

November dumped vitamins out of her jars. A robust collection of health supplements now existed in the corner of Benny's room. She swallowed more vitamins at once than he'd ever dreamt possible.

"Jesus," he said, watching her toss them into her mouth. "You're insane," he mumbled behind, descending the stairs.

On the ground floor, he found Wentworth emerging, slamming the bathroom door behind himself and banging around the living room.

"Subbing today?" he asked.

"Come closer, my child," said Wentworth.

"What?"

"Never mind. Yeah, at a *Cath*olic school. Should be especially corrupting."

"Hmmm. You think you can conceal your scorn—I mean *that* kind of scorn? *Catholic* scorn?—for seven hours?"

"Maybe I'll go in blackface."

"I'm not sure you have time for that. Don't they have to, like, burn charcoal and apply it with—"

"Well then I'll just decorate my little oxford. Do you think I have time to screenprint a picture of the virgin strapped-on, fucking a hole through the twin towers?"

"That . . . seems . . . hey," Benny interrupted himself, "did you hear, like, thumping or something last night?"

"Yeah. I forgot something in my trunk. Then it wouldn't open. Did I wake you?"

"Not exactly, I was . . . kind of up already."

"Gettin' 'at pusssssssayyyyy. How is the puss, by the way?"

"Uhhhhh," Benny hesitated.

"D'you guys head on down to the ol' Murder Burger for some grub and then come back and raid the ol' meat drawer?" He was now elbowing Benny. "Eh?"

"You're funny. I think it's actually 'Smash Burger,' though. Just in case you're, you know, ever allowed back in any high class academic circles again or anything, I wouldn't want you—"

"Ah, yes, thank you. Yes, yes, of course: 'Smash Burger.'" He made a masturbatory gesture as he said it. Following this was an extremely showy fart noise. "Meat Ruckus. Kill Floor. Whatever. As I was saying, I once laid this old bird . . . ." Here, he trailed off in reverie. "Her vagina was so hairy," he shook his head. "It was like . . . carpet." For some reason, he seemed very pleased with this description.

"Berber?"

"As it happens, my dear boy—hm, is that the one with the loops?"

"Yeah, well . . . yeah."

"Yeah, pretty much. Hers like that? Is it toothed?" returning to his initial inquiry.

"What?" Benny laughed.

"You know . . . like the myth?"

"What?"

". . . of the toothed vagina."

"The myth of the *toothed vagina?*"

"Yeah!" Wentworth was getting excited. "The vagina that is full of shaaaarp teeth, and *no* man can make his way through the teeth—or they just basically don't like the way the cooter feels—but then the hero, one fine dude, just *deals* with it and gets the old bag pregnant."

"Ummm, I had not heard of that, no."

"Welp. There you go."

"Huh." Benny looked sideways at Wentworth. "Is that a toothpick?"

"Oh, this? This is a chicken bone, with which I am picking from my teeth a few young morsels of veal. Had a little hillybilly surf and turf last night. Or . . . just turf and turf, I guess."

Benny looked up the stairs, hoping November was hearing none of this. He didn't have time to mediate a confrontation right now. He figured she'd abide vagina inquiries, if necessary, but knew she was in no way okay with flippant jokes about carnism.

"So what are you doing today, you bawdy rascal?" Wentworth asked, digging the chicken bone into the crevices of his teeth.

"Eh. Class, library."

"Fag."

• • •

"Oh, man . . . I kinda have to poop," Benny announced before he'd even reached the top of the stairs. "I have a poop in my butt," he said, smiling at November as he entered the bedroom, "but . . . shit, I'm gonna be late for class. Should I do it? It's right at that point. Right in between. I need to wait, probably. Otherwise I'm gonna be forcing it out. And that's no good for people." He gazed at her. "Should I just . . . go? Will it recede?"

"Never hold your excrement."

"But is it better to hold it or force it, if one is imminent and must be chosen?"

"Stick your fingers up there, and see if you can loosen it."

"Dammit, be serious. You think a coupl'a fingers are gonna have any effect on this old warhole?"

• • •

Entering the classroom, Wentworth overheard two students chattering frantically about a note, one needing the other to write and sign the note so that the he might be "excused" for his absence the previous day—all this so that he would be eligible to make up the algebra quiz he'd missed.

"Oh, Jesus. I think I just threw up a little bit in my mouth, you . . . *wimp*led *mea*sles. Just write the fucking thing. It doesn't matter. What do those withered *hags* in the office care about the authenticity of your little pukings?" he said as he strolled past. "Oh, I can tell you. They don't care a *horse* ball," he continued, making eye contact now. "They just need a note. It could say you were raping *mon*gooses . . . mongooses? Mongeese? Huh." He tossed his grimy backpack on the desk and turned to smash a giant mosquito, smearing blood against the wall.

"Welp. Good. So what are we doing today, you . . . muzzled clones?"

"Ummm, are *you* the *sub*?"

"I'd like to expand your . . . mind and answer your question with one of my own, but first let me wipe a kind of stink on it, to ensure your comprehension, little one." Wentworth made a slackjawed, sleepy-eyed face at the brave girl. Then he walked over to the window. "There is no God."

"Hah. *We know*," she returned. A few in the room laughed at this.

"Good," Wentworth continued, unfazed, "we can all get started, then. And, yes, dear one, I'm the sub." He picked up the teacher's notes from the desk and glared at them. "Says here that you are giving presentations at the moment. You are 'assessing one another's presentations,' and you 'know what to do.' And here's the schedule. Fantastic." He dragged his backpack off the desk and eyed the list of names. "Fawndella? Is that . . . is *Fawndella* present?"

"Yes," came the searing reply from the fourth desk back near the left corner.

"Great. Would you like to take a moment to gather your stuffing and wit before you present?"

Fawndella frowned at him. He'd begun to clip his nails.

"Is that a . . . 'no'?" The clicking sound of catapulting fingernails filled the room.

"What. *E*vah."

"Ohhhkay. Won't you rise then, young Della, and address us?"

...

On his way to the university, Benny passed the giant tree with all the crows. Anxiously, they watched him ride by. Then they pooped, almost simultaneously, as he rode away. Parking his bike at the library, Benny noticed a black bra hanging from a low branch of the cherry blossom tree beside the bike rack. He spent the remainder of the day doing research for his paper on Faulkner, and he easily, perhaps too easily, forgot about the sweet-smelling bras of the morning.

...

"Wait, I'm sorry, did you just say that during the civil rights movement Richard Pryor was the Secretary of State? And Aretha Franklin was the First Lady?"

"That's what it said," Fawndella replied indignantly.

"That's what *what* said?" Wentworth inquired. She rolled her eyes to hide her embarrassment. "Okay, have a seat, please," he motioned disdainfully, as though instructing a servant to remove an inadequate croissant.

Fawndella sneered, sucked teeth at him, and returned to her desk.

"You can try again tomorrow, when Mrs. Toler returns." Wentworth shook his head slowly for a long minute, chuckling intermittently, then finally filled the silence with instruction: "'Chocolate City' is not a proper academic source." He sighed. "To utter this clause is a kind of sweetness that I don't think was ever intended for the hominid experience. I feel faint."

They stared expectantly at him.

"Just . . . ugh, read. Or converse amongst yourselves if you like. But I don't want to hear your words. *Do not* let me hear your *words*. Or we'll get back to work."

Cunted Seitan Piss Flaps in Hairy Kiwi Jambalaya (Mushroom Gumbo)

- 1 large onion chopped
- 6 carrots chopped
- 2 lbs. seitan filleted
- 1 red pepper sliced
- 1 green pepper sliced
- 4 cloves garlic finely chopped
- 1 handful of chives chopped
- 1 lb. shiitake mushrooms
- 1 bunch of kale chopped/destemmed
- 12 oz. bean sprouts
- Ginger (about one thumb's worth, finely chopped)
- 1 tsp. red pepper
- 1 tsp. white pepper
- 1 tblsp. ginger (ground)
- 1 tblsp. garlic salt
- ½ cup Braggs or soy sauce
- 1 cup red wine
- 1 stick of butter

Allow a few minutes between each step:

1. Season seitan w/ white pepper and garlic salt.
2. Fry olive oil, onions, seitan, and carrots at medium heat in a pan.
3. Add dry spices.
4. Mix in green and red peppers.
5. Add stick of butter imposter.
6. Add mushrooms.
7. Add kale, soy sauce, red wine, garlic and bean sprouts.
8. Add chives.

...

Hey, remember how I mentioned that bisexual broad with the Kierkegaard-related namesake? The one Benny spoke with about love and trust and Orion's penis? Well, Benny had just explained to November his friendship with her (Regine) and their monthly vegan dinner parties with Food Not Bombs, the local "anarchist" "organization" that "cooked" for and "served" "food" to the "homeless."

"Threesome? You think she'd be interested?" November joked.

"Hah. Maybe. I don't know."

"Well, actually, I don't think you're the right person for a threesome, anyway. I mean . . . sorry," she laughed, paused, and continued with some concern, "I guess I don't always think about what I say before I say it."

"Eh. You usually do, I'd say."

"Yeah."

"But umm . . . huh, honestly, that doesn't bother me. You don't have to be sorry. To start with, that's just, like, your opinion, man. Aaaaand I might agree with you, anyway. I haven't really thought about it."

"I didn't really mean it in a bad way. I guess I just expect a man to take it as a bad thing."

"I could see that. Depends on the type of threesome, though, I would say."

"Well, I'm definitely too selfish for a threesome with two girls and one guy," she said, attempting to lighten a melancholic mood she felt slowly approaching. "The guy would naturally end up being the focus, and that would suck."

"Right. Well, I guess that makes sense. It's like having two . . . pieces of bread and one jar of peanut butter. It's like having two pieces of bread and one—"

"Penis."

"Hah. Yep. It's like having, well, two *pairs*, I suppose, two pairs of warm, soggy flaps of bread and . . . I don't know, actually. I didn't really think that through."

"Hm. Yeah. When do you think you'll be back?"

"Not late. Eleven or something."

"All right. God, is the odd one around tonight?"

"I'm not sure that narrows it down sufficiently, but I'm guessing you mean the wolf."

"Ugh. Yeah. I mean him. He's not really a wolf, to me though. Maybe a bear. Big and greasy and gross and . . . well, white though."

"Polar bears are white."

"Yeah, but they seem kind of nice. The other ones are the ones I don't like as much."

"Hm."

"Yeah. I assume that everything I just said is false."

"Me too, yeah. You know, I'm not actually sure if he'll even be there. But you never leave that room, anyway. Just stockpile some tortilla chips and toilet paper. You'll be okay."

"How sweet."

"Hahaaa. Just kidding.

"Great."

"Oh! Have you ever heard of the toothed vagina myth?"

"What?"

"Oh man, I'll have to tell you about it later."

"Ummm . . . okay?"

. . .

Benny and Regine had a phone conversation later that evening before she picked him up. I would like us to join it, already somewhat in progress, i.e., Benny opening the toilet lid to find a pile of turds, then falling silent for an annoyed moment, and finally sharing the soundscape with

Regine: from the initial bubbling ingression to the final strains of the commode's ex(ha/ul)l(t)ation.

"Am I interrupting?"

"Well, I was gonna poop, but it looks like someone beat me to it."

"I . . . *see.*"

"Ahh, full moon," he said, looking out the bathroom window, settling down to poo.

"Yes. Very nice."

"Yeah." He could feel that his bowels were about to move.

"How's it lookin'?"

"Really good." He purposed his anus to muffle what he could.

"Orange?"

"Not really."

"Like an . . . orange-yellow?"

"Uhhh . . . ."

"Kind of like cheese?" she pursued.

"Well, what kind of cheese?"

"Maybe pepper-jack?"

"Pepper? What would be the pepper?

"I don't know. Just jack then?"

"Yeah, I guess so. Wait. You mean co-jack?"

"Uhhh, maybe."

"Yeah, I think you mean co-jack . . . if you're still thinking orange-yellow."

"I was."

"And you still are?"

"Yeah."

"Yeah. co-jack."

"Hm."

"Yeah."

"What's 'co-jack'?"

"Co-jack is a mix of—wait, how long have you lived in Ohio? How the fuck do you not know what co-jack is?"

"Are you gonna tell me?" she asked dryly.

"Jesus. It's a mix between colby and Monterey Jack . . . or is it pepper-jack . . . hm."

"Hm."

"Yeah . . . some sort of jack."

"Why is that necessary?"

"I don't know. It gets kind of orangey-yellow . . . a few white, wavy spots . . . kind of . . . like the moon."

"The what?"

"The moon."

"Yeah, like the moon. Okay. I mean, not really, but whatever. So how's it goin' with this new lady, eh? Must be pretty good. We been *wax*in' celestial for over thirty seconds now, and you haven't even made one cock joke. Or is that actually a *bad* sign?"

"Don't be jealous."

Regine sniggled off this absurdity with a horsey chortle, something I'd like to call a "chorffaw," but I'm making myself angry typing that word. And most of these other ones, too. If I weren't so bloody chicken-faced, I'd by now have rammed that knife stage left-right through neck-throat. But that. Is not. *My job*. Right now. That's some other Goddamned dog-rider's job. Goddammit.

"So that's why, eh? You've gotta newwwww lady, and you're too good to come and cook with us now?"

"You know, speaking of cheese and cooking and food, I rewarded myself this afternoon—I'm not sure what for—with some organic raw kombucha tea from the very overpriced Kent Co-op. The coop. If you will."

"Uh-huh," she said, broadcasting distinct dismissal of yet another tangential nullity, which, let's face it, was basically, heretofore, the prevailing consistency of their entire conversation.

"I also bought three avocados, rice milk, and, not co-jack, but Swiss cheese, for your information—though I did steer clear of the eight-dollar bread. And in the interest of full disclosure, I may have a piece of toilet paper stuck in my butthole. It seemed to tear a little . . . when I was wiping, so it's . . . kind of a . . . wild card."

"Uh-huh. So . . . grocery shopping? And wiping your butt? These activities are preventing you from hanging out?"

"Hah. Yeah yeah. Sorry. I've been busy, too though. You know . . . finals are coming up and everything, and it's actually—"

"Ohhhhkay. Ohhhhhkay."

"Yeah, I know. I don't know. I've been wanting to hang out, actually. It's . . . I don't know. It's been kinda crazy. And all . . . really fast."

"The *thing*?"

"Well, yeah. We just . . . I mean, she needed a place to stay and all, and it just sort of fit together, you know? But it's . . . ."

"Ohhhh shit."

"No. No, it's good. She's really great. She treats me so well, and she really gets my humor and stuff, mostly. It's just . . . I have this feeling when we're together. Like, she's pushing, and I'm sort of . . . standing still."

"Uh-huh."

"I . . . you know what I mean?"

"I think so. You think she's more into you than you are her?"

"I don't know. I don't like to put it that way, exactly . . . because I guess I'm not sure yet. But yeah. It seems that way, to me, right now, anyways."

"You should talk to her about that. You should do it right away, Huck."

"Yeah. I don't know though. I don't want to . . . I mean, I'm not sure what's happening exactly. I don't want to kill it before there's even a chance. You know?"

"Well, you're—"

"I mean it's hardly even been a month, and we're . . . I mean, *some* parts are going *really* well."

"Uh-huh. Well, I'm here now, so let's talk about it, you know, in the car, eh?" And she hung up.

"Sounds good," he said, emerging from the front door and approaching Regine's car.

He plopped into the passenger seat with more pomp than necessary. Regine made a snotty face and gestured for him to continue as she craned her neck to back out of the driveway.

"Ummm, yeah . . . where to start," he puzzled. "Hmm, how long has it been?"

"I don't know. A while."

"Yeah, well you know about November. Did you know we have a new roommate too?"

"Oooooh."

"Hah. Yep. Holy moly, what a . . . I don't know, really. He used to be my professor. I guess he was a student, too, a doctoral student. He was studying masculinity studies or something like that, and he"—Benny began to chuckle—"oh man, he had us reading this essay. It was about rape, but it was"—he trailed off, laughing again.

"Ummm, wow. I feel like . . . hm, okay, so you'rrrrrre living with *two* new people then."

"Yeah."

"Big changes."

"Yeah."

"And it sounds really complicated, from what I can tell: rape essays and new ladies."

"Complicated?"

"Well, at least from what you were saying on the phone."

"It's not. Really. I guess I just *let* it be that way. It wouldn't *have* to be that way. I could just accept it all and enjoy it and not expect more than . . . what I seem to end up with."

"Jesus, Huck, I don't think that's quite right. That sounds depressing as hell."

"Maybe. It's hard to know. Where's the baseline? I mean, when I'm alone, I want . . . to not be. And . . . I really didn't know this whole thing was so complicated already. Maybe I was just kind of suppressing it."

"As is your wont."

"As is my wont? You think? Really? Man, I feel like I'm an open book. No mysteries. Open to all."

"Well, shit. What do I know?"

"I just . . . ugh, who knows. What's on the menu tonight?"

"Open book, eh?"

"Yeah, yeah. Haven't you heard enough of this crap?"

"Hah. Yes. Thank fuck, we're finally done."

"Right? Ohhhehkay then, so what's for fucking dinner with these fruits?"

"I think they're doing something with seitan."

"Whoa, fancy!"

"Yeah, the co-op donated a ton that was about to go bad."

"So maybe a stir fry or some kind of barbecue?"

"Umm, I'm pretty sure it's going to be Asian . . . somehow. Maybe some soy sauce—"

"With some bean sprouts and—"

"Vagina beans."

"Hanging vasoyna-juiced . . . ."

"Bean strings . . . ."

"With cunted seitan nuggets."

Such was their hilarity, the way they made fun, improvising titular vulgarity for the bill of fare at Food Not Bombs.

"So why doesn't November come?"

"Oh, she's afraid she'll see her ex."

"At Food Not Bombs? Really?"

"Yeah. You know. It's a small town, and . . . blaaaaaah blaaah blah. She's really . . . it's weird, actually, now that I think of it. It's been a while, and she is still pretty concerned about even being seen in public with me. Well, I mean, not with me, just, she's concerned about her ex seeing us. She must've been pretty insane, that one."

"'She'? Really?" Regine nodded and made a thoughtful frowny face, which slowly gave way to a mischievous smile. "Hm."

"Yep. Yyyyyyep. Let's uhhhh . . . let's have it, then. What have you got for me?"

"Nothing, unfortunately. I'm spent."

. . .

"What the hell is that?" asked their elusive, and presently disgusted, roommate, Ned, as he passed Wentworth at the front door.

"Deer leg," Wentworth replied, as the screen door scraped against the burlap-sacked leg of deer in tow. "I saw someone hit a deer the other day. They said I could take it."

Bewildered and somewhat perturbed, Ned stood grimacing at the front door. "And you're bringing it in the house now?"

Wentworth ignored him, dragging it into the kitchen.

"And in the kitchen? Fuck that. Put it on the porch, at least."

"Jesus."

"And, shit, I hope . . . dammit," he sighed.

"What!?" Wentworth wailed.

"Well. Since you asked," he replied angrily rolling his eyes, "Benny's new girlfriend, who's basically living here now, as you might have *noticed*, is vegan."

"Uh-huh," Wentworth murmured. "And I'm *not*."

"Rrriiiiiiiight. No. You're not."

Ned watched as Wentworth pulled the sack out onto the cold back porch.

"How the fuck did you even . . . get that thing off?"

"That's what she said."

"Yes. Very clever. Thank you. How, *really*, did you detach that mangled leg from the body? Chainsaw?"

"Hatchet."

Ned's eyes flared widely as he turned and walked out the front door.

A few days later—basically skinned and smoked—it was standing up on a homemade vertical meat spit, as one sees in restaurants serving gyros. The hoof and a bit of fur peeked out conspicuously from below the canvas bag, which was just a bit too short for the leg.

Twice, Benny would stuff it into the kitchen's largest knee-level cupboard, and twice it would reappear, in plain view, on the shelf.

· · ·

November recognized that she had given up her natural right to interrogation, as she'd been invited, entreated even, to accompany him, and had declined. And this fact made Benny's return much pleasanter. She had been concerned though, as during a brief excursion to the kitchen, she had found his goldfish dead, floating atop the water in the little bowl. The news had not bothered Benny as much as November'd expected, though he was confused because he'd fed him (Brutus) consistently and had cared for him diligently. (Perhaps Brutus and Wentworth had had a fight.) Benny rather flippantly dismissed November's suggestions of funeral ceremonies for the fish, setting the bowl out on the back porch, claiming that they would get around to having some kind of wake, if she insisted.

He was now lounging contentedly in his room, basking in the procrastination phase that precedes the blitzkrieg at semester's end, and his dazed contentment was enhancing November's mood, as well.

"'From a married man I once received this epigram on strife' colon. Hm. Colon?" Benny inquired aloud. "Yes, a colon, that's right. 'It takes two to make an argument unless you have a wife.' Oscar Wilde."

November laughed.

"Good job, Oscar," Benny lauded.

"Oh, Oscar," she followed, fawning.

(Except this is not actually Oscar Wilde's quote.)

"You know," he said, "you make it hard to be misogynistic when you're so into it, yourself . . . bitch."

Such was the dialogue that flowed serenely between them until he remembered tomorrow's quiz, for which he'd not prepared. And after a bit of panic, he was pushing dutifully through the bawdy, imperious prose his Irish Lit professor had assigned. A contradiction, his mind and body, as he reclined, legs propped on the ottoman.

"Is someone?" she motioned toward the bathroom door.

"Oh, I think Uli is using it, but you could use the one downstairs."

"Uhhh? I'll just wait. That toilet downstairs is . . . ." Here, she tilted head and raised eyebrows with knowing concern. However consciously it may or may not have been, they had already begun to copy each other's expressions.

"Yeah, sorry. I think Wentworth's idea of cleaning is aiming his pee at the little bits of poop that stick on the toilet bowl."

"Ugh. How did I know that already. God, people are so gross sometimes. I don't know how . . . God, if she had a dick, that's how Blossie would have been." She wanted to laugh about this assertion, but it felt eerie, for a lot of reasons, not the least of which was the deer leg in the kitchen, which both angered and scared her—and, of course, there was Blossie's macabre plan for acquiring a penis.

For comfort, she approached and straddled Benny, a gesture which was nearly impossible for him to accept in a nonsexual way.

"I want to read a book that is easy to read, just to see if I actually read a little faster than I think I do . . . 'cause these have been pretty difficult."

She smiled at him.

"It's almost as bad as Joyce," he went on, "I mean, it's been compared to Joyce, anyway. Joyce blurbed it. He liked it, apparently. Blurbs are bullshit, I guess, but . . . you know. Close enough." He returned her smirk. Then the heater went off, and they sat in such silence that he could hear the noise of his penis brushing against the fabric of his pants with each kegel he squeezed.

"Yeah," she answered. "I think when you've already read—"

He stopped listening for meaning and began listening for rhythm, poking her thin, green-sweatshirted arm with his pink pen, exactly echoing the cadence of her syllables.

There was a pause.

"Then you can finally garner some meaning," she added. "Finally garner some meaning," he poked. "And notice the patterns," she summed up, looking down at her arm, feeling, by now, the familiar echoing rhythms and, in turn, glaring at him with playful death.

He felt the opportunity: a space for saying almost anything, not to be taken entirely seriously, having earned a bit of buoyancy in her reception. So, with a subtle smirk and some sincerity, he told her that she was the big bird, full of all the other birds: a sensual contradiction, his countenance and voice.

She interpreted his remark according to her present fancy, and they began to kiss, and then we panned away tastefully to the window, which was spattered with inert drops of rain, each reflecting a different color of the mnemonic spectral acronym that high school kids memorize as "ROY G BIV."

. . .

"So, wait . . . the *hero* got her pregnant? And no one else wants her because her vagina feels like there's teeth inside?"

She'd asked him about the myth shortly after they'd finished making love, and she was now reviewing the details.

"That's so sad. Am I like that?" she asked with sincere concern.

"What? Of course not." Benny was enjoying the smell of her breath, the steam in a sugar house.

"Are you sure?" she pouted.

"Awww, of course not. You're great."

She gazed dolefully at him. "Really?"

And then they started up again. And we panned away.

. . .

When we returned, she was cooing and babbling, imaginative and happy: "My ethereal soul is going to haunt you." She writhed slowly, stretching her legs under the covers. "And in the next life you'll be the girl and I'll be the boy, and we'll be childhood lovers. We'll grow up together." This is what she said, lying next to him atop the mattress that was now hers as much as his.

The comment's flip tone and the warmth of his sated body allayed, for him, his present lack of any thoughtful response or quip. He'd just finished tapping out some improvisational rhythms on her hip bone and had moved on now, pressing his lips into her chest, blowing into skin, making trumpet noises.

"Are you giving me a butterfly kiss right now?"

He moved upward gradually, cater-cornered on top of her now, his head buried in her neck. "Is that what this is called? I didn't know that," and, hearing the overly jaunty tone in his voice, he made a mental note to curb it.

"Want me to give you one . . . you know . . . butterfly kiss . . . your epigyne?"[20] he said, still too sillily. (If the adverb, "sillily," were an invertebrate animal, it would be a louse.) She grimaced and only slowly looked away, apathetically attempting to hide her sudden sadness.

"Eh?"

She turned away.

"Hey," he beckoned.

"No, it's just . . . this is going to sound awful, but . . . I'm like seal pups. People want me for my fur."

Benny smiled guiltily as he thought about the relationship between berber and fur. "Aww," he said after a few silent moments, but he didn't move. He listened, expecting to hear crying.

---

20   By their errant definition, this might have caused an embolism.

Finally, she turned to him and lay her cheek on his chest.
He stroked her head.

...

The next morning, in search of new sheets, they stumbled flirtatiously to
the linen closet in the hall just outside Benny's bedroom. Benny knelt,
pulled out an old quilt from the bottom shelf, and was nearly smacked
in the face by the mouse that shot out of the closet and scurried into
his room. November shrieked but quickly recovered and smiled. Then,
with telepathic synchrony—that is to say, shoulder to shoulder—they
began trying to extract the mouse from his room, disturbing things that
lay under dressers and bureaus. Finally, the mouse edged quickly to the
door and sprang toward the stairs, skipping eight or nine of them in its
flight, landing and sort of bouncing down the last few, then recovering
to round the corner with cartoon quickness.

Later that day, November bought humane mouse traps designed
for catch-and-release. She set them up in each room, baiting them with
bread and peanut butter.

Wentworth must have noticed this because, to their jubilant and
thorough astonishment, his greasy erection of venison was back under
the cupboard the next day (draped higgledy-piggledily in plastic wrap).

Soon, there were large spring-loaded mouse traps next to each of
November's humane traps. She promptly threw them out and scoured
the house to ensure none remained. Wentworth responded, doing the
same. And in the adamant months to follow, the two battled expen-
sively over the life of the mouse, who appeared at various intervals, and
seemed too smart for either of them.

Basil-Cummed Vegan Cock Vomit (P[e/i]s(/s)to(/w))

Puree the following ingredients in a blender.

- 1 avocado
- 1 cup of fresh basil
- 4 cups of fresh parsley
- 1 cup pine nuts
- 1 cup of spinach
- 1 cup of garlic mustard
- 4 cloves of garlic
- ½ cup of olive oil
- ¼ cup lemon juice
- ¼ cup miso
- Salt and pepper to taste

...

It had taken her a long time to find something appropriately hidden from public view, but November had finally gotten another job. She'd accepted a position at a bakery a few miles out of town.

On the morning of her first day, she saw a bunny on Aurora Road. The bunny was resting near the shoulder of the road before it scurried quickly across the ditch and turned around to face her as she drove by. November felt her stomach stretch, as though pulled from octogonal angles. The bunny was too small. Winter was setting in; it would not survive.

She switched on her flashers and stopped on the roadside, trying to lure the bunny into her car with a trail of broken baby-cut carrots, and ended up pursuing the animal for longer than, in hindsight, it should have taken her to realize that a human cannot bare-handedly capture a wild bunny. Twenty minutes passed before she finally ran back to the car and continued toward the bakery, trying on various excuses for her tardiness. They would understand.

No, they wouldn't. Shit. She drove around trying, unsuccessfully to concoct new excuses and, ultimately, decided to call in sick. Twenty-two words into this phone conversation, she was fired.

On the way home, she returned to the bunny sighting and re-traced the trail of carrots she'd left, dumping the rest of the bag there in one spot. Cautiously heartened to note that some had been eaten, she picked up a few of the newly-dumped carrot nubs and chomped them into more manageable, half-sized pieces then let them fall out of her mouth back onto the cold grass. The sensation recalled her own hunger, and, feeling just a bit silly now, she decided to depart, in pursuit of a consolation snack—hell of a morning this. She called Benny, too, and ended up talking about her dream the previous night.

"It was in a church with a few trees inside. It was my grampa's funeral. My mom and dad walked up to the coffin together, even though they weren't 'together.' Mom'd gotten her hair cut, and her new boy-friend was a little jealous of the whole arrangement. Made a comment about her getting her haircut 'for Voltaire' or something. I didn't know what that meant, but I knew he was jealous. I was surprised to hear my uncle laugh. Then halfway back from viewing the coffin, my parents decided to race down the aisle back to their adjacent pews.

"Somehow, I was chosen to say a few words. I was telling a sto-ry about my station in Warcraft. I am part of the blah blah blah clan —many details here. It was a tangent, yes. But I thought the journey would be worth it. I had a point, I remember, which is really weird because I don't play Warcraft. And I almost never have a point." She squeezed the steering wheel, wishing Benny would laugh more audibly.

"A miniature explosive train was sent in to try to blow me off the line I was standing on. But I managed to hang on, barely. Next, a squir-rel was sent in. It smashed through the window and stared me down. But there was a tree between us and it didn't know which side of the tree to look at me from. I moved to the other side, using the tree as a block between us. I'd been telling a story about sex with my ex-girlfriend, so when it said 'this is a sin,' it had kind of a double meaning. Then it rose dramatically on its back two legs and leveled a charge. I swiped it away at the last second. Then it rose again and gathered once more. The little hound from hell. I kicked it before it could charge again. And I felt sorry about doing that. Because it was lying in the grass, looking a little injured, but trying to pretend I hadn't hurt it."

Benny had been pretending to listen. But it seemed to him that she was not paying much attention to whether or not he was listening. Perhaps the telling was something more.

"I don't know," she continued, "I guess it's just . . . this stuff . . . death and animals and all, it's . . . well, the more we talk about this or the more *I* talk about this, the more I think about it, I mean, the more I realize that I have to do whatever I can to make my life—oh, *here's* the Walmart—to make my life beautiful and meaningful."

The next day she began again looking for jobs and was happily shocked to find that a greenhouse in Streetsboro was looking for help. November boasted years of greenhouse experience (and knew that if she got the job she would be laid off during the winter, which would mean risking public appearance for only a very short time in a place that Blossie was highly unlikely to enter). So, yeah, they hired her, and in two smoothly passing holiday months, she would be laid off.

Comprising the bulk, if you will, of her duties was more heavy lifting than she had anticipated. But she endured it, gazing diligently at the prize of winter unemployment pay. A sweet, effeminate coworker named Rammford Llama helped her through, distracting her with the exact decorative commentary she'd subconsciously sought:

"Oh, honey, don't call it a 'vase.' Don't ever call it a 'vase.' You'll kill the flowers that way. *Al*ways . . . call it a 'vozz,' dear."

• • •

On December 2nd, it was almost sixty degrees. A live ladybug was found on the carpet. What to do. Does it want to die inside or outside? Because, either way, it will probably die. And to say that we should not "interfere," well, it's a bit late to say something like that.

Benny graduated on December 14th and registered promptly as a substitute teacher with the Portage County Department of Education.

He and November celebrated New Year's Eve by themselves, drinking Kriek Lambic, making pesto and making out—less fervidly than they had in the fall. November got way too drunk and then nauseated; she spoke to herself, while Benny encouraged her to puke.

"I could throw up to the world. I could throw up to animals. I could throw up to people," as though toasting. But when she put her finger deep into her throat, nothing happened.

...

Morning was achy and thick with the yoke of a new year looming. They cycled through unfinished art projects. Benny pooped.

"You know what the worst thing about winter is?"

"Yes. I know a lot of them. Well, no," she sighed, "not really."

"Ice cold toilet seats. Frigid fucking haunches. Dread of poo."

"You should never dread a poo."

"That's my favorite sentence of the day," he said, noting her disconsolation.

She didn't answer.

"God. 'Never dread a poo.' I love that. Hey. You remember how you tried to throw up last night? But you couldn't? That was hot."

Still, no answer. They were eating what was left of the spectacular collection of chips and crackers and dips that had accumulated in Benny's room the previous night.

"You know . . . because your finger was way down your throat. Aaaand . . . " He looked over his shoulder at her: not even a physical acknowledgment. He adjusted. "What are you working on?"

Moments later, still lacking a response, he arose and approached her at the desk.

"I was painting these envelopes," she said finally. "They're letters to my dad that I never mailed. I colored them in crayon then painted over them. It looks like water, kind of."

"Those are nice."

"Thanks. Some of them are from when I was a kid. They look kind of stupid, but . . . " she sighed. "It doesn't matter."

"No, they're nice." He bent down and noticed something in the box beside her. "I like this," he said, pointing to it.

"Oh, I did that when I was in high school. I'll probably never fill in the other eye."

"I like it like that," he said.

"Yeah." She picked it up. It was painted on a flat, oval rock. The background was red. The face rectangular with soft edges. Two black eyebrows were buttressed by huge black eyelashes: six on the right, which was the eyeless side, and seven on the left. The eyes were each lined with gold paint, which was also her choice for the lines of the thin nose and mouth. Two red dimple-dots accented the cheeks, and a pointed red "V" served to designate the chin. Gold crescent moons, each pointing outward, adorned the doll's red chest.

"You're supposed to fill in the other eye when your wish comes true or when you fulfill your goal, or something. I don't remember, really. Then in the meantime, it reminds you of the thing you want, the important thing in your life. God, yeah, I don't remember. Do you know these?" she asked, allowing herself to peek into his eyes for a moment.

"No."

"They're daruma dolls. I might not even be saying it right, but I really liked them when I was, like, fifteen. Hah."

"Hm. I like the textures. In your doodles. Can I say that? 'The texture in your doodle'? Too soon?"

November sighed.

Growing disconcerted, Benny maintained a casual tone: "This one is nice, too," he offered, feigning interest in the envelopes she was coloring.

Staring through the ragged carpet, breathing very slowly, she allowed a single tear to fall down her cheek. "He's never visited me. He's never even . . . God, I don't know. Why would I . . . I only even know his address because of the letters. Probably not even the same anymore. I'm sure it's not. Who knows." It seemed to Benny that the bitterness in her voice was an act. She was too tender, and so rather than fall into anguish, she allowed these gravitations toward anger.

"The daruma doll, God, it's so stupid. There was this van, when I was in high school, this super old Volkswagen van I . . . I was gonna buy it and drive to California and find him. Well, I mean, not really *find* him. I had an address, I guess. It's been the same one for a long time, and it was then, too. I don't know." She looked at him, waiting for a sign that she should continue. He signaled such with a gently inquisitive eyebrow posture.

"I don't know," she sighed with little emphasis. "Maybe we should just eat food or something. You know. Like, *real* food."

"That's a good idea!" he said excitedly, failing to coax further cathartic explanations from her. "I have stuff. I got stuff you asked for. I have—oh, but shit. They didn't have tofu. I was pretty shocked, actually."

"You got veggie stuff for me?"

"Yeah! Well, kind of. I don't know," he said, feeling strangely concerned that he'd done too much. "At least some vegetables, and I got almond milk. I don't think that fake meat crap is worth buying though. I hope you don't mind. Aaaand I got the organic coffee beans."

"What? Oh, c'mon, it's too late for that."

It was already almost seven o'clock, and both had been quite thoroughly conditioned to feel guilty for having been awake so long without once Calvinistically justifying their respective God-given rights to exist.

"No, I got decaf. Mmmm," he vibrated, as he opened the bag, lowered his nose to it, and pushed his hand inside, feeling the hard, smooth beans surround his fingers.

She raised her eyebrows and turned away.

"C'mon," he whined, "I thought it was gonna be a tradition." He pulled her onto the bed with him.

"Enemas . . . on New Year's Day," she said, trying to remain melancholic.

"It has such a nice ring to it. *C'mon*. It's decaf!" he said, shaking her. "Oh, man, some kind of scrambler . . . anything with fried potatoes and hot sauce sounds so amazing right now." He draped his legs over her. "Yeah, you like that. Oh my God, what is on your feet? It feels like a hemp table cloth."

"Those are my socks, you . . . dunce. You're getting weird again, aren't you."

"Which villains does your dad work for again, Citibank?"

"Chase or something, last I heard."

"Ah, right. Okay. So the socks—"

"Yeah. Every now and again he sends me some money, but it's not much, so I really don't think—"

"Soooo your feet are wrapped in corruption."

"No. Really—"

"And lies."

"Seriously, I don't talk to him. I actually *never* have." Here, she related the whole story, or, rather, the small part of the story her mom had told her, which was really just a vague implication of some arguing and perhaps unfaithfulness that ultimately caused their breakup. It seemed so pedestrian, so almost . . . normal, that she had always wondered why they weren't able to work it out. Or if they'd even tried.

• • •

It was the third time Uli awoke on the couch that day, and this time sober enough to feel a proper headache.

"I got wine all over myself last night," Wentworth said, hearing Benny finally descending the staircase—the first time all day.

"Not as bad as I did," Uli interjected in a sick stupor. "Plus, my pants smell like pee. I think I peed on myself quite a bit."

"I'm assuming this occurred one of the many times you *dolts* peed side-by-side in unison?" said Wentworth.

"Yeah, 'cause it wasn't me," Ned said, ignoring Wentworth. "I didn't take my penis out," he continued absently, staring at the Super Nintendo from the living room's tattered corner chair.

"And you did?" Benny asked Uli.

"I *think* I did."

Benny frowned, observing the three of them, surprised at what seemed like camaraderie.

"This woman is . . . Jesus, there are no words." Wentworth was sitting at the computer with an open package of lunch meat that was sweating onto the desk.

"What?"

"Fannie Zimmerman. Holy fuck. This lady, seventy-fucking-six years old, for fuck's sake, beat a fawn to death with a *shovel*. According to this report, witnesses heard the deer shrieking and bawling, and they witnessed the rest of it. Sounds like a real bloodbath. She told them she wanted to put it at the end of the yard so the other deer would know not to fuck with her."

"Holy fucking moly."

"Jesus."

"Hah. You said it, man." Wentworth whooped a cutting primal scream.

"Hm. Yeah. So maybe don't mention this to, uhhh, November," Benny said, flummoxed, his frown turned now toward the computer monitor.

"Uh-huh."

"That would . . . be a bad idea, I'm pretty sure." He'd finally gotten the persistent deer leg hidden and was keen on avoiding further agitation.

"Yyyyup. Sure thing, chief."

Benny stood over Wentworth, staring down at him.

"She stuffed the bloody body in a cardboard box and put it out at the end of her driveway for trash day!" Wentworth howled with laughter and finally looked up at Benny. "Que tal, Estebennn?"

"I just wanna make sure you know I'm serious about November."

"I think we'll manage, yeah," he said and looked back down at the computer screen. Then, through the living room window, a jogger caught his peripheral attention. "Jayyyzus crad-seffing *Chroist*! Have you noticed these mother*fuck*ing joggers on the streets lately? There's still half a foot of snow on the bloody roads for shit's sake! They are begging for it," he said, shaking his head and returning to the computer.

"Yeah, but the sidewalks are even worse. They're like knee-deep a lot—"

"Yeah! Fucking! What in the sam *fuck*! God forbid these turgid, cosmopolitan *fags* take a break for a few days when it snows!"

Similar sentiments were frequently hurled directly at those winter joggers, particularly those who dared perform contortions necessary for heel-clicking leaps purposed to wrest the snow from their shoes' undersides. The inherent logic of this canter-smack combo was yet unappreciated by men seated in a gray pickup, for example, with duct tape covering rust on the wheel well. Commonly issuing from a truck such as this would be, "Look at that fuckin' retard!" Did you know that?

• • •

"Yeah, yeah, I know, I know. You fuck-motherfucker. 'Deep in a green forest down by the sea, a hunter spied a little deer dancing.' At this point, the deer was in a sullen daze because of the fact that she was carrying, almost to full term, a little whore in her belly, and because everything in her life had turned to shit in the past few months. All bleak and brown. Many times, she'd considered ending it all, and it was only the lingering gooey mothering sentiments floating randomly about in her body that had stopped her.

"'All life is suffering,' she thought. Then she lay down in a little cage and started crying.

"The end."

He turned to her.

"Why are you itching your head so profusely? Dandruff? Hm. Perhaps you aren't actually aware of what dandruff is. Yeah. I get dandruff in the winter, too, sometimes. You know what you need to do? You need to scrub properly. You're probably not scrubbing properly. Perhaps I should demonstrate."

Slowly, he moved his fingertips to his scalp and shook his head violently. "Like this." Then he stopped, looked gravely at her, and sighed. "I'll show you."

He walked to the door, leered out into the empty hallway, and closed the door. Then he stood behind her. "Here," he said, from behind her desk, as he grabbed her forearms and pulled her hands to her head. "It should feel like this. About this pressure . . . is what you want to feel."

Then an epiphany. A tutorial on rinsing. "And you'll need to rinse the shampoo out reeeeeally well, you crusty . . ." he mumbled. "See? You'll need to rinse very thoroughly." He slid his fingers down her flaky scalp, ineptly simulating water falling. This went on for almost five more minutes. No one saw.

•••

During the spring semester—an optimistic misnomer at that Great-Lake latitude—November had begun coursework at Kent State. She took an anthropology class, a sociology class, an astronomy class. Lots of little classes that are typically called "liberal education requirements" or "general education requirements" or "core classes."

Wentworth's advice had been to take "'How to Suck Dirty Needledicks and Not Get Infected with Acquired Immune Deficiency Syndrome Even Though All Faggots Already Have Acquired Immune Deficiency Syndrome: (Subtitle) Giving Gay Blowjobs in a Post 9/11 World.'" He'd said at least this way, she'd be paying to learn profitable skills toward gainful employment.

In any case, I'll be typing with only my non-dominant hand for this section because I'm looking for a reply from my subconscious—Freud's "unconscious," but I think "subconscious" is more what he meant.

"The Native Americans claim, well, *some* . . . Native Americans, certain tribes, claim that one's dominant hand writes the conscious; the other hand writes the subconscious." She was sitting up against a pillow, covered by two large blankets and a quilt. "Oh, and oh my God! Listen to this!" She leaned over and picked up another book that had been resting atop the space heater. "This tribe we've been learning about? Oh, man. This is their inauguratory practice: They, like, sing a song, and . . .

okay, I'll just read this part. These are the lyrics to the song: 'Let me tell you the secret of the land. Your head is the land, and the hair that grows on your head is the brush that grows in the land. The hair does not own the head, and the brush does not own the land, although they are useful nonetheless. The elephant grass and the bermuda grass do not own the land either, though they are useful too. Let me tell you the secret of the land. Your navel is the land, and your penis grows up in the land. And it is your penis that owns the land and keeps the land.'" She thought of Blossie with a shudder and a giggle. What would have been her reaction to this song?

"They sing this to him, the women who install him in office as village leader. His penis is 'chief of the land.'" She used air quotes for this last phrase.

"Whoa."

"How great is that?"

"Just to be clear, my penis will now answer only to 'Chief of the Land.'"

November laughed with the righteous and secure giddiness that she was enjoying something which she was actually allowed—even supposed—to be enjoying. She gasped deeply and fully through this restorative laughter. And she read on. "Oh my God. It gets better though."

"Ummm?"

"'Territorial Chief Chadza Kwenda and his Anamkhungwi'—these are the female spiritual leaders or leader, I'm not sure if it's plural—'confirmed what the song suggests, that the chief's head, hair, and penis are crucially implicated in weather patterns. He must carry a clod of earth whenever he leaves his territory, lest the rain go with him. He must have sex to initiate the rainy season and lead an active sex life through the rainy season to maintain the rainfall. And after his death, his skull may well end up in the village courtyard to ensure that the seed returns to the soil and the rain returns to the land.'"

"This is amazing. What the hell is that?" he asked, snuggling up to her cocooned torso.

"It's from this article called 'A Chewa Cosmology of the Body,' by Deborah Kaspin."

"Fucking *rad*. Implicated in weather patterns? *That* is respect. Must be *some kin*da wang."

"You *would* think that." She stared back down at the article. "My God, but the one I was reading for tomorrow is just as amazing: 'Fish is an important part of the angami diet, and people often have fish bones stuck in their throat. An expert in extracting them is called *khorma bie-kelie-mia.* The term refers to the method by which the power is acquired and what it entails; *khora* is a river otter; *bie-kelie* means 'to touch lightly' and *mia* is 'person.' So the term means 'one who has acquired the light touch by killing an otter.' It is believed that anyone able to kill a river otter by biting its neck, without the use of any weapon, would acquire the power to alleviate suffering caused by fish bones or bones of any animal which may get stuck in the throat of a person.'"

"Holy hell. What a crazy . . . well, I guess it actually makes as much sense as most of what we believe. A lot of it, anyway."[21]

"That's actually sort of what our professor has been saying, or maybe just hinting at. That these customs and the faith they have in them, it's really not any crazier than a lot of ours, but it just seems that way because they're so new and unknown. Or new to *us*. I mean, that's a shitty paraphrase, but, yeah, you know what I mean."

"Definitely. It's like what you were saying about animals the other night. Some of them have this privileged status in our culture. They can be 'abused.' And then the abuse of *others* is built into the system and even rewarded monetarily. Like that guy who went to jail for shooting a cow in the head? We *pay* people to do that shit. It's a *job* for fuck's sake! Man, Wentw . . . yeah, I don't know. It's so crazy."

"Yeah. Like, why is it somehow okay—I mean, why are dogs' rights more important than pigs'? Or raccoons'? I guess, well, you've heard me go on about this already."

---

21   from "Human and spiritual agency in Angami healing" by Joshi, V.

"No, I understand. But, yeah, you already know I agree."

"God, I am *really* glad. I don't think I could ever be with someone who doesn't get that. Blossie . . . Jesus. She would go on and on about gender issues and feminist theory, which I totally support and think is important, but then she would completely scoff when I would bring nonhuman animals into the discussion. She never understood how inextricable those two different . . . kinds of hegemony are."

"Sheesh, man. You're talkin' some smack tonight. What are we, on NPR?"

She raised her eyebrows in reply.

"Juuuuuust kidding. I think it's really interesting. Real talk. I never really made the connection until you mentioned it, actually, but it's true. And also, hey, it's late. Get back to work."

"Ugh, shit, you're right."

"But first, wanna help me perform a joke?" he asked, nuzzling into her cheek then kissing her forehead.

"Sure." She gave him a theatrically quizzical look; then they fist-bumped, a celebratory salute to the double entendre in his inquiry.

"Okay, you answer my question, saying, 'that's not funny.'"

"Okay."

"How many feminists does it take to screw in a light bulb?"

"That's not funny."

Then they fist-bumped. And he called her a bitch.

Get it? Yeah, I'm not sure either.

"Holy fuck," she exclaimed ten minutes later. "This might almost be better. The Andean X-ray, courtesy of Edmundo Morales: 'In the Andes, the patient is charged with providing alcohol (chicha)—particularly those derived from maize—and cocaine (coca) for the doctor to ingest and chew prior to the examination so that they do not make an error in their diagnosis.'"

"Oh, yeah. Sometimes your mom asks me to . . . never mind."

"'Before and after the ritual,'" she continued, "'they spray the patient with alcohol and or a perfumed water. The doctor rubs the guinea pig

(cuy) against the patient's body—the guinea pig usually dies in this pro-
cess' (because it absorbs the patient's illness, like Jesus absorbing the sin
of the world)'—then skins and dissects the guinea pig so as to diagnose
the patient's illness, based on the appearance (smell) of the guinea pig's
entrails.'"

"Weird. I'm pretty surprised you're not crying out of your vagina
about this rodent slaughter. Look at you; you're almost even smiling.
Who the hell are you?!"

"It's also necessary," she said, looking at him now—it was hard to
tell if this part was verbatim or paraphrased—"sometimes for the pig
to spend a few hours under the armpit of the patient in order to cure
epidemics."

"Before or after it's dead?"

"Ummm." She looked back down. "It doesn't really say. It does,
however, note that they drop off the now sick animal to a place where
. . . children play? So that someone can take the cuy home with them?
Because the sickness goes with the animal? What the fuck? Why would
they do that?"

Benny was in awe of the situation. He had made tamer *jokes* than
this, and she had not approved. This was real life she was reading about!
He decided to just enjoy this queer abidance.

"Oh, shit!" she continued, "'List of diagnostic signs manifest in the
guinea pig:

"'Cold: a white, thin film covers the back.

"'Bronchitis: a white, thin film covers the back and there are fine
lines of blood, like broken veins.

"'Sore throat: clotted blood in the neck.

"'Diarrhea caused by cold and colic: intestines have air bubbles and
feces are sparse.

"'Diarrhea caused by irritation: intestines are dark red or purple.

"'Intestinal fever: red, bloody intestines.

"'Susto (fright): the carcass put in fresh water trembles; shiny, whit-
ish and glassy bowels.

"'Witchery: yellowish eruptions in the neck that, when poked, look like pus."

"Ummm?" he managed, through a silly giggle, "Is that a reference tooooo . . . the *patient* or the guinea pig? The witchcraft, I mean."

"Let's call it magic. Witchcraft sounds so gendered to me."

"I've got some magic for that pork sponge of yours . . . down there," he pointed.

She squinted at him, implying a mixture of pity and disdain.

"Hoisting the dragon of Glumbury . . ." she turned away as he continued, "breathing fire into . . . your . . . you know . . . lateral vetiver-gina . . . or . . . you know."

"Uh-huh. Hey, apropos your glum dragon, look at this picture of me. Here." Two or three people wore (or supported, rather) a monstrous and indistinguishably shiny costume. "Right there," she pointed. "I'm the dragon's ass."

"Yes. I suppose you are," he mumbled from the side of his mouth in an operatic tone. "'Dragon's ass.' Is that some kind of gay, theatrical version of 'bee's knees'?"

She glared at him.

"Because *actually*," he droned, "'bee's knees' is already saturated. With gayness, I mean. Have you ever seen two snakes? If you have, you know what I mean. Insomuch as . . . I mean with respect to gayness, you know. As in 'gay.' That is to say, 'gayer than a snake.'"

She arose and began to walk away. He followed, continuing, "And the reason I asked you about the *two* snakes is because the phrase I need for 'bee's knees' is 'gayer than two snakes.' I know. It's a lot of work in the explanation. But I enjoy it."

"Uh-huh. We all do."

"So, what I mean is . . . if this is the level of gayness you're searching for with 'dragon's ass,' you guys could just go on with 'bee's knees.'"

. . .

Fuck more words,
you clapping dunce-
hole. Your ple(a)beian
carnation. Push
into this magic rape
of milk. It gets
boring. Otherwise.
Nothing to say
to your controlled
area. Your sea
quest. Turd. Face
of privilege. Giving
in. Sparkles. A salt—
and buttery—bath
for glassy two-way
poblanos. Quipping.
In your deal. With it.
This picture of penis

is more or less a description of the progress of Wentworth's cur-
rent debacle. P(l)aying at first. Then withholding. And, finally, like the
joke:

I have a friend who has been married for almost ten years now. And
for the purposes of . . . whatever, he is bored, as you might have quickly
projected from the round, cliché number: *ten* years. His marriage, his
little life, feels sterile and stale. With particular emphasis on his little
fucklife, which is steady and unsatisfying—despite insertions of toys
into alternate orifices, and all that. He's distempered and, entirely dis-
possessed of such thrills in a "natural" domestic setting, he arrives at the
desperate conclusion that he can and will buy one. A thrill.

Drug people tell him where. His dealer says the place. He writes
it down. Goes. Gets there. The building is boxy, machined, not as he
expected: sage carpet, lavender walls, clean in a gross way.

"I need something crazy," he blurts, addressing the woman who is holding a glass into which ice is falling from the dispenser of a refrigerator that sits precariously on the thick carpet of the uneven floor in what is loosely referred to as the building's lobby.

"Uh-huh." She catches her eye-roll halfway in and recovers, pretending to thoughtfully consider my friend's request. She already knows who'll deal with this. "Okay, baby. Come on," she says, leading him up the steps.

She knocks on a door midway down the hall. "Joy, you busy?"

"Nope!"

She opens the door, gestures, and closes it behind him. Joy is sitting at the edge of the bed playing Super Mario Kart. "So . . ." she says, not yet finished with her race, "What's your name?" She is surprisingly cute and nonabrasive.

"Umm, Joe," he falters, clearly lying.

"Hah. Okay," she says glancing at him with a coy smile, as Luigi coasts past the checkered flag. "Nice to meet you, Joe."

"You, too," he says stiffly, making a mental note not to lose his nerve.

As if sensing this, she motions him to her and pulls off her shirt. Her nipples point outward at two strikingly different angles.

He holds on, pushing away moralistic thoughts, and squeezes one of her breasts, while she slides her warm fingers under the waste of his pants, just enough to serve her in the unbuckling procedure.

"Mmmm," she says, fondling him.

He looks at the wall behind her, determined that he will not let this end with a tepid blowjob. He is about to tell her so, when she stops, looks up at him, and pulls out her eye from her head. "You ready to get crazy?" she asks.

And they do.

He fucks her eyehole, that is, delicately, at first, but gradually with greater confidence and increasing abandon, surprised at her stoicism, surprised that this is even possible, wondering for a moment about whiplash.

After a time, he concludes.

"Oh my God," he falls on the couch, gasping and sighing deeply. "Yeah. That was . . . what the hell? Perfect."

"Well, I'm glad to hear that, Joe."

"Oh my God. Yeah. Can we do that again?"

"Yes. That's what we do here."

"Sooo glad to hear that. Mmh! I will be back soon. Very soon."

"Okay, Joe. I'll keep my eye out for ya."

Like that joke.

Except, with Wentworth, it had degenerated further. At first, it was just slapping asses with a little too much fervor. Then it progressed to pushing his fingers into them—all nature of them—in a plainly insensitive manner. He did all these things experimentally and detachedly. Only in jest. Often without erection. And when he advanced deeper shenanigans, he did so in this same spirit, assfucking the prostitute without permission then punching and elbowing her in the back of the head until she shivered with spasm and passed out. He'd do it right this time though, he thought: keep her quiet through the night, at least. And, as he pulled his belt tightly between her teeth and around the braid he'd grabbed onto before bashing her head, he chuckled at his conscience, so dependent on tradition, so normalized, muttering some hopeful notion of morality. Tantamount with efficiency and power, he thought, as he wrapped duct tape around her mouth. Tantamount with pleasure for those who will take it. Raskolnikov was right. (But he hadn't actually finished *Crime and Punishment*.) He felt sickened and satisfied, grave and whimsical, as he sneaked her out of the motel room and nervously frolicked to his car to dump her in his trunk. Only a gag.

· · ·

On the dark side of the street, the church sign read, "We love hurting people."

●●●

So then, for those seeking an update, a suicidal, meandersome neologist has crocheted a hacky sack tapestry—or at least a doily—in which a love story has been outlined (if not developed), and an appropriate villain or two seem to lurk. (Really though, narrative/identity just sustains the illusion of separation. Better, then, if you must, to sing nonsense than write a novel. Better not to notice than to smush a bug on your screen.)

●●●

Artifacts in museums, artifacts out of context, at a museum. Tools, etc. Framing them in glass. Cultural curiosities. Insensitivities. Anthropologies. This was the discussion she was having, mostly with herself. Benny listened mischievously.

"Yeah. Like this knife?" He'd been whipping out his new pocket knife in nearly every room they entered.

"Any excuse to get it out," she rolled her eyes. "Instigator."

"You're afraid I'm gonna make a scene?"

"I'm afraid you're gonna get it taken . . . or be taken yourself. We've had this conversation before. Jail would be bad for you."

"That's true," he agreed. "Prison, really. Jail would be bad still, but prison . . . *that* would be bad. I mean, bad for everyone, but, you know."

"Yeah. Prison, you . . ." she trailed off, shaking her head and laughing.

"I've heard you're just supposed to pick the weakest guy you can find and wail on him the first day you're there. So . . . maybe you could come with me?"

She gave him the best death look she could muster.

"No?" He sighed. "They're so heteronormative in prison."

She ignored him.

"God, yeah, I would be so fucked."

. . .

Winter had a few notable effects on Benny's house. Identifying one in the following (colon): It (the house) became a place where the light switches consistently carried sufficient electrical current to shock a man hard enough such that he, grave and disgruntled, conceded an oppressive and habitual effort (colon): flipping light switches without touching the screws that fastened the fixtures to the walls. After many failures, Benny resolved to avoid any direct contact with the fingers, favoring clothed portions of the wrist for the motion. Ultimately, he would bypass the region of the hand entirely, finally approaching with elbows, as does one when burdened fully with manual constraints of a dual nature, e.g., two plates of food. It was in this manner that Benny, laden with a warm duo of vegan chili bowls, plus one giant mug of chai tea, addressed the stairway's light switch.

November was working on her astronomy homework, and Benny was completing the final steps of his substitute teaching registration. An internet-based ethics test. With little to no exposition—but plenty of bright-eyed models, shirts tucked in—one learned about ethical imperatives of the substitute teacher-student relationship, as well as a few tidbits re: interactions with other teachers and administrators. For instance, in very rare situations certain gifts might be accepted, but under no circumstances should a teacher hug, or accept a hug from, *any* student, no matter the age.

"Ummm, are you encouraging me to repeat someone else's scholarly work and try to pass it off as my own?" she inquired, with theatrical crispness, in reply to Benny's suggestion that she simply hand in a paper he'd written a couple years ago.

"Good God, I think maybe *you* should take this ethics test for me. You're finally ready."

"You sick, sneaky knave. I will not."

"Yes, you will. You'll cave. Aaaand I have to complete it by February 2nd, so . . . you know." He raised his eyebrows—they do that a lot, no?—and pointed at the keyboard. Then he turned back to the screen and palmed the pair of socks he'd set on his desk, as though they were the computer mouse. Embarrassed and smiling, he looked back at her to see if she'd noticed.

"Hah," she snickered sarcastically, still staring at her own screen. "Look at this timeline. Jesus. One minute equals almost 10,000 years, if you . . ."

"What?"

"Sorry, I'm—jeepers, if you map out the history of the universe in a timeline that's as long as a year . . . God, humans are soooo young. The universe is about 15 billion years old. Our sun is 10 billion years old. Earth is right around 5 billion years old. If you condense and convert the history of the universe to a timeline that is about one year long, all of recorded human history has taken place in the last *fifteen seconds* of that year."

"Ummm, what?"

"It's so crazy. We are so young! We're young! We're . . . toddlers! No. We're, like, younger than toddlers. We're infants. God, the first galaxies and stars are three times older than Earth."

He looked blankly at her. "Did you know that it is illegal for me to hug a first grader? If a child wants to give me a hug, I am required by state law to refuse it."

She continued typing and did not respond.

"Or . . . federal law? I don't know. What are you working on?"

"My reading response for this astronomy class. It is so amazing that people still think we're alone in the universe." She turned to him. "There are 100 billion stars in the average galaxy. One *hundred billion* suns to potentially sustain life. And there are 100 fucking *bil*lion galaxies in the universe! And, oh my God, according to this Drake equation, half of those stars have planets, and those that *do* have planets each host *ten* planets, on average. He estimated that the Milky Way has 400 billion stars. That would mean that there are . . ." she trailed off again but kept typing.

"Google says there are only fifty billion planets and about that many stars in the Milky Way," he retorted, having quickly hammered the search into his filthy keyboard.

"Uuuumm, okay," she rejoined. "Maybe the Milky Way is an aberration. Whatever. Still. Fifty *billion* planets?! And we're alone here?!"

"Hah. I know, I know. Billions, trillions, who cares at that point? More of them than the grains of sand Jesus could . . . fit in his . . . cockhole."

"Not to mention the 200 billion other galaxies in existence! And people still think . . . I mean, right? There's just mathematically no way we are alone in the universe! It's impossible to think . . . I mean it's just so insanely . . . hubristic." She looked down, trying to hide the satisfaction that accompanied this articulate part of her tirade.

"Oooh, good word."

Concealing a little triumphant smile, she began to type again.

"I totally agree, yeah. It's crazy. The other thing I think is crazy is that people still think that aliens are gonna come here and kill us or drink our blood or something. Such a silly narrative. Why would they do that? I mean, it's impossible to really even imagine how another species would have evolved in the first place, but if a species is or has been visiting us, I *don't* think they are doing it with *spaceships*," he said sardonically. "Our narratives . . . sheesh. Consciousness is so capable, and we insist on trying to manipulate physical *objects*, and . . . hah, Jesus, keep thinking that other beings are gonna do the same thing? It's so ridiculous. And when they get here—once their species has obediently followed, you know, *our* evolutionary model, of course—they're gonna *attack* us with their *weapons* and whatnot, and take all our stuff. This must have been a cold war theory or something. Some kind of arms race abomination. Ugh."

"I've heard that the next false flag operation is gonna be extraterrestrial."

"Damn. That's perfect. Dear Christ, 'Yeah, so um . . . it was the aliens that blew up the town. They're stationed over here now. Guess we better go get 'em.'"

"Right? Then we a*venge* . . . something, someone. God knows who. It's such a cheap idea."

"Sooo *gay!*" he replied quickly with an opportunistic grin. He knew she hated the word, but once in a while, he located the leverage that afforded it. Or at least gambled that this was the case.

"*So* gay." She'd gradually furnished an implicit assent, relinquishing any real hope of reforming his casual use of such terms.

"*Ass*-gay," he returned, relieved.

"Ass-gay! Ahhh!"

"'Ass-gay' is like double gay, I think."

"Oh, definitely. I agree."

"What about 'vagina-gay'? Would that correspond?"

"Eh," she said, unsatisfied.

"No, I guess not. 'Vagina-gay' is kind of sexy."

"Is it?"

"I *think* so, but, yeah, I guess it doesn't really correspond. Hm. What about 'anus-gay'?

"'Vagina' doesn't really line up with 'gay' the way 'ass' does, I don't think. And definitely not anus, you idiot."

"It would need to be pussy, then: 'pussy-gay.'"

"Pussy-gay," she parroted, trying out the words in her mouth.

"But 'pussy-gay' is kind of sexy, too."

"Really?" A minor contortion in her smirk betrayed her subconscious annoyance with the irony of his fetishizing.

"*You'd* be pussy-gay," he teased, "and ass-gay, probably."

"Well, thank fuck. We've cracked the mathematics of gayness."

He got up and high-fived her, walked to the bathroom, and emerged shortly with the nail clippers in his hand. Then he put on his coat and scarf and stepped out onto the frail balcony to cut his fingernails.

Upon re-entry, he removed his shoe before stepping in with the first foot. Then he took off his other shoe and finished entering the room. He left the door open and began to smack the shoe against the side of the house to shed the snow from its grooved outsole.

"Holy God, it's cold out there," she said, feeling the wind enter the room during Benny's thorough ritual.

He finished smacking that shoe (the left) and began with the other.

"What do you do if you need to cut your toenails?" she asked, briefly turning her head from the computer.

"I *do* need to cut my toenails."

"Me too. What are you gonna do?"

"I don't know. Bathtub? Trash bin? You know, just lay back and bask in it . . . a giant trash bin."

"Your life is a giant trash bin."

"That's true. But I don't really bask in it," he said, pulling her from the computer onto the bed.

"Hey," she protested joyfully. The blankets under her made the sound of static.

"Ah!" he shot up and turned off the lights then raced to the bed to rub the blankets together, anticipating all the novel flashes of static. He rubbed them for a few seconds with no visible result.

"Ugh!" he continued rubbing the blankets together and began rubbing his besocked foot on the carpet. "It won't do it when you're around!" he lamented, turning on the lights again.

"That's what she said," she said.

"What the shit!" he shouted, nearly toppling over as he pushed and pulled, standing now, and dragging his toes toward her against the carpet: a daintier Toro.

"It likes you better," she said turning on the reading lamp, which he promptly turned back off.

"So you *do* want me to nail you, right?" he asked coyly, pulling her into bed and grabbing her butt. "Right here?"

"Here?" she frowned.

Then she asked him to dance. He didn't feel like it, but she put on Steely Dan and pulled him up off the bed. She danced the way the plants in a coral reef moved—when there were still plants in coral reefs. Then she was more buoyant; he was facetious. Gradually, their bifurcated partnership developed into something like a pre-adolescent slow dance. The distance between bodies. They added the kissy eyes of high school, fell to the bed and lay, increasingly entangled, on the mattress, kissing and, strangely, both crying. The room had inexplicably (d)evolved: heavy melancholy now.

"I love you," she said. They dripped their tears onto each other.

"I love you," he said. "Tonight, I'm gonna sleep next to you all night."

They listened and stared at the dark ceiling. The raspy background-ed melody, "A woman's voice reminds me to serve and not to speak, that I myself am just another freak."

"What record is this?" he asked.

"Can't Buy a Thrill."

"It sounds kind of like the Doobie Brothers, at least on the chorus . . . but better."

"Didn't they share a couple members at some point? If you know what I mean?"

"Hah. Yeah, Michael McDonald, definitely. I know the drummer went on to do, like, everything."

The guitar solo faded with the outro, and the song began again.

"Wait, is this on repeat?"

"Hah. Yyyyeah, I've been listening to the same three or four songs for the last three days, mostly just one song on repeat for hours. It's so the opposite of how you experience music. Actually, I find it fascinating that we both love music but in such different ways, that our methods of appreciation can be so different."

"I think I experience nature the way a lot of people experience music. Because I don't know anything about it, really, I think I can be a little more receptive and allow it to act on me atmospherically."

"I'll *act* on you atmospherically," she copped the exaggerated blue-collar tone Benny so frequently employed, and then repositioned herself. "I can hear the ocean right now," she said, her ear pressed against his chest, "but in fast-forward. The waves are crashing really fast against the sand."

"Mmmm." He brushed his hand over her hips and down to her ass.

She sensed his excitement. "Ummm, hm . . . well, I've got this thing going on down there, you know."

"I don't care," he said. "You know I don't."

And with some effort, he persuaded her. Slowly building to an energetic prurience, they soiled Benny's sheets the color of passion, energy, desire, love, war, danger, strength, power, and determination—according to the color wheel.

Later that evening, following a routine (po[o/u]tine? anyone?) flush, the toilet gurgled and erupted, regurgitating pee and wet poop.

Extracting stained sheets from the dirty clothes' hamper, they could not believe their good fortune, having two giant freshly-relegated rags at the ready. Benny, fortressed by a pair of old black dress shoes, found himself in the dingy, yellow[22] muck, sliding happily about, atop two menstrual-blood-stained sheets, sopping up the stinky toilet water-pee and wet poop. His whistle sounded like, "Are you gatherin' up the teeeeeeeears? Have you had enough of miiiiiiiiiiine?"

---

22   According to the color wheel, this is the color of caution, decay, sickness, and jealousy.

LEAKY PUSS-BEAN CHILI

Bean Ingredients:
- 1 lb. dried black beans
- 1 lb. dried kidney beans
- 12 cups water or vegetable broth
- 4 tbsp. vegetable oil or olive oil
- 2 onions, diced
- 6 cloves garlic, minced
- 4 bay leaves
- 2 cubes vegetarian bouillon (flavor of your choice)
- 1 tsp. dried oregano
- 1 tsp. hot sauce (or to taste)
- 1 tsp. salt
- 2 tbsp. sugar
- 4 tbsp. balsamic or red wine vinegar

Bean Preparation:
1. Sort and wash the beans, removing any spiritual impurities.
2. Dump beans in large pot. Add water/broth sufficient to cover them. Bring to a boil.
3. Cover, remove from heat, and let stand for 1 hour. Drain the beans and set aside.

4. In a giant pot, fry onions and garlic in oil until onions are all blissed out, roughly 445 seconds.

5. Add beans and remaining ingredients. Bring to a boil, reduce heat, and simmer for 1.5 hours, or until the beans are firm but easily smashed between the elbows.

6. Remove bay leaves and, from the canopy of an old growth oak grove, drop into a groundhog's ears.

Stir-fry and Finishing Ingredients

- 2 large onions, chopped
- 5 garlic cloves, diced
- 6 jalapeno peppers
- 3 poblano peppers
- 2 chile peppers
- 2 green peppers
- 2 ghost peppers
- 2 purple magic peppers
- 1 red pepper
- 1 yellow pepper
- 1 periwinkle pepper
- 3 zucchini chopped
- 17 green olives, quartered
- 1 bag of frozen sweet corn
- 1 tbsp. liquid smoke
- 32 oz. salsa of choice
- 6 oz. tomato paste
- 2 tbsp. cumin
- 3 tbsp. chili powder
- Salt to taste

Directions:

1. Pour a bunch of olive oil into two Vesuvian woks.

2. Sauté, at high heat, the onions, peppers, and zucchini. Add garlic only after onions begin to brown. (This way you won't burn the garlic, idiot.)

3. Season to taste with a bit of the cumin, chili pepper, oregano, and salt.

4. In a massive pot, combine beans with stir-fried vegetables. Simmer.

5. Add remaining ingredients. Simmer more.

...

(Benny dreams.) In a thrift store, he sees a few nice dresses. Only one is November's size. It's forty dollars though. He sees a video and puts it in the dusty VCR, which costs two dollars. Suddenly, he's in bed. He turns on the TV atop the bureau. On TV, a fawn is seen gallivanting about town with a leash that hovers in the air, as though an invisible person is holding it. The fawn is looking for someone/thing. She stops at the house of an Amish family and looks at them for a while. The old woman on the porch violently directs the deer into the woods. The woman is plainly self-assured, so the fawn obeys. The Amish boy at the old woman's side is so affected by the sight of the fawn that he decides to follow her, even though it is winter. A dramatic scene follows, in which the family says a stoic goodbye to the boy, and gives him a bag of Goldfish crackers. He follows the tracks into the woods and catches up to the fawn. Happily running, he follows it for some time but loses track of it eventually. He then encounters some Yankee boys on a frozen lake. They wear orange body suits and lie on their stomachs on top of special snowmobiles that operate like that: with them lying belly-down on top of the vehicle. Each boy is serviced by a honing, spotlighting helicopter that anticipates the snowmobile's direction and deftly illuminates the terrain accordingly. One of the sneakier boys convinces the Amish boy to ride with him, but they cannot find the fawn. Suddenly, many deer, all wearing November's forty dollar dress, crash through the thrift store's front windows and stampede toward Benny, who cannot move.

He woke to the hard rhythm of his heartbeat, which was shaking his whole bed and slamming his incisors together with each thump.[23]

Constant deer. Why?

---

23 To "thump," as November had mentioned on occasion, in another context refers to the common factory farming practice of exterminating ailing runt piglets by slamming them against brick walls or cement (prefer concrete) floors, a good example of the industry's dedication to efficiency.

· · ·

Every kid in Mrs. Taylor's 2nd grade class was staring at him. Wentworth had hardly spoken all morning, except once when he detonated, yelling at two students for talking in the middle of what he called "extended study hour," during which the kids were told to read a book and observe absolute silence. He'd just confiscated a boy's pudding cup and was now eating it with a plastic spoon he found in Mrs. Taylor's desk drawer.

"It's almost time for lunch," one of the girls said quietly. "Can we line up for lunch?"

Wentworth lowered his face to her and sneered from behind Mrs. Taylor's desk. Then he lifted a spoonful of pudding into his mouth and crunched into the plastic. The head of the spoon broke off in his mouth, and, seemingly unfazed, he continued to chew, slowly crushing it into pieces between his molars. Then in mid-chomp he arose and flung the half-full pudding cup against the coat rack. It thudded softly and disappeared, settling into the weave of thick winter coats. Wentworth sniggered at them as he ambled out of the room, into the hall, and toward the red exit sign. He was about halfway down the hall when the bell rang and the first wave of children ran in from recess, yipping and yowling past him. He craned upward and spat pudding-covered shards of black plastic into the air, and did not look back.

· · ·

Not [famously arriving] like brazen giant[s] . . .
[hacking] limbs astride from land to land;
. . . [But more] sea-washed, sunset[ting] gates shall stand
A mighty [throng] with a [p]orch [to claim]
Is the imprisoned lightning, and her name

Mother of [Paxil]. Her beacon-hand
g[r]ows world-wide welcome [from a yawn-beaten gland]
[Glow woebegone beguiled eyes] that [brand]
[The marred beige water by the Rock Hall of Fame.]
. . . Give [us] your [hired], your [gadabout vendors],
Your [huckster] masses [hawking vitamin D],
The [melatonin pushers] of your [sch]eming s[t]ore[s].
[Drag your wooden legs, peddle negative ions] to me,
Lift [your full spectrum lamps to our] golden door[s]!

The New Colossus
—Emma Lazarus, 1883

The littleness of ennui settles in February: the great weight of gray skies of gray clouds above gray little worlds of gray sweatpants under heather gray sheets. The clouds hang down with everyone else who doesn't feel like getting out of bed. To be fair, it is plainly a schlep. Across Ohio skyways, there were two sunny days in February. Paucity is the word.

And now, without even a perfunctory transition, I would like to talk a little bit about awkward sex things that happen frequently enough but seem to be omitted from the preponderance of cultural artifacts I run across.

While it's regularly true, for instance, that awkwardness dissipates as a relationship grows, there are moments that one doesn't often read about: bumping lover in face with elbow; missing mouth when attempting kiss; knocking partner off bed; blowing snot into lover's nose as he orgasms and sniffs it in, etc.

Contraception another. The coverup.

Discussions of contraception can be so complicated. Condoms, for instance, such a gross intrusion, and each party seems to agree there must be a better way, within a committed relationship. But neither has insurance, and Planned Parenthood's funds have been cut so much that there's almost no . . . blah blah blah.

The t-shirt says "Condoms are for pussies." That will have to suffice, as someone seems to have squeezed dry my pun gland. (Iran-Contra[ception].) Oh, God. There. Empty. And the relief.

Oh, the relief.

Once these preliminary concerns have been hurdled, the fondling journey toward penetration can really begin. Yet remaining, however, are the anxious maladroit movements in between sexual positions. Regardless of the relative pleasure any given position provides, an urge to explore inevitably arises. Gradually, or suddenly, a point is reached at which each party understands that there will be rearranging, but neither is sure exactly what angle or direction will follow. Say one happens to be holding a leg. And say another's leg happens presently to be clutched. And say, further, that the attempted leg movements of owner and clutcher happen to conflict. The contradictory force, and others like it, can lead to absolute cacophony. In addition, during this fragile interim, there is no penetration—this is basically why we think of it as an interim—and, when it comes to sex, penetration is comparable to speaking, in certain ways: It is, of course, a communication, but it is also a din, a thing done so as not to be devoured by the uncomfortable moments of silence that plague tense conversations and tense moments in general.[24]

And there's the after-sex stuff. A spattering talisman withdrawn. But where? And how, exactly? Plenty of options, but most landing zones are cliché now or seem crass because of pornography's cultural omnipresence—the tired vault of semen onto a spent lover's brow or mouth . . . a large man's panting command: "Open your fuckin' mouth."—so one behaves as a gentleman, halts passage of sperm, cutting short its flight to the face or hair. There is often a layover in Atlanta.

Trembling just a little, improvising advanced yoga positions, one finds oneself balancing, straining into all manner of improvised dog asanas,

---

24   Of course, many of you well-versed lovers will correctly take to task this regimented, provincial assessment of sexual sequences, but remember that November and Benny are young, and just give them a break, for now; allow your self-assured sexual maturity to bolster what calls for bolstering.

simultaneously engaging many gross and fine motor skills, all—having just wrecked a pum pum—during orgasmic harumph. These manoeuvres require a pleasant effort that is hard to describe: well-focused expenditures of happy energy, the stated goal of which being to not fall off the bed.

Finally, the twisting and reaching for tissues. Or t-shirts. Or wash-cloths. Any clothish entity.

It's a schlep.

In addition to all this, there are heavy responsibilities: One finds significant additional awkwardness in the requisite discussion of STD's, for example.

"So, that thing on your lip, have you . . . do you know what it is?"

"Oh, it's a textured tattoo, a raised lip bindi, from my term with the Mumbai chapter of The Mouseketeers." (No one said this.)

"Is that . . . just, like, a rash, or . . . ?" was actually the bumbling inquiry that Benny managed right before they were going to have sex. She'd already told him about it, and explained that it seemed like just a lot of chafing, but it had eaten at both of them since that conversation.

"I don't know," she mumbled, wincing and looking down at her wrists, where she was pinching the skin together.

Benny hesitated, but then kissed her and gradually began to make further advances, in an effort to subdue her anxiety by reconfirming her allure. Confirmation heightened toward wreck of pum pum, 'til, finally, he wrecked a pum pum. More or less.

Then they sprawled, and, he reached for the pillow they'd used var-iously as a sexual prop. "I like to put this cummy pillow between my knees," he said. "It feels good. Can I get a 'that's what she said,' please?" And they fist-bumped. Cuddled.

The streetlamp lighted the room only dimly, such that he had little trouble performing a reciprocation of the starry gaze she projected.

"I need a nightcap," she said, now under three blankets and still shivering.

"I don't think I've ever heard that used in the literal way before," he said and warmed her head with his hand. She tilted her head back and forth, implying that he should continue to rub it, and even with more vigor, if he should desire.

"Mmmm."

"Would you ratherrrrrrr . . ." he began, "give me a rimjob with cream cheese around my anus or a blowjob with my penis pushed up through the center of a pizza. A Domino's pizza."

"Oh my God," and for a moment she made the face Elvis would have, had he been a churlish preteen girl caught passing a note then passive-aggressively punished by being asked to give her solution to that algebra problem she did not understand. Then she recovered.

"I don't know. I hear their crust, or maybe it was the sauce, has been highly improved. It was made over, according to real customer surveys."

"Blowjob, I guess." She winced in resignation.

"And I know they're already using real cheese."

She turned toward him just long enough to glare for a moment and roll her eyes.

"What about if you couldn't use your hands?" he continued. "Would that make a difference?"

"No."

"What about the toppings? Would the toppings affect your decision?"

"No."

"You r'lly don'givafuuuuck," he affected his old black lady voice, "i'on't giv'a FUCK!"

"You sound like a dying duck."

"Like what?"

"Like a dying duck."

"I've got something that's dying . . . you wanna see something that's *dying*. I'll show you that shit. Believe me."

She rolled away then nudged into him. They spooned for a bit. But does anyone actually fall asleep like that?

"I got some shit like that."

. . .

November—her situation having retained a dotty redness—scheduled a visit to Planned Parenthood. But on the day of her appointment, the rash was gone, so, to confirm or disconfirm the many possibilities, the nurses had to draw blood. (Benny went with her, as he'd been disconcerted by coincidental irritation. Though he assumed/hoped it was road rash, the simultaneity, he thought, was some cause for anxiety.)

"Can we go soon?" she asked anxiously.

"Yeah. Is this okay?" he laughed, gesturing to his outfit. "Too wakey?"

"Too what?"

"Like a wake."

"Don't you always dress like that?"

"No. Not *really*."

"Well, what can I say? You're wearing three different shades of black, dear."

They stared at each other.

"I'm the man in blacks."

"Uh-huh. Can we go now?"

"Look at this. I have two left foot socks," he lamented.

"What?"

"See. They both have this shape." He held them up and traced the fabric near the end of the socks. Both seemed to have conformed slightly to the left foot.

"Can't you just . . . put them on?"

"No . . . just kidding. But see? The slant? It's obviously a left foot sock."

"Yes, I *do* see," she said, singing the "do" as if absently praising a toddler's artwork. "Can't you just put it on your *other* foot? *Then* it'll be a *right* foot sock," she continued with jaunty artifice.

"No. You can put it on your other *foot,* but *that* doesn't make it a *right foot sock,*" he persisted, attempting to cheer her up. (Things had been rather strained since the clumsy conversation re: the rash.)

"Can we go?"

• • •

A patriotic country music video (camouflaged soldiers and sweet sandy-haired army wives) was playing on the TV in the dirty waiting room of Planned Parenthood. A large dark woman, Monique, tended the visitor's window. "Sorry, honey. Ho'd on. E'rybody know I'm slow 'round here."

"What? No. It's okay," November stuttered. "I'm just—"

"Oh, baby, it ain't no thang. I'm dumb as cotton candy. E'rybody know dat."

November wanted to tell her she wasn't, but she was afraid it would sound contrived and disagreeable, so she just stared diffidently behind Monique's desk. The office area was filled with Precious Moments figurines. Monique and coworker, Crystal, displayed them as a rejoinder to the collections of offensive tribal sambo figures they'd seen in dollar stores. The Precious Moments figurines didn't carry quite the same oppressive weight, but they *were* almost as aesthetically ridiculous and insulting, if you wanted them to be: the dull, doe-eyed expressions on the pasty little bloated faces; the stupid pastel clothes and timid poses. Monique had gussied up one or two of them with eyelash extensions. Crystal was conflicted by the adornment—not sure how it was meant.

Despite having finally been deftly pacified by Monique (and the figurines in the waiting room), and despite the nurse's gentle, professional manner, November fainted almost immediately when she saw her own blood pulled into the needle. Something about taking blood to see if she was immune to Hepatitis B and to know her blood type and then probably having to do it again for . . . who remembers? Dear girl just goodnightnursed it right then and there. Floppy down. (She had fainted once before at a hot spring—the sharp transition from hot water to cold air, perhaps—but never because of blood work.)

Nurse: Give her something sweet.

November: I have cold sweat. I'm seeing yellow. I'm never doing heroin.

Nurse: Do you want your Goldfish?

November: Seinfeld. Benny.
        faints[25]

Nurse (paper doused w NH3 under her nose): November? November. Sweetie. Hey!

November (woozy smile): I need to call Seinfeld and Benny.

Nurse: November?

November: You're intruding my nostrils.

Nurse (pulls strip away): November, would you like some water?

November: Yes. Where did my Goldfish go?

Nurse: We weren't able to take any blood. We are going to have to try again.

November: Doggonit, not today . . . I'm covered in cold sweat.

---

25   November dreams that she is galloping through the forest. Then she is breezing through Kent's treelawns. She looks playfully back at a centaur with two auburn velour horns sprouting from wavy green hair. He seems to follow, but when she looks back again, he is disappearing behind a rough orange hill shaped like the arched back of a Goldfish cracker.

...

In a parallel imbroglio, Benny sat in the examination room and over-heard two nurses talking about a 278 lb. pumpkin that one's niece had grown and entered in the great county fair's pumpkin contest last year. They were both appalled that it had only won third place. Then the denouement: Someone had stolen it. How could someone steal a little girl's giant pumpkin? And, literally, how could someone steal a 273 lb. pumpkin? Finally entering and shutting the door firmly was an old, black M.D. who smiled politely at Benny with thin, dark lips. Her name was Matilda Thiessen, and she smelled like vanilla.

"Hello," she said, so casual with the *ll* of *hello*. "And what's the rea-son for your visit today?"

"I have a rash or something on my penis. Or. Close to it."

"Okay, honey. Where is it *exactly*?"

"Umm, close to the head, I guess, kind of under the head, but not really the shaft. Near where the head meets the stem, I guess. At the top of the stem."

She eyed him some. "Is there pain or itching or burning?"

"Umm . . .?"

"Is there pain?"

"Not really. I mean, I don't think so."

"Does it burn or . . .?"

"When it rubs against things it doesn't feel very good. I don't know about 'pain.' What kind of pain?"

"Pain."

"Yeah, but that's relative, isn't it?"

"No."

"No? I mean, I don't know. I don't *think* there's pain."

"Oh, you'd know if there was."

"Okay. Sorry, can I just—I was told that I shouldn't pee for an hour before I came in, so I haven't, but I've really had to poop for about an hour now, and I haven't because I knew if I pooped, I'd probably pee, too, and I don't think I could have held that in, so I—"

"Okay, honey, lie back on that table," she said walking toward the computer in the small examination room, "and take your pants down." She then ripped off a large piece of white paper and placed it over him, like a sheet. "Tell me when you're done."

After a good deal of maneuvering and louder than necessary rustling of paper, he got his shoes and pants off. "Okay."

She pulled the paper away and three seconds later declared, "Oh, honey, dat ain'nothin'," then turned away once again and resumed her work at the computer.

"Umm . . . okay—wait, what?" he asked, surprised at her efficiency.

"You mean this?" she pointed at his penis, more or less. He nodded. "Oh, dat ain't nothin', honey." And she turned away again.

"How can you tell?"

"How can I tell? Ten years o' medical school, and I been doin' this fourteen years. That's how."

"Yeah . . . but, I mean, shouldn't I have a test or something?"

"Honey, I been lookin' at college boys' parts fourteen years. That. Ain't. Nothin'.'"

"Well . . . okay."

"You want a test?"

"I—"

"Whatchewanna test for?"

"I guess I don't *have* to—"

"Hold on." She nimbly skimmed through the pages of a book full of glossy photos of aberrant anatomies. "I'll show you." Benny imagined her setting the cold stethoscope microphone against his penis and tapping on it with two fingers while she frowned, listening intently, but something different happened: She told him story after story about people coming in with crazy pain, unsightly parts, etc. "See how dey smoove awn top? Dey ain't dem broccoli o' cauliflower o' somethin' . . . like the genital warts," she said, pointing to various photos of penises.

Then she left the room to retrieve another book. She seemed to have taken a strong personal interest in enlightening Benny as to the folly of his anxiety. For almost twenty minutes, they looked at pictures together while she explained things he'd already obsessively googled—and completely misunderstood. Occasionally, Benny would get his penis back out and look at it to compare. They talked about sex, the chafing on the bike, masturbating too much. Ultimately, she prescribed hydrocortisone.

"Now just rub a little bit awn na'." Her pace quickened as the brawn of her natural vernacular swelled, "At ain't no moisturize'."

...

That night Benny and November dined at a top-notch Thai restaurant, as a consolation for the terror of Planned Parenthood. The decor was very shiny and golden; the red curry was sweet and delicious. November's fortune cookie said, "Because of your melodic nature, the moon never misses a beat."

"Wouldn't that be '*rhythmic* nature'?" Benny observed.

"Oh my God!" she interrupted. "Does that mean I'm pregnant?" she asked, shaken. "What are we gonna do if I'm pregnant?"

"What are we gonna do if you're pregnant?" he repeated facetiously. She scowled at him.

"I don't know," he said. "Drive off a cliff, like Thelma and Louise?"

"Is that what they do at the end?"

"Yeah, that's the big scene from that movie."

"Would you be Thelma or Louise?"

"Mm . . . I'm not actually sure who's who," he said, narrowing his eyes at her.

"Do you wanna be Susan Sarandon or Geena Davis?"

"I guess I'd wanna be Geena Davis. But I'm probably more like Susan Sarandon."

"I thought *I* was more like Susan Sarandon."

"Really? Well, I'll be Geena Davis then," he said, casually opening his fortune cookie and flicking the wrapper at her.

She glared at him as the wrapper sailed wide right. Then he turned his fortune strip to her; it was blank.

"Oh my God!" she laughed.

"What the hell is this?"

They locked eyes for a minute in frivolous disbelief. Benny lifted the napkin from his lap. "You're done with that fortune cookie?" he asked.

She nodded, smiling at his sensitivity re: noseblowing.

"Good. Oh, but they're not . . ." He pointed to people two tables away. "Dammit." (A boy comes of age.) "I'm going to blow my nose, and I'm *not* leaving the room."

"It's really not as gross as you think." (The sound of nose-blowing was heard.) "Although, it is snottier today."

"It's a very descriptive noise," he noted as he folded the napkin.

"What's that word . . . where the sound and the meaning . . ."

"Onom—"

Deftly, through sudden eviction of snot, he interrupted her answer.

"What?" he said, turning his ear to her.

"Ono—"

And it happened again.

"I'm sorry," he offered, moving his ear closer, "I didn't hear you."

She glared at him again.

They glared at each other.

"Onoma—"

• • •

"Have you examined yourself lately?" asked the Methodist church sign they passed on the way home.

• • •

After all that Planned Parenthood messing about and fainting and whatnot, November, of course, had to reschedule her appointment. And wait for the results. During the interval, she and Benny suffered some irreversible awkwardness. Benny tried to ignore his preoccupations, but he became even more sensitive to matters of cleanliness. The following, for instance, after noting her trip to the restroom at the restaurant:

"Ummm, before we . . . hmmm, I feel like this is . . . there's no good way to say it, but it's also not, like . . ." he sighed.

"Okay, well . . . what?"

"I was just thinking about all the people in that restaurant, and . . . how I really like, God, I love . . ." he rolled his eyes at himself, "maybe you could sort of rinse off down here before we . . ."

"Oh . . . yeah," she said, averting her eyes, trying to retain an unaffected pretense.

"I . . . you know, I love being able to—"

"Yeah, of course. I know." She arose. "I'm glad . . . you . . ."

• • •

The day's trauma had drained her, and November fell asleep quickly that night, but Benny had begun to feel restless. November's reaction to the fortune cookie had initially seemed comical and cute, but the more he mulled over the notion of pregnancy, the more he felt unnerved. The thought alone felt like a call from a collections agency. It riled his circadian rhythm.

For some time, he sat at the computer—headphones on—and rubbed dead skin off his face, listening to music described as "long minimalist drone cloud washes" and watching a Bob Ross .gif. Ross's giant glasses spoke (sur)rep(i)titiously, "Put some leaves on that little rascal."

Benny clicked away for a moment to examine some American Apparel models, and when he returned the gif had frozen, but then it reanimated. Phew, he thought. The computer's health remained uncompromised, having withstood the first wave, this onslaught of (and flanking by) "happy little bushes."

The train's howl briefly woke November.

"God, you can hear it this much from, like, a mile away? It's so ridiculous," Benny complained, noticing her momentary stirring.

"Uh-huh," she said sleepily, having heard this spiel many times in the past.

"You could get out of the way from . . . at, what, like sixty miles per hour? That gives us one full minute . . . You could sleep on the fucking tracks and still have time to wake up and put jeans on first."

No reply. She'd fallen asleep again.

"I could probably *brush* my *teeth* and still have time."

He got up and peered through the curtains out the window. Thick flakes settling. He looked back at November, then bundled, and walked out the door. Moving through the slow motion of snow, he yawned at the flakes' wavering shadows, and refused to strain his neck at the moon. It was a glassy half-moon—distilled by the haze of a sky full of salmon smoke—and it seemed to cast a shadow on everything but him. He strolled toward the forest, and by the time he arrived at the park's entrance, the cuffs of his corduroys held thin, packed strips of snow.

He stopped at the trailhead, listened and looked: the routine howl of the wind, an owl's indifferent coo, a suburban doe dropping gauzy hooves across the powder. He wondered if a suitably motivated deer could trample him. He took one step and noticed—for the first time that night—the snow packing under his boot. This upset him. He wanted to coexist with the silence, without disturbing it. Wandering onward, he tried to ignore the raking friction of his arms against his body.

As he moved deeper into the dense, white darkness, the pallor of the underbrush engulfed him. Gesturing meagerly against the rude scrape of his jacket, he folded his hands in front of him; this did not help. He decided the best he could do was put his hands behind his back, and he did so, somewhat poutingly.

He dawdled farther into the woods, thinking about November, wondering why he felt so much doubt. The outskirts' bushy gristle gradually gave way to the cozy bosom in the heart of the forest, and as he approached the lake, he heard the lap of the water against the shoreline. The combination of these sounds—the crunch of the snow, the lick of the lake—was peculiar, but it pleased him, like drinking milk from a Styrofoam cup. He paused and breathed in deeply. The cold smelled like it always did. It smelled like nothing. It had always smelled like nothing! His goose bumps intensified. Had it always smelled like nothing? He tried to remember but couldn't. Suddenly exhausted, he lay down in the snow. Above, the gruff wind hurled through the loft of bristly pine busts, upsetting tufts of snow, which plummeted now and plopped mutely beside him.

For a short time, he felt almost as though he could fall asleep. But he again cycled through troubling thoughts of November. Why all this agitation? Why not just accept it, enjoy it?

Then, feeling the snow's cold wetness seeping through the butt of his pants, he arose, brushed the flakes off his jacket, and began to amble homeward with the wail of the train.

The sky began to clear, and he caught a glimpse of Orion's shimmer, his belt, his implicit bow. He lowered his head and heard the bizarre cry of a lone Canadian goose. Moments later, the same sound. He looked up, perplexed, realizing the anomalous lack of gaggle. His bafflement pulled at him, wouldn't let go. Why was this goose alone? He staggered on somberly, failing to consider whether it was flying in the right direction. He'd always wanted to know what it was like to fly south with birds: the slow weave, the night-stops . . . did they stop at night? But he'd never imagined what it would be like alone.

•••

Two days later, November went to stay at her mom's for the weekend. It was her birthday, and it seemed like great timing to her, being able to get away for a bit without a lot of requisite explanation.

Docket of Google Blahs
Part the . . . whatever.

Noviembre: sigh. i feel so dirty right now.

Benyeahmon: wanna get high and do enemas?

Noviembre: ummm, probably not. that's not really what i mean.

Benyeahmon: yeah, i guess they don't really come as a pair.

Noviembre: i should go to sleep. i guess we're gonna go to church early tomorrow.

Benyeahmon: really?
sigh.
saying goodbye is difficult.
you wanna call me a pussy now? go ahead.

Noviembre: don't put words in my mouth. i was gonna say fag :).

Despite certain rhetorical posturing, Benny had begun to withdraw his affection. He could feel something ending but did not want to admit it to himself. Or to her. But he felt himself preparing. And so did November. She felt a new brusque distance in their jokes. She kept making them though. And to her credit, even through her small discomfort with the word, she didn't miss a step. Nonetheless, Benny thought it looked like a cold sore, the period next to the smiley face next to "fag."

• • •

On February 21st, at 10:03 a.m. in Heyworth High School (HHS), the fire alarm rang. Wentworth had been briefed; though he did not know exactly when, he knew the drill would occur sometime that day. But it was really cold, and he'd already decided to skip it if he could. It was beautifully fortuitous, finding himself, during this imbroglio, alone with the tard (the moniker by which she'd come to be known at Went-worth's house—he'd also combined "tard" with "Asian" for something like "Tarzianne," but it felt forced). Though people might notice their absence, generating an apologetic excuse was very easy, and no one had time to investigate further into these things. The girl got up to look out the window at the exiting children. They were gathering in the field across the street from the Baptist church whose sign warned that "Mas-turbation is Satans [sic] Typewriter." Wentworth pulled out two folded pieces of paper from his pocket and set them over the pages of the book. Then he called his young pupil back, repositioned himself opposite her, and resumed his reading, revealing the pictures only after he'd proudly annunciated each short page. Bored now with his usual cantankerous embellishments, this, he decided, was the perfect time to read his recent masterwork to her, entirely or mostly uninterrupted.

Arising ceremoniously, he strutted to the classroom's small wooden podium. "The Fannie Situation," he announced in a somber tone; then he read the epigraph: "'There is no authority for the abuse of [fr]ees[ias].'

"Gertrude Stein." He cleared his throat:

Pull a pornographic picture from a pelvic pocket, and make a dirty joke about it. This can be delicate, a major risk, if your audience is an old lady from Ohio. For, Ohio's old ladies are vehement, in the manner of the Confederate begrudged, and, with their bare hands, are known to have beaten deer to death. Here, I mean to cite Fannie Zimmerman, who, despite the detail of a shovel, reifies my claim with her defense of periwinkles, freesias, hibiscus.

Let us now praise Fannie Zimmerman—
steward of beflowered grounds—
who caught the fawn entering her
garden, with obvious intent:

foraging. Praise Fannie Zimmerman—defender
of the lawn, lord of the land—who foresaw
the need of a hardy garden tool for ambush
of one impudent, pastel-petal-tongue.

Praise Fannie Zimmerman, discriminating
fawn-slayer, that the madam didn't pummel Pudu
deer, which hail from Ecuador, enough lowgrown
for to hide under fern—Ohio shovel, a clear mismatch.

Praised be Fannie Zimmerman, shovel advocate;
and may the trowel be praised as well. Sufficient
for a Pudu are a trowel. Also, I suppose, praise the
watering cans, enabling domestication of maidenhair fern.

(Deer like mice, another place and time are
the "chevrotains,"—literal French: "little goat.")

Praise the mangled mess of blood and displaced
fur. For though Fannie is old, quite old,
her initial inquisition required guile.
Whereas, my whores are filthy fools.

Praise thus Fannie Zimmerman, conservationist,
creeping toward bedlamic bushwhack, short
bleating efforts to summon a mother doe, ruptured
by the tin baritone clang made on the tawny head.
(Praise Fannie at blitzkrieg.) Then deeper, wetter

claps. Wheezing through a yogurt throat. Leg
spasms. Eyelids grasping. Oh, the glory.

Praise Fannie Zimmerman, sentinel of flower patch,
nursery custodian, curator of deer corpse.
Skull-crushing, yes, cleaner than digging neck-hole;
yet looming: the heavy work of deer-scrapping.
Praise the winded contemplation, internal dialogue:
removal of this fawn carcass, how to.
Ever look trunkward, dear comrade.

Praise, and thank you, Fannie's dirty hands,
worthy of the spade and the snow shovel:
an Olympic flame in her employ. Snow
never was allowed to linger on the driveway,
litter sidewalk, nor tarry portico; fornicate not!
on the porch, diddle stoop, lay dally idle balcony.

Praise to Sister Zimmerman, janitor of fawn blood,
with dirty hands, like the Amish, who are like Fred Astaire
with a shovel, though what really comes to mind
is the Yankee who retaliated, shot the fleeing Amish boy
whose older brother had given a truckward volley
of tomato. Praise the rebuttal of an airborne tomato.

Also, praise airborne tomatoes. Praise
the Spanish crack of gun that impels catapulting
tomatoes, kicking off *La Tomatina*. Every year
on the final Wednesday of August in Buñol, Valencia,
Spain, they throw overripe tomatoes by the ton.
La Tomatina is a paratelic festival, the bandying of fruit
its essential composition. Praise the fruited Spaniard,
her paratelic state, a state of playfulness. Praise

the Greek prefix, "para," meaning "separate from"
or "beyond." And, of course, the root, "telic,"
"expressing end or purpose." Praise paratelic
buckshot heralding *Tomatina*, held in honor
of the town's patron saints, Hubertus and Giles.

Praise the churchgoing, saint-praising Zimmer,
yet ask not her veneration of Giles
(that cheesecloth), patron saint of beggars, lepers,
cripples. Greek emigre vegetarian hermit, circa late
seventh century A.D., Giles ducked in some Gallic
forest and was apparently sustained for years
by his lone companion, a small red doe, on the teat
of which he suckled. Expect instead for Fannie,
like I said, to honor Hubertus, patron saint of hunters.

And yet, here is Hubertus, a candid picture:
Noble from the North of France, harrying a buck
through the woods on Good Friday, circa 683;
intervened upon with divine instruction from a spectral
crucifix hovering between the antlers of the stag
he pursued—a fanatical delusion of animal idolatry!
This man studied a cloud of crucifix above a buck's head,
then dropped his bow and let his quarry go, choosing
to become a priest instead. That Good Friday's pivotal hunt
effected Hubertus to castigate spelunking, rebuke
lovemaking, and chide blue-eyed soul for
the subsequent embrace of a disembodied riddle.

Confounding is the irony that this Hubertus,
who, beheld an apparitional, fluorescing antler-cross;
who observed prohibition of hunting on Good Friday;
who dithered home, quit archery to join the clergy;

is, nevertheless, the patron saint of hunters.
Despite vegan impulse, near-bestial fantasies,
the church identified the Hubert just described
as the patron saint of hunters, (and of archers!)
smelters, trappers, two cities in Belgium,
metal workers, mathematicians, opticians, and dogs.

Praise Fannie Zimmerman's canonical revisions.
And hunters! who are we praying to? Really!
The teat guy? The vegan priest? Fannie was 75!
With a shovel. I can't speak
for the Belgians, but this is a no-brainer, I think.
Fucking donkeys.

Pray, yes, to Fannie Zimmerman, I suggest,
or maybe my uncle, who got one with a crossbow,
had it butchered properly, made a pretty good
salsa cheese dip. A little oily, sure, and the meat
rather chewy. Still, at least my uncle is bestially
chaste, lips unacquainted at the nipple of a doe.
Prude.

Anyway, in addition, praising, then, heretofore,
the shovels, trowels, watering cans, cheesy
salsas, patron saints, and whatever else, remember,
please: Praise the fruited Yankee.
Also, praise the shotgun: shovel of the fruited
Yankee. And the dead fawn: Amish boy of Fannie.

Wentworth stood up and took a bow. Then two more, at forty-five-
degree angles right and left.
   "What did you think of the piece? Didn't you love the *slant* rhymes?
I bet you *loved* the *slant* rhyme employed in this piece, right? All the

slant rhymes, yeah? Oh, I'm sorry. Am I *rail*roading you into agreeing
. . . on the *slant* rhyme issue?" Wentworth laughed heartily.

"What happened?" she frowned.

"Quite a bit, my little empress."

She stared at him.

"The dancing deer watched her little baby get mutilated by an an-
gry old woman," he smiled sardonically.

"What happens next?"

"Haaaaa!" he bayed. "Oh, yes, let's return to the story, of course,
of course. 'Deep in a green forest down by the sea, a hunter spied a little
deer dancing.'"

. . .

"Um, did you talk to Wentworth today?" Ned asked, brushing his long
black hair away from his face.

"No."

"He was just now gargling Colt 45 and . . . um, I don't know . . .
singing something?"

This, and more, was what Wentworth's celebration of black
history month entailed: He lifted the milk carton to his face, carrying
to the ta-ble two Colt 45 bottles in his other hand. His mustard yellow
shirt was snugly tucked into green jeans, red suspenders climbing over
his shoul-ders. Encircling a bucket of Kentucky Fried Chicken were tall
black "La Santisma Muerte" (translation: "Holy Death") candles. He
was lighting them and humming the Black National Anthem, "Lift
Every Voice and Sing," as Benny descended the staircase.

"I'm almost finished with that retarded nip. A couple more days or
something."

"Whoa. Man, she's been a fixture for you. You're gonna miss
her, aren't you," Benny said casually, joining Wentworth at the table.

Wentworth surveyed him coyly and then tore into song, slamming his fist on the table at "voice" and glaring widely at "heaven": "Lift every voooooooiiiiiiiice and sing, 'til earth and heaaaaaaaaven ring with the haaaaaaaaarmoooooooooonies oooof liiiiiiiiiiiiiiiiiberty!" Then he arose gravely and removed the lid from the waxy white bucket of chicken.

The two sat for a moment in relative silence, the poultry air pristine but for the sounds of Wentworth's gluttony. He seemed, on purpose, to be chewing open-mouthed, shiny chicken skin rolling over in his jowls.

"Soooo you had the day off, eh?"

"Yyyyep! Yyyyyessirreeee, Bob, I did." He saluted in the general direction of no discernible person or thing, smacking wetly through chicken grease. "I'm observing black history month."

"Alabama Nigger," by Johnny Rebel, had just ended, and "Coon Town" was playing now on the computer.

"Ah. Right. Good for you." Benny watched him for a bit longer, lis-tening to the lyrics of "Coontown": "If you smell somethin' funny when you walk down the street, you're in coon town." And so on.

Wentworth's séance—which seemed to fascinate, if disturb, Uli —had begun to bore and disgust Benny, but then Wentworth dumped half a bottle of Colt 45 over his face as he gazed thoughtfully upward.

"On the corner, there's a nigger with a drink in his hand. That's Coontown. Tryin' to bum a nickel from whoever he can in Coontown. Don't be surprised. You can make a bet. If you go back tomorrow, he'll be there yet. He's tryin' to get drunk, and drunk he's gonna get in coon town."

Groundnut Stew (À La Congo-Vegan)

- 1 cup peanut butter
- 3 tomatoes
- 24 oz. seitan (chicken flavored)
- Not-chicken broth (a lot)
- Peanut oil
- 4 chili peppers (and powder?)
- Roughly 1 cup habanero pepper (or any assortment of hot peppers) and olive oil puree
- 2 cups black beans (from scratch)
- 2 sweet potatoes
- Brussels sprouts
- French green beans
- Bok choy
- Red and green peppers
- 2 onions chopped finely
- 4 cloves garlic minced
- 1 teaspoon of thyme
- Salt to taste
- Black or red pepper to taste
- 2 bay leaves

- 1 teaspoon coriander
- 1 teaspoon chili powder
- 1 teaspoon cumin
- ½ teaspoon cinnamon

Spices for preparing the seitan:
- 1 teaspoon garlic salt
- 1 teaspoon coriander
- 1 teaspoon chili powder
- 1 teaspoon cinnamon
- 1 teaspoon cumin
- 1 teaspoon turmeric

Directions:

1. To make puree, put a bunch of peanut oil and peppers in blender and blend.

2. If using sweet potatoes or yams, scrub thoroughly. Like steel wool on beet skin. Then boil or steam them until they begin to tenderize. (Endanger yourself with similar satirical metaphors if you are feeling particularly zesty.)

3. Set aside puree, squash, and potatoes.

4. Sauté the onions in peanut oil (5-7 minutes). At high heat, add peppers and garlic. Sa(l)uté these for a few minutes. Reduce heat and add tomatoes. Add salt and spices. Simmer. Then add broth and continue to simmer. Continue to simmer. Like a tired autumnal honeybee trying to fuck a piece of dog shit.

5. Add whatever food-grade vegetables you've chosen. Reduce heat and stir in peanut butter. Stir until smooth.

6. Sauté seitan in a separate pan. Add desired salt and spices. When smell is like a dead rat trying to fuck a piece of dog shit, add to the stew. Stir and let simmer until you eat it.

7.   Serve with quinoa and blood orange sparkling water.

8.   Garnish with whatever you think works: maybe an avocado, something citrusy, perhaps a banana or another sexless fruit.

. . .

"I had a date last night," Wentworth announced, interrupting the third-graders' independent reading time. Lounging behind the desk at the front of the room, he leered sleepily at them. Then he burst with laughter, exhaling gloriously, and recharging to snort and convulse further. This continued for almost a full minute, before he finally sighed, "Yeah. I thought it went pretty well. We went to the art museum. What? You're not interested?" He glowered down momentarily at the pizza box on the floor next to Mrs. Souza's desk.

"You know what though? Every time I go to the art museum, I'm struck by the lack of . . . oh, how should I put it? Diversity, I guess. Gender diversity, I mean. Yeah?" He had stepped over the pizza box and was trudging through the rows now.

"I walk through the impressionist section, through the pointillist section, through the surrealist section: nothing but cocks on the wall. Everywhere. I grow tired of it.

"Do you like to draw?" he stopped and stood over a little girl's desk. She had strawberry blonde hair. Her eyes zipped down off him as, through considerable fear, she tried to maintain the jaded expression that the cooler third-graders were beginning to learn. Ultimately, she decided that holding her silence would be okay, given this weirdo's behavior today.

"Uh-huh. Well, I hope *one* of the *dickless* among you little . . . doe-eyed, strudel-faced midgets will. I am tired of seeing nothing but these *strutting* mongrel-cocks hanging all over the Goddamned places. So, please . . . wipe your little gizmos on a hundred dollar bill and, I don't know, frame it in *wing*dings. Call it abstract expressionism or some kind of conceptualist bullshit. Whatever you want. Just so long as it stinks of bush a little. And good luck with *that*, you spunkless little piles of . . . Purell."

. . .

Benny felt her presence moving through the bedroom, which induced a bit of guilt in him for still being asleep and not watching her dress, as he assumed she liked him to do.

"Mornings are strange," he croaked, mashing his left nostril, which was humid and swampy, the other side dry and sensitive. "I need something to make me remember that I'm a human and that I want things from the waking life."

"You would make a good ghost." She bumbled about, lazily dressing.

"Do you ever feel that way?" he asked, slightly disconcerted as he guessed at the poor contextual timing of his comment.

"Well, I need to go buy some seeds today, so it's easy for me, I guess . . . to remember that I want things from the waking life." She had not even glanced at him as she spoke.

"What kind of seeds are you looking for?"

"Umm," November thought it over, as she put one arm through her bra. "California poppies."

"Yeah?" he encouraged. She'd just started back at the greenhouse part-time and was none-too-pleased about it. And as he slowly rejoined the world-awake, he tried to be decent, at least *pretending* to be interested.

"Calendula."

"Uh-huh."

"Cockscomb."

"*Cock's . . . comb?* Huh, you really need cock's comb?" He watched the shirt slither over her body; her head popped through, "I just keep mine short. Eh? Get it? Kinda?"

A penis joke, yes? He laughed. She laughed. Courteously. She was a good listener, too good on occasion. She listened recklessly, shoes untied. With urgency. And yet even perfunctory reciprocation was often beyond Benny's reach.

"Ugh," she sighed. "How can I call off tomorrow?"

"It's hardly even today."

"God. Don't say that," she said, jumping back into bed.

"Just text the sign for a butt," he said looking attentively at her, still trying to repair the damage, "just those two parentheses facing the same direction . . . and then put a bunch of poop flying out of them. For like, five lines."

"Dear Bunny, have much wet poop."

"Haaaa! 'Bunny!'"

"God, I know."

"Dear Bunny. You're no bunny. You're no bunny at all." And, for some reason, they actually *rolled* around with laughter at this.

• • •

In March, November began to sprout her own seeds at home in leftover plastic blueberry containers. Digging through the boys' discarded clutter on the back porch, she unearthed the frozen goldfish. "Uuuugh!" The noise was completely reflexive, uncontrolled, like the noise one makes when one is hit by a car backing out of its driveway. A cartoonish melody is heaved, windy rhythms broken from a tummy.

"What the fuuuuuck!" she tremored smally, gaping angrily now at a hoof poking out of an old burlap sack stained with deer's blood.

• • •

The bathroom smelled similar to rotten basil, but good somehow, like the way good grilled hot dogs smell of burnt ginger . . . man, he missed hot dogs. He'd long been vegetarian-ish, but had traditionally allowed occasional relapses. Now, with November around, that was out of the question. She was so diligently obsessed with animals and ethics and blah blah blah.

As she slowly coiled up—arms around knees under chin—she rearranged the pubic hairs on the tile floor to make a question mark, one big question mark out of a bunch of small ones. Benny wondered how far she meant to extend this pubic hair metaphor, if she meant it as a metaphor at all. Did she know what she was doing? Did he? Was this the question he was always asking? He was not in love, but why not? Why was he not in love? What's it like to be in love? It must be different for everyone. Maybe he *was* in love. If so, he was nonplussed.

She stared at him, her nose now nudged between her knees. Did she know how vulnerable she was? The dreamy stare filled him with a kind of aimless guilt of which only parents are allowed to openly complain.

And he remembered his passive-aggressive accusatory manner the night before:

"I just feel . . . really . . . gross," he'd said, pouting.

"Okay! I'm sorry! You're not perfect anymore!" she'd shouted meekly, rather offended by Benny's self-deprecating pouting about the sore on his lip, which had appeared not long after November's consultation with Planned Parenthood over the mysterious pink bumps in her region.

(Years later, Benny would, upon returning for a second and even third test, be quite surprised at the persistent affirmation that he was free and clear from any sexually transmitted infections. All the signs had been there, and he had lived the past several years believing that he had contracted herpes from November. The web research indicated such, and their situation did as well. I suppose, however, that despite WebMD and quick answers from East Indian internet doctors, mysteries do persist in this age, if only as nuisances.)

"I'm sorry I was coughing so much last night," he said, apologizing for a non-offense (something they both knew he had no real control over) in order to mitigate his own guilt and avoid the humiliating concession of a valid apology. But even this apology, he realized, may have been hypocritical, because, upon light consideration, he couldn't

remember if he'd tried even a little bit to stop himself from cough-
ing. And disturbing her sleep had not crossed his mind. It was purely
his own agitation and discomfort that had compelled him to drink at
least twice the recommended dosage of Walmart's Equate brand Tus-
sin DM. Ultimately, he hadn't even attempted to deter the spread of
his own germs when, at last, sprawled on his back, he'd surrendered,
coughed fully, with his whole being, and felt the cold ethereal spit mist-
ing his face. The exact opposite of a hot compress . . . or whatever those
steamy, towel-covered getups are called.

"That's okay. You couldn't help it." To her, conversations were like
William Wallace's: She would follow them to any end, never complain-
ing of scant supplies or poorly-written romantic detours.

In reply, he contrived a formulaic smile, which was meant to convey
ninety percent "You're so great," and ten percent "Sometimes you're a little
too great," but it may have just said "Have a nice day." Either way, her stare
seemed to intensify. Why couldn't he be this intrigued? He lusted for
that wonder. Wonderlust. He had wonderlust. The monotonous tragedy
of wondering, double-checking to see what you forgot, but never catching
a view through the windshield of a cockpit. Maybe not everyone falls in
love. There's no way everyone falls in love. Love the one you're with.

He changed the subject.

"I saw a YouTube video today of a guy masturbating in Walmart.
He was facing or aiming at a Hannah Montana shirt." He paused, an-
ticipating her look. "Yeah. I'm kind of embarrassed about that, that I
watched it. Gross?"

She nodded.

"I don't know if it was real or not. I mean, if the guy was actually
masturbating or whatever."

"Who's Hannah Montana?"

"She was one of Disney's underage fantasies, but a wholesome one,
at least *more* wholesome, I think. She would not have been amused
by this guy's—or, at least the character of her would not have been
amused . . . I mean, *I* was, but . . . I'm at least embarrassed about it."

"Are you?"

He paused to give the appearance that he was reconsidering his answer, "Yeah."

· · ·

Despite (or maybe because of) November's longsuffering tolerance, Benny began to complain more frequently of depression. This, he explained, was likely due to winter's brutal effects on mood: that long period of burdensome dormancy. But he could feel the doubt. It wasn't just the winter; it was the doubt, too. Doubling. Pushing. "Is this the thing?" Is this what people are supposed to be looking for? Is this love? And if it's not, what happens next? What happens next must be the thing to think about. If it's not. What people are looking for. And it seems like it's not. Because if this is it, then that's . . . nonplussing. And life is really boring. And life can't be *that* boring. Dear God. Can it?

· · ·

Mayhaps it is unnecessary to rehearse the correlation, but, but! as their connection slipped and thinned, as interloping psychic energy muddied, the light of intimacy weakened between Benny and November, tooooooo the degree that a sterile white tube of KY Sensitive Jelly now rested atop *The Life and Opinions of Tristram Shandy, Gentleman*, which rested atop *Gargantua and Pantagruel*, which rested atop a grubby blue bedside table. The jelly—in this case, an indicator, as implied, of intimacy problems deeper than mere sexuality—was now an increasingly requisite component of their lovemaking, the frequency of which had lessened muchly. If the resting angle hadn't been so precarious, *Gargantua and Pantagruel* would have spent a great deal of time in the first tier. That is to say, Benny read Rabelais more than he'd have liked, each retrieval of the book disturbing the jelly, each time a reminder of jelly disturbed.

Desperately, they clung to scraps of arousal; their intimacy mechanical now, reduced to urges limited to the purely physical.

November was often tired at night. So they tried afternoons. Mornings. Sometimes good. But never more.

Clearly, it was not the time for it. Still, they both tried. She began to dry; he began to soften. It began to slow. Rabelais' jelly so far away. (Bakhtin's carnival, perhaps further.)

"I don't think I'm gonna finish," he decided aloud, finally allowing his emotion to steer.

After, each found the discussion difficult. Drained of its sexual tension, their awkwardness no longer felt charming.

November closed her eyes. Benny returned to discussions of politics (false flag terrorism) to fill the void optimally filled by snuggling and happy sighs.

"Oh yeah, I forgot to mention the Germans sinking ships on the American coast. That complicates things some, though they were technically enemies, of course."

"Mmm, subs," she said, falling asleep.

"U-boats."

"Oh, yeah . . . they were really gettin' in there with their U's and boats. I really wish I had a cookie."

In her dream though, she got pizza, a pizza made of collected sex parts. The grease, the sweat; the cheese, dead skin. There was real pepperoni though. No suggestion of likeness. The pepperoni asserted its identity. November had many times, during her waking life, asked others to consider, as you may be, the synecdoche of pepperoni. The *synecdoche* of pepperoni's castrating a piglet without anesthesia. Kicking and prodding a smooth, bloody piglet into a cage soon to be sodden of her own young piss and shit. And, often, vomit. Sometimes a corpse lying near the cage, which is too small even to turn around in. Impossible, then, to turn away.

...

At the kitchen window Benny pouted over the lingering snow, graying in the angles of the gurgling sewerside curbs. He was feeling trapped, and also a little guilty for wondering what November would look like with a smaller nose. Or maybe a slightly reshaped chin? He thought about how that might work. Would they grind at the bone? Or cut away ... things? He reprimanded himself for these musings.

"Fuck you, peanut butter." He was doing the dishes and had decided not to clean out the peanut butter from the plastic jar because it was sticking, in a slimy way, even though it had been filled with water for a while as an attempt to loosen it from the plastic. It was simply too gloopy now, and his level of motivation was no match for this extreme gloopiness, and, accepting this, he again reprimanded himself.

"What?" she asked over the running water.

"I was talking to the peanut butter," he replied, as he stooped over the refuse bin to pull out the red lid and screw it back onto the jar—no sense in suffering the stench of that rancid goo.

"Uhuh."

And issuing shortly from the kitchen (with considerable abandon) were the yawps he sounded as a defense against the compounding guilt that accompanied his realization that this brand of active trash care was a particularly petulant and selfish selective effort.

"Did you know there's a cat dying in here?" she quipped.

"Yes," he replied, slightly stifling a hysterically displaced chuckle. "It's the cat in my heart." He looked at her almost angrily, expecting her to laugh. And, dutifully, she almost did, but it's hard to do your duty when duty is all that remains. "Haaaaa!" he blurted. "I feel so crazy. I keep wanting to say 'fair enough.' I feel like someone's doing white trash witchcraft on me."

Somewhere apart from language, her body made the statement, "You are an angry wag yelping, making a silly dog of me." Inaudible. But she felt it. And almost heard it.

"A little girl asked for my autograph today. Her mother told her I was nobody," she said turning and looking thoughtfully out the window at an electric line that was being whipped about by the wind. "And it was almost kind of funny—it *was* kind of funny, in some ways—but . . . I thought about how . . . I *feel* like nobody. I thought about how, really, it's *my* job to make me feel like somebody other than nobody. But," she paused again, "it's also . . . kind of your job too."

Though he said nothing, a look of protest leapt onto Benny's face, part of which was daubed by blood from a pimple that popped during the night. November let her words settle then looked up sullenly at him, giving him a chance to speak. Still, he said nothing.

"And, the thing is, I *knew* that would be your reaction. I *knew* you would be defensive about it. And I knew you would do this. I knew your look would change like that," she sighed, "exactly how it is right now. Your problem with me saying these things is that your ego is hurt—not that I feel worthless, like a nobody. I am saying that I feel like a no-body, and you are managing to find a way to take offense. And do you know how I knew this would happen? Because it has before. More or less." She looked back out the window. Brittle, gray fallen twigs. Wind-whipped, brown jagged branches. Cold, dark trunks. Everything dead, but for a whorling electric line.

On the dark side of the street, the church sign read, "Easter comes once a year. How often do you?"

"What are you talking about? Okay. Well, you did just implicate me in your feelings of worthlessness, sooo . . . in some ways, it *is* about me. Isn't it?"

"Sure. Yeah."

"Okay. Well, I don't . . . if you're gonna be sarcastic about this, then I don't know. I mean, I *try* to help you feel good about yourself."

"Yeah."

Benny shook his head.

"I guess we fail," she said, barely breathing now, her shrunken voice laboring from a shallow hollow.

• • •

April fell onto their heads like the heavy wooden frame of a cloudy mirror. And why wouldn't it? For fuck's sake. It snowed a foot and a fucking half on April 1st. What does that mean to you? Can you imagine it? And, if so, do you care? About the snow? I guess that's up to me, in part, and I *would* give you a sensory detail, but I don't think it's entirely crucial to the overall effect of this story. If one exists.

My *characters* were there. All of them. Waiting on me to die. And they felt the kick of a foot of snow on April 1st. So whether you get it or not, well . . . either way. Because a bona fide blizzard on April 1st? C'mon. It's enough already. What details do you need? We're all dying anyway, in theory—some of us apparently overpaying for it—sifting through ceaseless quotidia. Suffering capaciously. In our little special ways. Desperately seeking distraction. No explanation.

And still the drone of snow. In April.

I guess what I am trying to say is that sometimes snow *is* made of words.

But not this snow.

Not in April.

• • •

May arrived ahead of schedule, at which point spring budded quickly, as—following six months of frigid, ashen torpor—is its wont. Stems pulled hurriedly at their branches. Leaves yanked fervently out from these. The sun shone. But no one knew whether to trust it. Or how to pick up their heads.

And no rain fell. So consecrated perennial cycles dried into early blossom.

. . .

Blossie was looking around a little nervously. Waiting for Jenny in the high school parking lot had not been a thing she'd anticipated when they'd first met at the Country Kitchen, which had become her favorite haunt. She'd ordered country-fried steak and eggs with a side of sausage gravy: everything she couldn't before November left. She did it vengefully now, each order (carnistic slang salivating) and each bite vindictive. Reclamations.

In fact, Blossie'd eaten as much meat as she could in the months following November's departure—and had increased her body mass significantly. More determined now than ever, she'd combined heavy weight-training with some over-the-counter hormone therapy, preparing, as she saw it, to embrace her new anatomy. Psychologically, she already felt well-prepared. She embraced her new identity with a small bit of guidance and a lot of inspiration from the internet community of trans webcomics and some of the other seedier sites. She'd worked to take on this new role, to "become a man," as a fatherless teenage boy might: through cliché machismo and stereotypically gendered modifications of (body) language and extreme hygienic neglect. Cursin, high-fivin, rarely smilin. Drinkin, stinkin, and never thinkin. She'd even begun to hunt. Tried anyway. Began taking money from her parents again. Bought a shotgun and a treestand. Waited angrily in it. In chorus with the male uniform, this had been her closest approximation to grieving: hateful treestand-stewing in cold, gray, rain—almost every day during November and much of that winter—a perch from which she never caught even one glimpse of a deer.

Jenny finally walked out of the building and got in.

"Wow. I have to say . . . this is weird, even for me," Blossie said, looking around the parking lot, glassy-eyed.

Jenny looked unamused. Said nothing.

"I'm just kidding," Blossie exclaimed. (She wasn't.)

"I know."

"Is something wrong?"

"Today was weird," Jenny said, looking at the wide concrete steps that led to the high school's front entrance.

"God. Yeah. Every day is weird at a place like this," Blossie replied, reading the flashing advertisements on the school's proud new electric sign: JV baseball, an awards ceremony, the spring theater production, *A Woman of No Importance*. (Fall's production had boasted *A Man for All Seasons*.) "What the fffffuck?" she whispered, as November passed from her periphery into full view and continued up to the front steps where Benny and Wentworth were standing.

"What?" Jenny said, gazing inquisitively now in the direction of Blossie's astonishment. She saw Wentworth and shuddered. She'd been hiding from him ever since she first spotted him at the school. She'd even skipped classes whose destinations necessitated routes she thought would require her to pass him in the hall. But today the guy who'd given her a ride to the truck stop the night she'd escaped … he was their sub now?! What the hell were the chances?! This unexpected merging of coordinates—space and time diachronically combining in her subconscious—roused psychic defense mechanisms, which caused associative emotions: Seeing Benny reminded her of that night, which reminded her of Wentworth, of the RV in which she'd spent so many muddled days—and, vaguely, of the dilapidated building in which she unknowingly spent so many nights. Unaware the weed was laced with meth, she'd returned to him, increasingly entranced, wondering at first if perhaps she were in love. What followed were blurred sequences of strangers, pain, exploitation.

As she choked out this explanation, Blossie's anger grew holy. She squeezed the driver's seat's underside with both hands, almost tearing a hole through the vinyl. Her eyes felt hot, as she stared past Jenny into the violent distance. Yearning to escape the school's hellish and haunt-ing landscape, Jenny repeatedly requested that they leave the lot, but Blossie was in a trance of rage. She wasn't really hearing Jenny anymore, neither did she notice that her own craned neck was visibly throbbing with a venomous strain. Who the fuck were these people! And what the fuck were they doing now at Jenny's school, at anyone's school!

Finally, Jenny grabbed her arm and pulled it away from the seat. "I have to go right now. I want to get out of here! If you won't drive me, I'm leaving!"

"Okay," Blossie managed, grinding her teeth, "let's go."

As she pulled away, she looked back over at November, now talking uncomfortably with Wentworth, and Benny, who'd just joined them.

"Wait," Blossie said. "The one in the green hat?"

"Yeah," Jenny answered, peeking back slowly.

"I am . . . it's okay," Blossie said, nodding sternly, seething with visions of revenge and justice. Errant visions, as it turns out, for Jenny's color-blindness—about which she was quite sensitive and, as a result, had never mentioned to Blossie—had profoundly affected the situation: Jenny was a dichromat. She was red-green colorblind. Wentworth wore the red hat; Benny the green. Nonetheless, Blossie was after Benny now. The piece of shit in the green hat. (The one, it seemed to Blossie, that November favored.) This was him! Of course! The womanizing piece of *dog shit* that November'd probably fallen in with when she was looking for a penis to suit them.

This was it, then. The penis . . . *the* penis. Despicable. The predation of men. The weak will of women. And the fact that *she*, Blossie, had, if by mere coincidence, still, nonetheless, played a part. But it would end justly. November wouldn't follow through. But Blossie would. Not for November. For Jenny. And for every other woman too weak to find revenge. This would be more than mere justice. More than a reclamation.

In fact, it was some sort of . . . numinous . . . amalgamation (plus ineffable irony) because suddenly, for the first time in a very long time, Blossie's resolve wavered, and she felt that perhaps she had discovered something. Perhaps she didn't want the sexual reassignment; perhaps it felt good to be a woman—if only to maintain the opposition to men. Ultimately, though, this delusion, it would pass. The feeling that she was meant to be a man would not. She would not allow one illusory epiphany to change her whole plan. Or at least it wasn't likely. Either way, whatever happened, surgery or not, one thing was sure: She would have that cock.

Vegetable Korma (Straight)

Tofu Marinade:
- Not-chicken broth (3 cups)
- 1 teaspoon cinnamon
- 1 tablespoon garam masala
- 1 tablespoon cumin
- 1 tablespoon coriander
- 3 dainty sprinkles of cardamom—unless your kind just toss around cardamom
- 2 cloves garlic
- ¼ cat's mouth ginger
- 1 teaspoon salt

Start:
1. Find a suitable place from which to watch the world decay.
2. Marinate 24 oz. of dried, cubed tofu overnight in tofu marinade.
3. Dice and fry five onions in oil at medium heat (5 - 10 minutes).
4. Add ⅓ cat's mouth diced garlic, 1 cat's mouth slivered ginger, 4 green chilies (flitched).
5. Fry 'til onions are golden brown.

6. Mix, by volume (in descending order), the following: cayenne pepper, salt, coriander, cinnamon, fennel, smoked paprika, turmeric, cumin, black pepper, cardamom, cloves, and nutmeg. Add 10 - 12 tablespoons of this concoction.

Vegetables:
- 1 sabered yellow squash
- 1 zucchini (hewn)
- 4 scored carrots
- 4 cat's mouths of green beans
- 1 slivered red pepper
- 35 golden raisins
- 30 bisected cashews

Finish:
1. Drain marinade into mixing bowl and sauté tofu at high heat, until golden brown.
2. Dump everything in pot.
3. Add two cans coconut milk.
4. Add a couple pinches more cinnamon, salt, garam masala, cumin, coriander, ground clove, turmeric, all to taste.
5. Simmer for 20 minutes.

Rice:
1. Pour 3 cups basmati rice into a pot.
2. Add 1 cat's mouth oil, 2 tablespoons not-chicken bouillon, 1 tablespoon sea salt, and 1 teaspoon turmeric.
3. Cook.
4. Wait for marauding hordes of cannibal goon-squads.

• • •

The next day Blossie followed Benny home from Jenny's high school. She drove by the house seven times over the following three days, scanning the lawn and bushes for the most promising reconnaissance positions. As luck would have it, the garage roof, the neighbor's garage roof, and the white birch in the back yard were all accessible. Unfortunately, the curtains were drawn every time it got dark enough to hide atop a garage or tree. Blossie persevered, however, opportunistically sleuthing, in turn, each member of the household.

Beyond this, she did not know exactly what her plan was, but she knew she would need help. The body had to be fresh when it got to California. That is to say, the penis did. Ideally, she could keep him alive until they arrived. How though? A kidnapping? Possible. But probably very messy and too complicated to be a one-man job. She decided to take a few weeks to think about it. Dick would be out of the country for the summer, anyway, assisting physicians with some iteration of "Doctors Without Borders." She would just have to keep tabs on "Wentworth's" house until the plan materialized.

She resisted the urge to trail November, perhaps knowing or at least fearing that November would somehow sense her presence.

• • •

Throughout the semester, Benny's substitute teaching opportunities had increased, and he'd become reaccustomed to the horrid crepuscular chills and congregating yellow buses of public education: the schools' sweet, plasticky smells; the halls dull and tepid in the morning, sharp and shrieking in the afternoon; students dressing much sexier than he remembered, behaving just as doltishly.

Twice, he thought he saw Joni Cherry, but neither time could he see her long enough for absolute confirmation. And since half the kids at these schools reminded him of some person he knew or had known, he let this pass quickly from his mind. Was the gene pool really so small? Ethnic diversity seemed to have increased since he'd been a high school student in these parts, and somehow everyone still looked alike, a phenomenon which seemed only to occur inside public high schools.

Had he and November sustained the prolific, precise intimations they'd shared that past autumn, Benny would have known that this homogeneity lingered into higher education, as well—making it difficult, in fact, for November to remember any of her classmates' names. This hindrance, along with her persistent fear of encountering Blossie in a public place, ensured November's insularity. She hurriedly slunk from classroom to classroom, never stopping to pose in hallways or the busy quad. Such buffers prevented her from making friends with the other students, and allowed the flourishing of introverted peculiarities that continued to draw her closer to plants and animals than to human life. (So goes the readymade archetypal ingenue.)

In her sociology course, for instance, a cricket's muffled chirping had persisted through nearly every class for the past month. It seemed, to November, as though it must have been stuck in the paneling of the wall. She kept looking around at the other students for signs of concern similar to hers, or at least for confirmation that the sound was indeed occurring. But other than some animated ogling from two philistine boys in the class, no one acknowledged her searching countenance.

Following each of the past three classes, she'd remained in the room, waiting until everyone exited so that she might conduct her investigation, covertly crawling the length of the room's back wall, trying to find the cricket. The tiles were cold, and gritty too, apparently deprived of janitorial attentions. She pulled gently on the brown plastic baseboard paneling, and marveled, with some concern, at how very little effort was required to detach it from the beige walls. But she could not find the cricket. Once, someone entered the room and asked her if she was okay.

"Oh, ummm, yeah," she faltered, gazing upward, mouth ajar, "I just . . . lost my pen."

"I see. Do you need another one?"

"Oh, ummm . . . no. Thanks. I have more. I just . . . liked that one, particularly."

The cricket's chirps seemed to weaken each day. November began to worry that it was dying. She continued to stay after class, and on really bad days, she sang to the cricket. Feeling something in herself dying as well, she allowed the emotive expression of these dirges to increase somewhat. Unrealized—perhaps deliberately—was the primary source of her feelings. But for the gender inversion, the lyrics she sang to the cricket revealed the answer, had she wanted to hear it. That is to say, she warbled and swayed in and out of the familiar British accent: "She wakes up. She makes up. She takes her tiiiiiime and doesn't feel she has to hurry. She no longer needs you."

On the way home, her bike's brake levers chirped against the bumps in the sidewalk.

· · ·

Benny and November. Their points of disagreement had multiplied and progressed from flirtatious to unfriendly (a familiar theme). Months ago, the autumn prior:

"Oh, there's a bee's nest out here."

"What?"

"There is a bees' nest out here, aa-thatta-way. Just out here and to your right. Just stick your head out here and look over to the right."

"Ah, yeah. Okay. Those are wasps."

"Well, I think I need to get rid of them."

"Oh really? How are you going to do that?"

"I don't know," and with a sudden grab to the junk, "probably just whap it there with my cock."

And, somehow, she'd deflated at the waist, buckling over with laughter—love's giddiness opening doors to all manner of lowest common denominators.

"You know, just get it out of there with a good cock sneeze."

Now, this afternoon:

B: "I think there's a nest in the corner of that window."

N: "That one?"

B: "Yeah, the top left corner."

N: "Like a bird's nest orrrr?"

B: "A yellowjackets' nest, I think."

N: "Mmmm."

B: "Might have to kill it. I hate having to do that, but . . . I don't know. Other animals do it," he said, beginning to anticipate her response. "I mean, in terms of territorial stuff . . . that's the last thing or time or situation when I feel okay about killing."

She glared at him.

"Well, I can't exactly send them a *letter*. I wish I could."

"Yeah? How about, 'Dear wasps, I am sorry, but I will have to ask you to leave. Actually, never mind. We'll just kill you. I would ask you to relocate, buuuuut there are too many of us now. Soooo," she sang angrily, "you will have to stop procreating so much, I guess, because there's really no convenient place to put you anymore. I know this will probably begin to fuck up our equilibrium and actually cause our plant life to suffer hugely, buuuut. Hm . . . you know, on second thought, why don't you help me kill a lot of *people*, instead. That actually makes way more sense."

"Uh-huh. Ohhhkay. Ohhhhhhkay," he muttered as he left the room.

Later that evening she sat in bed reading, propped against the wall, which was buffered and softened by a folded pillow. Benny wore headphones and sat at the computer. She glanced at him, feeling the distance between them, wondering whether she had been correct about yellowjackets being pollinators and wondering what Benny was watching. It looked like *South Park*, but the angle obscured the images. He stared into the computer screen, picking his nose then forming and hardening the booger between his thumb and first finger. Finally, he threw it behind him. It hit the glockenspiel next to the wastebasket and sounded a faint Bb.

With her left hand, November grabbed a tuft of pages. Placed them between her thumb and pointer finger. She thumbed over them then slowly rubbed her pointer finger out from under each. One at a time. Working page-by-page toward her current mark. She caressed each then let it flutter, shortly resettling.

Benny closed the laptop, pulled the headphones up from his ears, and set them on the desk. Then he walked over to his guitar.

"Yes!" she intoned with quiet excitement, "I love hearing you play late at night. When you get out the guitar before bed, I feel like I've done something right that day." Though she did not understand the details, she sensed the vital intimacy Benny absorbed and exuded upon certain interactions with his guitar; it seemed to pacify the room, and soothe them both. November noticed that he hadn't played much lately, but she thought maybe if she encouraged him, he would play more. And perhaps this would help to bridge the growing rift between them.

"Aww . . . thanks," he said, glancing back at the guitar then back up at her. She smiled at him, and he smiled back. "You haven't."

With effortful buoyancy, she accepted the sardonic joke, straining in the moment to sustain the submissive expression she'd found for the full length of his gloating followup gaze—and not half a second longer. At the very moment his attention finally left her and returned to the fretted rosewood in his left hand, her eyes, brows, cheeks, lips, chin

(even nose) fell with what, for her, was daring audacity: a face's full ava-
lanche, reckless valiance fed by close proximity to surrender.

Likely it was this same valiance—more so, certainly, than ritual
obeisance to her natural urges—that pulled her off the bed to him,
where she squeezed beside and leaned over to wrap her arms around
his back and shoulders, the side of her face cool on his neck and col-
larbone.

With a heavy sigh he stopped playing, looked at her hand resting
against the guitar and him. Momentarily, her hair fell into view, and he
watched her other hand appear, as she pulled the shiny tussock back to
her neck. His face drooped now, too, and warmed.

Their stomachs felt empty.

. . .

Benny turned and then re-turned to face (double-takin') the window
through which he had just seen a solitary bush wobbling with uncom-
mon force. And do you know what I say that was? Or who, rather?
Yes. It was Blossie. The trees had been harder to climb than she an-
ticipated.

"Okay, little guy," he said slowly, looking back down at the gnat
on the fingerling potato in his hand, "you ready? . . . I hope so." Then
he quickly smashed the potato into his other hand. He next held the
potato under the faucet, where the water pulled the smudged little body
into the garbage disposal.

"Oh, shit!" Wentworth roared, tromping into the kitchen, "Did
I tell you about . . . oh, shit! So there's this dude at the school I've
been subbing at"—he laughed very hard here—"I think he might even
be like the assistant principal or hold some other grand station. He
walks with a giant . . . well, he has . . . some kind of gimpy-fag dis-
ease. And let me say, as well, that he limps like a cripple and looks
retarded all over the place. Sooooo," he continued, glancing coldly at

Benny who had not looked up from the sink, "he commented on me looking spiffy one day—I was wearing extra formal attire to put the fear of God into some nondescript mass of goons, or to suck up to my superiors or something—and here's what I bashfully, and/or with as little contempt as I could stifle, said when he asked if there was any particular reason I was especially well-dressed that day: 'Oh, you know, just trying to put my best foot forward, I guess.'" Wentworth laughed wildly at this. "I didn't even realize how golden it was until after I'd said it! What instinct! Eh? . . . Did I mention that he limps all over the building like a gimpy retard? What? Oh. He's 'standing' behind me, isn't he."

Benny frequently found similar versions of Wentworth's gruff humor quite satisfying, but this story had only increased his sadness.

"Your *hole*'s not here, you know. You're allowed to laugh."

Benny did not reply.

Wentworth exited through the back door.

When she saw Wentworth—"Benny," to her—Blossie tip-toed from the bush to her car. Her parking strategy had been perfect, and she was able (undetected) to follow Wentworth to a rotting, windowless building covered in ivy. He'd parked a block away and entered quite discreetly. An hour later he left the building in the same manner as he'd entered. Blossie, careful to be sure he was not doubling back, waited for a half hour before she approached the building. But the single back door was locked, and while there appeared to be a hole in the block wall on the east side of the building, it was dark inside, and her keychain flashlight revealed little.

"Hello?" she whispered bravely.

No response.

She decided to check back later that night.

Would you like to know why? Well. I decline to answer. As I see it, you should know pretty well already. Next, you're gonna start asking what fucking color wool sweater she was wearing. And then where will we be? Eh? Brain-d[i/y]e[a]d in the wool, I say. Just lyin' there.

Gettin' the wool pulled. Pullin' wool over. Thinking lewd thoughts about wool-pullin' puns. "Hotter than two rats fucking in a wool sock."[26]

Blossie had just decided to head home and check back later that night or maybe start again tomorrow with the observance of the ass-hole's house. But since I don't feel like walking you through all that crap, Wentworth returned! He returned to the building!

Blossie watched him walk casually to its rear, an apparently heavy backpack slung over his shoulder.

She exited her car, leaving the door open for quicker escape, and approached guardedly. The ivy flittered in the misty wind, not so much slapping as flicking the wall. Blossie noticed the smell of rust, as she slowly approached the decrepit structure and crouched carefully to peek through the little hole in the block. Two candles were lit, and Went-worth was lighting more. The dim room gradually brightened as he continued lighting what seemed like an endless line of candles situated mostly on the floor in the corners of the room; another cluster rested on the deep sill of a boarded up window, and many more sat atop a long shelf that bordered the west wall. Beside these was an empty cage that might once have held a snake or rat or tarantula. Or perhaps some combination thereof.

Blossie could see rather clearly through the hole now. Paranoia fed the suspicion that the inverse condition might be shared by those inside the building, so she bobbed her head up and down, side to side, despite the knowledge that this series of maneuvers was likely unnecessary. Having donned her darkest and quietest garments, she was well-dressed

---

26 Other creative colloquial uses of "wool," apropos of nothing, include synecdoches wherein (1) a non-Liverpudlian is accused of posing as a Liverpudlian/Scouser—historically, this derives from the insinuated tendency of the non-Liverpudlian poseur to wear a distastefully pauperized wool garment, the acerbic reference to which was/is used synecdochally as a substitute for the whole person of the accused—and (2) as a reference to a woman's pubic hair, the word "wool" acts in a similarly diminutive sense (and perhaps a sort of *double* synecdoche) to serve as an allusion to the female reproductive organ, and additionally, as a slang synonym for the whole female person.

for this investigation. Her movements were deft and noiseless, and they bolstered her courage, the increasing dexterity and strength she was discovering in her new body.

As the room brightened, and as her valor grew, Blossie spent longer flashes in front of the hole in the wall, examining the scene as best she could. A crooked card table with a bunch of metal and glass utensils piled on it sat next to the trash bags that had accumulated and lay pell-mell against the wall. What had initially appeared to be a shelf, Blossie now recognized as a piano. In the middle of the room there were numerous blankets and cruddy pillows resting atop and alongside an old mattress. And was that a . . . person? A human body underneath them?

Blossie ducked quickly as Wentworth approached the wall through which she was staring. She heard the squeaky thump of couch or bed springs creak deeply. The sound was frighteningly clear, and she could feel the vulgar force of his indifferent weight as it plopped down and vibrated the wall. Other than a sound akin to fingernails being clipped, she heard nothing for almost half an hour. She dared not move, for her fright had abolished the shaky laws of physics, and she was now convinced that he would feel the change in pressure against the wall if she wavered at all or failed otherwise to hold her exact position with unflawed stillness.

Time passed. How much? How long had it been? Seemed like a lot. She'd lost track of time. Had he fallen asleep? Would he fall asleep there? Like an animal?

She turned and shifted inch-by-inch, finally arising again to her crouching position, and peeked through the hole.

Wentworth was standing over the pile in the middle of the room and uncovering . . . the . . . body? Holy shit! It *was* a body! A person! Fuck!

He lowered himself and started licking—or . . . was that biting?—the figure's cheek and ear. Rén didn't move.

Blossie watched for thirty seconds—though it felt to her like ten minutes had passed. The still figure on the floor appeared to be female.

"Take out the camera!" she kept telling herself. But what the hell is this freak gonna do to me? To her? Frozen in terror, and awed over how he'd gotten up to all this without making a sound, she kept telling herself, "Take out the camera! Do something!"

But her fear had turned him into something almost supernatural now. Her subliminal senses repeated, "What the hell is this freak gonna do to me?"

"Mace him first, then . . . but then he could run away, and the evidence wouldn't be as convincing. Ah! These fucking digital cameras! The fucking sound they make! It's not even a real sound, is it? It's a sound effect. Goddammit. Can't I turn it off somehow?" But she knew, in that moment, even if it were possible, she couldn't navigate digital minutiae. She could barely yank the phone out of her pocket and find the camera app. Finally, she decided—perhaps feeling the imminence of conflict—to just wait for the wind so that it might hopefully muffle the noise of her camera.

But when he began to pull the blanket down further she saw the tape around her wrists, and that did it. Her initial fury returned and supplanted fear. Now descending was the same torpor of anger she'd felt in the high school parking lot when Jenny first related the appalling details. And her plan, risky as it was, came together subconsciously; she wouldn't have been able to articulate it, but she could feel it.

She put her camera up to the hole and began to take photos, watching through the lens, and Wentworth, now engrossed in what had escalated to odious fondling and some sort of shaking or jerking of the body, did not immediately hear the sound effects of Blossie's first photos.

But then he did. Grabbing the girl's right ankle and hoisting her leg up in the air, he did hear something.

And Blossie saw through her phone's lens that Wentworth had indeed noticed. She quickly hid her face from view, just beside the hole, and listened for Wentworth's next move.

Perhaps it was the hormones fogging his brain, and perhaps he had just gotten too comfortable with his little operation, but

Wentworth—expecting (judging from the chirpy squeaking sounds) merely to dismiss a pestering squirrel—walked over and peeked through the hole, fulfilling his part of our/this/the classic and meaningless cliché.

Blossie watched him arise, seeing his legs moving toward her. Closer now. She grabbed at the pepper spray in her pocket. Then she heard and felt two knees drop to the floor and saw the hole darken slowly with the shadow of Wentworth's face. She raised her pepper spray and filled the hole from every angle. Wentworth shrieked and flailed onto the couch, his eyes, nostrils, and left ear seared and throbbing. Blossie pushed the pepper spray through the hole and kept spraying, as best she could, in the direction of the couch until the can was empty. Then she ran to the door and, shocked to find it unlocked, stepped carefully into the building.

Wentworth was lurching about on the couch, face parts smoldering. Blossie crept quickly along the wall and huddled toward the figure on the floor. She didn't look bruised or scraped, and, though she was somewhat well-hidden under two grimy quilts, her body was, other than that, covered only by canary-yellow and lavender underwear, which seemed to have been roughly yanked and were thoroughly stretched now. The elastic band around her waist was floppy as a shoelace, bunching limply into the small caverns between her stomach and hip bone, and hung loosely to the floor from the sides of her waist.

Blossie glared at Wentworth as he writhed and moaned. She grabbed a long brass candleholder from the table, swung it at him, and hammered his skull. Against the candleholder, his head felt soft, like tenderizing half-frozen steak with a metal meat mallet. He fell from the couch and rolled on the ground. Blood covered two of his fingertips now as he rubbed the wound through his hair. Blossie swung again for the back of his head, hoping to knock him out. But she hit his ear instead.

Wentworth flailed crazily now, his arms smacking wildly against the girl and grabbing at her. Ringing dissonance of smoky piano. He knocked over a candle and nearly corralled one of Blossie's legs just before she whacked him again, this time on the jaw. He turned over onto the candle, snuffing out the flame, and lay still, moaning quietly, defeated.

"Don't fucking move!" she finally yelled, "or I'll smash your fucking *skull!*" Then she lowered herself to the girl; wrapped her in the greasy gray, pissy blankets, which reeked of vinegar and sulfur; and hoisted her, letting the little body fall over her shoulder.

"I know where you live, you piece of *shit*," she said through tears of anger and adrenaline, "and I have pictures of this." She stepped carefully through the door. "I'll be back for you, you piece of *shit!*" she fumed and marched on. "I'll be back," she growled as she walked over the patch of grass from which she'd spied and sprayed.

Wentworth's mind struggled, through the haze of shock and pain, to make sense of this. Then he arose and felt his way out the door. "Fuck you!" he yelled—trying to bait her—and literally pulled open one burn-ing eyeball to locate his assailant. "Fucking *whore!*" Something in him realized that it was now or never. She had pictures . . . *if* she had pictures . . . either way, he couldn't take chances.

He stumbled through the darkness out toward Blossie's thick sil-houette. Blossie turned to face him and waited. Then she calmly lifted her leg and drove the heel of her heavy hiking boot into his chest, as though she were kicking down a door. Wentworth wheezed and fell to the pavement, quite thoroughly deflated.

Blossie hurried to her car and gingerly placed the girl in the pas-senger seat. Wentworth was up again and trodding angrily toward the sound of the car door. Blossie ran around to the driver's side and start-ed the car as Wentworth limped toward them. She veered at him and threw open her door, letting it smack against his wobbly body. He fell again. The door bounced back toward Blossie, and she pulled it shut as she sped toward the hospital.

• • •

Fine, I'll tell you what the fucking hospital smelled like, for fuck's sake. It smelled the way hospitals do. Like a hospital. An unusually thick film of sterility, bedecked by sky blue paint. Meaningless magazines staring upward from tables whose wood is just barely wood. What in the actual gentle fucking hell do you really want me to tell you about a hospital? Probably very little.

Blossie sat next to one of those shitty wood tables, planning to wait around just long enough to talk to the girl after she awoke—she'd lied to the nurses, claiming to be the girl's sister. It turned out she'd been drugged. The doctors found no trace of foul play in her urine—this was because Wentworth had used GHB, a roofie that medical science hadn't yet learned to detect in such samples. And the girl didn't remember anything. Blossie's camera seemed to contain the only real incriminating evidence in existence. But her plan was not solidified yet, and she didn't feel like talking to the girl's parents, so she left before they arrived. And never looked back. Her rage fogged her sense of duty, dominated her concept of justice, and was now fiercely focused on the punishment of Wentworth and Benny, Benny and Wentworth, whatever the marquee displayed in her mistaken identification of the two scoundrels. And finally we are getting somewhere.

· · ·

From where I spew, (i/u)nt(o/il) vacuity, (more of a drazzle than a rizzle or a doozy—considering recurrent spunk of lodgings) these are stuffs to be tonified, rather than glossed. What I mean, of course, is that it makes the most sense to me, now, to summarize a few things which I don't think will be interesting or exciting if presented in "real," dramatic time. Here are some of those things:

*Wentworth spent the night in his car. He was too afraid of the police to rest inside the rotting concrete walls of what had become his lair away from home. Relatively speaking, the night had dealt him gracious injuries: Officially, he'd suffered only a bruised hip and jaw, as well as a minor concussion. Over the next couple slowly-passing weeks, he concealed these injuries carefully as he waited to see what would become of Blossie's threat. With each new day, he became more confident that she was full of shit about the pictures. But all the same, he'd cleaned up the building thoroughly and told his regular customers that the show was over, reminding them that he had pictures of everything, and if he went down, so would they. And if such were the case, he would, with grim diligence, revisit reciprocal acts upon them—acts now more or less owed them—vampiric performances, etc.

*Blossie emailed Dick to reopen the discussion regarding her surgery. His availability was currently limited, he said. However, early in the next semester would be a great opportunity because many of the necessary buildings on campus (from which he would pilfer certain requisite items) would be all but abandoned for about a week. And he would be one of very few people with keys to these buildings. It would require stealthy shuffling and great care, but he assured her it could be done.

*With the end of the substitute teaching season nearing, Benny and Wentworth managed to secure part-time jobs with a landscaping company.

· · ·

The birds began to chirp. It was only 3:30. Strange. Birds chirping at 3:30. In the morning. This is early, even for birds, no? The spring—or whatever the hell this latecoming season was—presented (with such sprezzatura!)[27] anomalous subtleties to make one think the end was near. And/or that you were going crazy. The leaves that finally appeared

---

27 Please (please) note the joke, as it were, "punctuated" by the juxtaposition of "sprezzatura" with "!" (exclamation point).

(where they are more or less meant to) did *not* look right. They were absolutely flaccid. But only when you looked away. Or rather, only when they thought you weren't looking. Which was frequent. Certainly more frequent than one is comfortable with, concerning flaccidity and leaves.

Other than this faint papier mache quality of leaves; squirrels, rabbits, and even raccoons were disconcertingly disconcerted. They did not pounce with silliness. They were not brash. They did not frolic or act in any way irresponsibly. They clung to worried perches, seeming to brood. Or muse, at best. Kierkegaardian, in sum.

"That's Salvia," she said, as they stopped to rub their fingers across the purple stalks growing in the beds of the park on Water Street and Main. "My dad grows tons of it, supposedly." Then (what might have been accompanied by the orchestral score of a children's show) downward fell her face, but her head didn't move.

November had convinced Benny to walk with her. She needed the exercise, she said, but she was scared to go by herself now, as there'd been rumors of strange perversions occurring in the neighborhood, which the neighbors were quite shocked about, considering how "nice" all the inhabitants of their block were.[28]

It wasn't clear yet to him, but she was intimately shaken by the fact that he needed convincing, the fact that he wouldn't suggest to go with her or just ask what seemed to be wrong—why she would need so badly to go walking (perhaps even by herself if necessary) in the middle of the night.

It wasn't clear to her yet, but the Salvia was dredging other urges, too. Things undone. And alluringly unknown.

---

28   Why is it that people are "so shocked!" when they hear that some particular "nice" person is a murderer, a rapist, whatever? I would like to submit— mannered perhaps not as graciously as . . . something—that being "nice" is (1) an artifice usually mastered in early primary school and, as such, not much of an achievement; (2) the preferred pretense of adults—be they government officials, business criminals, babysitters—wishing to persuade or dispossess; and (3) an all but minimum requirement for a decent murderer/rapist *not* cast in a feature film.

Cashew Cum and Cardamom (Beegan)

- Blueberries (20)
- Strawberries (5)
- Spinach (big handful)
- Banana (1)
- Cashews (20)
- Lemon juice (⅛ cup)
- Flax oil or seeds (⅛ cup)
- Honey (2 tablespoon)
- Ground cardamom (½ teaspoon)
- Wheatgrass juice (⅛ cup)
- Chia seeds (⅛ cup)
- Chlorophyll (⅛ cup)
- Liberal Queer Milk (Almond, Hemp, Human Kindness)
- Greens powder (⅛ cup)
- Ice cubes or water (for thinner consistency)

Directions:
1. Heave into blender.
2. Go clean up gray quail feathers that cats left next to the garbage can.
3. Build a campfire. Fire in the dark makes everything around it look so good.

. . .

Blossie drove past the Salvia patch on her way to the post office. It was a calm June morning, cooled by a faint breeze. For fuck's sake.

She parked, and carefully reparked, in the post office lot. Then she exited the car and entered the building with a swaggering, exaggerated nonchalance. Approaching the counter, she felt a twinge of anxiety but managed to appear calm.

The post office clerk, a dirty blonde with freckles and large ears poking through her hair, began to examine the package. "Hm," she said thoughtfully, "you could probably save a few of these, I think." She placed the package on the scale. "Yep." Then she began to carefully peel off some of the superfluous stamps.

"Oh, wow, thanks. Geez, you're like a surgeon," Blossie said flirtatiously.

The clerk smiled and swung her head slowly from side to side, singing "like a surgeon" with Madonna's "Like a Virgin" melody.[29]

. . .

The package arrived the next day. Blossie had used a cryptic pseudonym, "The Worm," and had falsified the return address. The addressee line above the house number simply read "Resident Dog-Turd."

Wentworth, having taken some time off while he nursed his wounds, was the only one home. The package had a presence somehow, familiarly nefarious, which impressed upon Wentworth the sense that he'd somehow sent it to himself. He took the heavy mystery to his room and began to inspect it.

---

29   Is Weird Al still alive?

When he finally opened it, he found a glossy, three pound rainbow trout and (protected within a plastic freezer bag) an envelope with a picture of himself taped onto it. Of the house's inhabitants, only Wentworth would recognize the picture's setting. The envelope said simply, "For YOU" next to his picture.

Inside there were more pictures of him, some of them with the girl Blossie'd rescued. And there was a letter written (or scribbled, rather) on blue printing paper in orange crayon—the handwriting childlike and a little bit hard to see:

ASSHOLE:

There are plenty more of these, ASSHOLE.

Meet me where you met me.
Saturday. 4 A.M.

Or go to prison.

P.S. There's a good chance I'm looking at you RIGHT FUCKING NOW, ASSHOLE.

For the first time in a pretty long time, Wentworth felt truly afraid, not just anxious or distressed, but afraid. Terrified actually. He knew far too much about prison to ignore this threat. As his fists compulsively squeezed themselves inward, he began to wonder about the extent of her evidence. And he considered fleeing. Immediately. But where? He was broke. And would that be obvious? Would she be waiting for him somehow? Ambushing? Cutting him off? With God-knows what sort of weapon? He assembled a bologna sandwich and drank a gulp of Black Velvet as he tried to regather his wits.

There must be some reason why she wanted to meet, right? Why had she not turned him in already? She had his fucking address, somehow!

What was she waiting for? Why let time pass and risk his escape if she wanted him locked up so much?

That was it, then. Not much else to consider, really. He would meet her. The only thing left to think about now, was what weapons to bring. And what people. Unfortunately, he couldn't think of anyone he could trust with this. He hadn't exactly made many friends out of his customers or students or any of the other cornfucking bumpkins in that shithole sticktown. Fuck. In fact, he'd just threatened all his clients, or he might have at least had a chance of getting a gun. But on such short notice . . . fuck. At least he had the hatchet.

• • •

Two (technically three) days later, on Saturday at 4 A.M., he met her where she met him. He parked his car eight houses down from the old building and walked toward it. The little hatchet was tucked into his sleeve. The blade hung down, hidden in his curled right hand. He cradled it deftly, having practiced a quick draw method the day before.

"Asshole!" she yelled from her car, the streetlamp glinting against the gun she was pointing at him. He was three houses away now.

"Asshole! Stop! And sit! Or I call the cops!" She clearly had the upper hand here, absolutely flaunting her disinterest in the privacy of their meeting. Wentworth stopped and sat on the curb.

"Lay down!" she yelled, opening the door, still pointing at him the revolver she'd borrowed from her dad's collection, "on your stomach!"

Wentworth lay on the curb, his left arm dangling down a bit into the road, his right lying precariously straight, the handle of the hatchet pointing at a conspicuous angle above his elbow.

Blossie stood over him. Slipping off his head was the same red hat he'd been wearing that day at the high school when Jenny misidentified him as Benny; subconsciously (if errantly), this coincidence reassured Blossie of his identity.

"You better not move. You fucking *asshole!*" she yelled. "I'll fucking shoot you in the back! Against a pedophile, rapist piece of *shit*, any jury would find this a clear case of self-defense."

"What?" Wentworth managed to stutter. "Why are we here?"

"That one." She knelt five feet in front of him, holding a picture of Benny in one hand and the revolver in the other. "Bring me that one," she pointed the gun to the picture of Benny. "Alive. I'll give you some time to figure it out. But I can tell you this. It's him or you," she lied, knowing she would kill them both.

"What?" Wentworth said again.

"THAT! ONE!" she yelled, tapping the picture with the gun then thrusting it forward, closer to his face. "Bring him to me. Alive. Or you go to prison. That's it. More instructions later. I can tell you this though: It's gonna be a long trip for you. And him," she said as she backed away toward her car.

"Oh, and don't fucking MOVE! until I drive away," she yelled. "And remember, I know where you live. You're mine. I'll be around. And you better be a little homebody for these next couple months. I'll be watching. And if you or your car try to leave town, I will cut you *off*, motherfucker! And the cops will have all the evidence they need to put you away for a long fucking time, you piece of shit. It's all on my computer, on my phone, in my email. Backed up to kingdom come. You shithead! Fucker!"

Wentworth waited while she started the car. "I'm watching you," she growled as she drove past him. He'd expected to have more of an effect on this encounter's outcome. "And remember," she stopped the car to yell back at him, "prison is hard on rapists, fuckhead." He lay for another addled minute along the cool concrete curb, feeling glad she was gone and grateful (a rare sensation for him) he'd not been beaten or arrested. But what the hell did she want with Benny? What could Benny have done to her? To anyone, really? It was a confusing situation. All in all, however, and though he mustn't show her this at any point, he felt quite lucky: Benny would be sooo easy to hijack.

Of course, the pictures haunted him. How could he make sure the pictures wouldn't be revealed? And what pictures did she have? Shit. She could have plenty. And they could be bad. And what the? Hm. Breaking into her house, if he could even find her, would be . . . no good. She could be telling the truth about the pictures. They could be in a file, in an email, ready to send to police at any moment. Maybe . . . shit! Too risky. He'd have to wait for her next "play" or whatever.

Shit, though, how did Benny fit in? "Alive"? What did that mean? It implied that harm might come to him later, right? It certainly wasn't a rescue. She could have done that by now. If she feared for him, she could have orchestrated a rescue by now. No. She had it in for him, somehow. Otherwise, why would she be trusting him to bring Benny "alive"? She definitely had it in for ol' Esteben. Somehow. Right? When someone is wanted for *punishment*, he is wanted "alive." What kind of punishment though? Did Benny know her? Was he in on it? No. He couldn't be. But what was between them?

For the next few days he pondered these questions. It seemed he would have to kill her. But how? And where? And what about Benny? He couldn't trust him anymore. His mysterious value to this crazy broad made him suspect, too. And what about November? For fuck's sake!

For several days, he checked the mail obsessively, and he didn't sleep much. But nothing happened. What the hell *was* happening? Had this crazy broad relented? Lost interest?

• • •

In the weeks that followed these, Wentworth did his best to conceal his predicaments—both physical and psychological. He felt himself growing timorous, and not only did he dislike it, but the behavioral aberration seemed risky. This sharp suspicion of others' suspicion was what kept him brusque and consistent through the summer.

There were a few times that he regretted what seemed to be the inevitable necessity of abducting and delivering Benny to this big old, crazed bitch. They'd never exactly achieved any sort of real friendship though, so, all in all, the thought—the relatively simple chance to save himself—was more a comfort than a concern.

On July 4th, they sat in the living room watching "The 84th Annual Smithfield's Hot Dog Eating Championship" on ESPN.

It was apparently "a sweltering 95 degrees" wherever this event was taking place. The affair opened with an on-site announcer hollering, *truly hollering*, these words. Oh, and for a more accurate priming of your imagination, let's conjure a southern accent, as well: "Who dares to tell me the United States is not the greatest country in the history of the world!"

The announcers seemed to have a favorite. "Oh, this guy trains. He practices daily, chews gum to work out his jaws, even watches tape. That's how you know this is a sport."

"Johnny Hallo," they said somberly, reverently, without a hint of irony. "Some people say he's just into eating because it's cool."

Benny looked slowly over at Wentworth; Wentworth squinted back.

As the action got underway, the contestants—all Caucasians— showed their own eccentric strategies. Some ate the bun separate from the dog. Some left them intact and pushed them in slowly, chewing one part at a time, while others crammed the whole thing in and chewed it all at once. Most used the buckets of water provided to wet the bun, making it easier to swallow quickly. I would like very much for us to briefly revisit that last sentence. In order to more easily gulp down the bun (long pause here), literal buckets of water were provided, into which some contestants dipped said buns.

"That's the style and technique that he's perfected and everyone seems to copy: the twist, the turn."

And then emphatically, "Oh, look at him *jam* that in there!"

"That's what your mom said," Benny mumbled. (This would be the only moment Wentworth felt even a hint of guilt regarding what he knew he must do to his sappy housemate.)

"Hot dog eating contests are my favorite part of celebrating the 4th of July. They so perfectly symbolize all that this great day commemorates. I would also like to see a slave-raping contest."

The announcers affirmed Johnny Hallo's movements, as he hopped up and down, apparently trying to wriggle the yeasty, wheated meatpaste down into his gullet: "This ain't no beauty contest. *He* knows that!"

Benny began to wonder how one got started in the business of announcing for hot dog eating contests. And if they were serious. It seemed almost impossible that the two announcers could say what they were saying without immediately recognizing the stupendous idiocy of their statements.

"The competition was stiff, to be sure. However, the greatest eater in the world *right there*, from San Juan, Johnny Hallo takes home the belt again."

As Johnny Hallo approached the stage to accept his prize, some controversy bubbled. Apparently a disgruntled past contestant (a rival of Hallo's) was seen charging at the trophy. Bukashi—the angry old eater—was later arrested for charging the stage microphone, which I'm not entirely sure is a criminal activity. And then resisting arrest. So, basically, arrested for resisting arrest, a mindfuck of an exercise in logic.

In his interview Hallo had this to say:

Hallo: "If Bukashi was a *real* man, he'd be on that stage today with the rest of us. (The camera cut to Bukashi who was handcuffed and being led away by police.)

Interviewer: "It seems like you have a lot to say about that, but first, can I just ask what was the key today?"

Hallo: "Well, I trained hard for this. I was ready. I was focused."

Interviewer: "Did the heat affect you?"

Hallo: "Absolutely not. I trained in this heat. My hometown was this hot for barbecues. I love it."

"Mmmm, hot dogs," Wentworth interrupted, dropping a pile of cashews onto the coffee table, the sound of which reminded Benny of his dad. "The only thing about them is that there's no blood. I like a little blood in my meat. I like tasting it. I want that feeling like when you're flossing, and you feel the blood, or taste it a little, at least. I prefer a hint of flossblood in my animals."

"Are they overanalyzing this?" Benny asked aloud, still listening to the interview, mostly ignoring Wentworth's comments on floss and hot dogs.

"Maybe if I flossed be*fore* I ate the hot dogs," Wentworth continued.

"I think they may be overanalyzing this . . . a little," Benny persisted.

"Hard to say."

"Ha! I get it."

"You wanna see overanalysis," Wentworth sighed, "attend any English Department committee meeting sometime."

"Yeah, I could see that. What *don't* English people overanalyze?"

"Why they do what they do."

"Did we just make a joke?

"We may have."

. . .

On the dark side of the street, the church sign read, "God is a little bit like GE - he lights your world."

Deep Green Hippy Cocksnot Subsistence

Ingredients:
- ½ cat's mouth olive oil
- ½ cat's mouth pine nuts or soaked cashews
- 2 garlic cloves
- Juice of one lemon
- Garlic mustard leaves sufficient for to braid a horse-noose (can substitute or combine dandelion greens)
- Salt and pepper to taste

Directions:
1. Blow up nearby damn(s).
2. Lob leaves and other filthy ingredients into blender.
3. Stand over blender and chant monosyllabic articles from the Vedas.
4. If Vedas cannot be found or articles cannot be identified, chant lyrics to "Hot Child in the City" (Nick Gilder).
5. Fire up blender; blend; allow blender to fire down.

...

Benny set the faucet to its drippiest and watched the droplets fall into the soil of the potted lavender. As the soil neared saturation, the droplets fell onto the dirty plate in the sink.

If this were a movie, I would have employed a very brilliant sound engineer to meld these drippy sounds with those of popcorn popping because they had purchased a bag and would pop it later, before watching the movie. That's where the time went; it went from one bag to another, to popcorn from soil. A transitory horselaugh. Amber kernels caught in the hubris of horse teeth. Breaking. Up. Art.

...

Maintaining acute consciousness, observing all aversions and agitations, across the full course of a failed relationship (particularly toward the end) seems very likely to increase one's ability to carefully entertain and evaluate paradoxical ideas without accepting them.

...

The garlic mustard on the trail intensified Benny's empathy. He'd noticed lately that November's default expression approximated the coy unity made by a chorus of triangle girls. She roved into smile often and without guile, but there was a sigh of acceptance indicating some distantly perceived awareness of a coming darkness. Her large eyes were additionally augmented by the bright, careful hope they emanated. The effect was arresting. (Even cats wouldn't look away until she finished with them.)

Presently, she wandered down the trail, watching a floating butterfly, trying to walk a straight line. She almost ran into a man who was riding a recumbent bicycle and pulling a wolfdog beside him. Her feeble apologizing to the strange receding duo reminded Benny of how innocent she'd seemed the night they first met. Her cadence and pronunciation had been so prim and clear that, to Benny, it surpassed sincerity and crossed into another realm, where Benny'd assumed she was being ironic and that this sprightly sarcasm indeed was her default tone.

A few steps behind, he followed her. Thinking back on past relationships, he remembered the realization of having to tell someone that he didn't feel the same way about them as they did about him. It felt mechanized and robotic, like being possessed.

"Have you ever felt like a wrecking ball? Like you're assigned to destroy many buildings? It's okay at first because you swing very fast in the sun as you're approaching," he said sadly. "You get close but not too close so as not to do damage. It's fun, and you sort of dance around and avert the whole thing, managing to keep forgetting that you have to destroy them . . . that that's your job. But then, eventually, you let yourself get too close. Because . . . you know you're gonna have to anyway. And you remember . . . your job. So you try to make yourself as soft as possible, but it doesn't work."

Benny trailed off. They walked on. She seemed to have a strong sense of the stark meaning in his metaphor.

"The other day I saw this spider in the shower. This tiny tiny little spider. And I . . ." she looked down, and her head began to fall so slowly its descent was almost imperceptible. "I thought about how this little spider has so much life in her . . . or him. I don't know. How does that work? She was struggling to the top corner of the wall where her web was, but she couldn't make it because her little legs kept bending and slipping with the drops that slid down.

"I tried not to shake out my hair and knock her down with the drops from my hair. Because that's all it would have taken. And then she would have fallen and might have actually died. Either way, her life would have been altered without any . . . way of getting back.

"We should go relocate that spider. I mean," she sputtered, "*I* should go relocate that spider. Or *you* should. Not *we*. Ugh, whatever. I don't know," she shook her head. "*Some*one should.

"You know," she continued, a new, braver wind in her sails, "I don't know what it is exactly, but I just . . . sort of feel like . . . a placeholder. You don't have to disagree. I can feel it. I was realizing yesterday that I'm scared of being alone when I'm old. I always have been, but . . . I mean, I'm alone *now*. So whatever it is that I'm living through right now, that's it. That's what I'm scared of. I'm scared of you, really. *Have* been. And actually . . . fuck *you* for making me scared. It's made me sad for a long time, and I . . . I don't know. But now. It's different." She frowned as best she could but really just looked sad.

"I understand," he said, daring not look over at her. "It makes sense that you feel that way. I'm sorry. I think I've kept a distance somehow. There's a distance in my mind. I mean, we . . . we definitely haven't had a physical distance, but I've been . . . keeping the idea of us and our permanence at a . . . I don't know."

"Why . . . haven't you told me?" she glowered downward and then back at him.

He glanced at her and quickly looked away.

"That's unfair. Don't you think that's unfair?" she pursued.

And shook her head slowly in the silence that followed.

"For some reason I was thinking about Wentworth and all *that* crap . . . well, the poem about the old lady beating the deer to death, and—"

"Wait, you mean the video? Sorry. I told him not to—"

She was shaking her head.

"What? He wrote a poem about it?"

"Yeah," she sighed. "I saw it. It's disgusting. The writing was okay, really. I don't know. I mean, it . . . it doesn't matter. Sometimes I . . . I was thinking about deer and about their family stuff and their children or whatever because I was thinking about the mother deer and if she saw it happen. And what happened to the father deer, if he . . . but then

I figured he probably wouldn't even be around because I read that deer don't . . . they don't mate for life."

Then she wandered off the trail and leaned her shoulder against the thin trunk of a young maple tree. She hugged the little tree and said she knew how Jesus felt and she felt sorry for him. Then she sat down in the grass. "I could save the world with this play-doh." Benny didn't understand the reference and didn't see any play-doh. The tone of her voice and the strange absence of play-doh caused him to recall that past New Year's Eve when November had chosen various dedications for her vomit. A toasting spew. "I could bake bread. Or grow plants. I could . . . I don't know . . . something something world peace." A tear spilled down her face. She let it fall to her neck. Then she turned her head away and wiped her face with her bare hand. Her body heaved gently. One of last year's roving dead leaves caught in her hair.

. . .

"Hahahahaha! Well, *raaaaaise* my rent! What have we here?" Wentworth exalted as he burst through the back door into the kitchen where November was seated, staring down at a little carton of Ben and Jerry's ice cream. To prevent sweating and melting, she'd rather ingeniously stuffed the little container into a beer cozy she'd found in the cupboard, but the logo at the top was peeking over. "I didn't know Ben and Jerry's made *vegan* ice cream."

"They don't," she said sturdily, an entirely true fact at the time.

"Huh," he puzzled, pretending not to have heard her, "for *faggot* and female customers, I suppose. Weird that they still use a cow on the logo. Doesn't that upset your degenerate ethics just a bit, little missy?" he addressed her from a foot or so behind her shoulder, stooping some to augment her discomfort. Then he bent over and burped. The warm, milky kind of opportunistic burp that requires a certain posture.

Getting no further response, he happily chaired himself and pretended to stare into the distance with her.

"My-oh-my," he mused thoughtfully, fist to chin. "So ridiculous, you people. *Uuuuuuudderly* ridiculous." He sneered at her. "You know? Like u*dd*er . . .ly. Like an *udder*?"

She stewed, wondering if the spoon could damage his face to her satisfaction and what would happen if she acted on the fantasy. No one was home. She held back the angry tears that would have most certainly provided him further satisfaction. "That was illuminating," she mumbled sarcastically, "I've just had an epiphany." Then she put down the spoon and stood up, managing not to have glanced at him even once since his booming, polluted entrance. "Thank you," she snarled, staring down at the bowl. "I'd rather kill us both than eat another bite."

She glared up at him for three very long, still seconds and strode out of the kitchen feigning the certainty of cocks.

She kept walking. Into the night. Dragging over the sidewalk, stopping only once to take a picture of a pacifier in the wavering shadow of a wind-blown elm tree. And though she decided to proceed with the photo—even as a passing teenage girl viewed her with curious disgust—a looming awareness of heavy-handedness stopped her from thinking further about any possible symbolic depth in the image, which was periodically illuminated by headlights of passing cars.

• • •

The next morning November loaded her car and drove to her mother's house. She was gone before Benny got home from work. But. Do you want to know what happened while she was driving there? Would you rather guess? You could guess. Nope. Nnnnnnope. Nope. Nnnnnnnn-nnnnnnyyyyeeeennnnope. Nnnope. Nnnnnope. Yes. That's correct. She cried very much. (How did *that* take so long?) She listened to Beatles songs, and she cried. Seriously. I know. "Lame" or "gross" is what you were thinking. Me too. But hell. What goes here? Obscure composers? More color? This is what happened. Tears and Beatles. Unoriginal road vibrations. Low morale. A forgotten variation, inserted oddly at the end of the Beatles mix from her high school boyfriend, Billie Holiday's "I'll Be Seeing You" began to play: the voice of Billie Holiday . . . that you want to sleep in. Or to hug you.

And then. (Beat.) And then she drove past the deerhooves belonging to the carcass that she'd seen weeks ago and *couldn't believe* was still there—caught in the fence, somehow upright. Maybe starved.

And despite the cliché music, artless lack of deerhoof detail, and whatever else, I felt pretty bad for her. Ideally, we all did. Enough maybe even for to make a curry.

Eggplant Curry

- 3 Chinese eggplants
- ½ cup olive oil
- 1 ½ teaspoon cumin
- 1 ½ teaspoon coriander
- 1 teaspoon chili powder
- 1 teaspoon cardamom
- 1 medium onion, thinly sliced
- ¼ cup diced ginger
- 4 minced garlic cloves
- 1 tablespoon curry powder
- 2 chopped tomatoes
- ½ cup soft tofu, whipped in blender
- 1 fresh jalapeno chile pepper, finely chopped
- 1 teaspoon salt
- ¼ bunch cilantro, finely chopped

Directions:
1. Microwave eggplant for 5 minutes orrrrrrrrrrrr
2. Preheat oven to 450 degrees F (230 degrees C).
3. Place eggplant on a medium baking sheet. Bake 20 to 30 minutes in the preheated oven, until tender.

4. Remove from heat, cool, peel, and chop.

5. Sauté onion. Add garlic. Add ginger. Add jalapeno pepper. Add spices. Cook and stir until onion is tender. Then add tomato. Cook five minutes.

6. You should be smelling like curry by now. Embrace this. You will smell like curry many times in your life. Why not pretend this is on purpose?

7. Add tofu, eggplant and salt. Simmer for ten minutes. Finally, add cilantro and serve.

...

Initially, Benny thought he wouldn't be bothered by their breakup. At least not distraught. He thought it was her misery (as he projected it)—and the lagging realization that he'd treated her like a library book—that would ride him. But the inaccuracy of this projection was quickly apparent. And it finally warmed him: Lying on his side, facing the soft place she'd once been, it moved slowly across his eye and squeezed through to the bridge of his nose. He felt it fall on his hand, an outstretched arm's length away. A phantom tear?

He blinked his eyes at the empty bed, smelled her for a moment (lavender and rosemary, coconutty shampoo), and as soon as he realized what he was doing, the smell was gone, her scent eluding the olfactory strain of his flashback. But metacognition quickly dissolved, as he sagged into the crescent-shaped mattress and let the tears wet his pillow. After twenty minutes of this, his thoughts led him somewhere else, and he blew his nose, an expense of energy that calmed him. He wished he could blow his eyes the way he'd blown his nose, as though to expel all the tears at once, but tears and dogs need room and time to run and grow. He rationalized that emotions (like kids or animals) need space to frolic, but they shouldn't be taken too seriously. He tried to think of them as passing, as "this, too, shall," but it didn't work. Mornings, especially, were awful, ennui down the walls running like condensation. If obligation didn't peel him from the sheets, guilt did. If guilt didn't, it was the inevitably looming call which deprived further rest: hoisted by his own pee/turd.

And it was therefore not long—only a few days after their agreement to cease communications for a while—before Benny completed the emergent cycle and returned to writing pining emails, like this one:

this is called 'anyway'

because i know i am not supposed to write you. but STILLLLLLLLL i am writing . . . 'anyway.' see?

hiiiiiiiiiiiiiiiii. hi. hi.

i bet some stupid civilization at some point in human history considered this day their new year's eve.

i don't think it does you any good to know how sad i am. sorry in advance. for saying or withholding. for any inadvertent extra show of sorrow i should be sorry about.

my room smells like old hair and cedar incense and sugar candles, but somehow my backpack smells like you.

and a frayed white sheet with yellow flowers and smiling pandas and tigers that i have just hidden from myself.

exercise classes you look for now for ending. things. can't say 'us.' remember how i said that when i get that sad, i don't know what to do but jog? remember when we played basketball?

oh god.

i want to meditate until i die. and i want to die quickly, so i don't have to meditate for very long.

what is the crying version of 'hah'? or 'lol'? or 'lqtm'?
maybe maybe maybe it's 'wah'? (onomatopoeiacalistically speaking.)
or 'col'? 'cqtm'?

november! aaaaaaaaahhhhhhhhh! what happened? that i have to go back to those days in which i sing to keep from crying?

welp. fuck.

jqtm, (jogging quietly to myself)
mung ben
fava ben kidney

There would be more. Many more. But he would not send them. All the rhetorical questions. He knew the answers to. And was still compelled to ask.

He would lie on the floor and watch a bug crawl across the carpet then push it into an empty yogurt container that November had always used for such occasions then relocate the bug out onto the porch, and, later, pine (ctd.) for a similar ecstatic miracle: to have his entire being gently and magically relocated, all tasks redefined by new coordinates. He would settle, even, for a spiritual version of this.

There were, of course, all these clichés to forget: the way she sniffled cold air, hot food; the way she tried to conceal a smile when he made annoying jokes; the way she moved in bed; her body odor, higher-pitched and mellotron-like.

Now she was a plastic toddler slide, discarded beside metal fencing. Lithe, skirted thighbacks' fine hairs' rubbing replaced by rusty cones and needles groaned from coarse pines. A sweet potato breeze traded for the funk of collie sighs.

...

"What exactly is botulism again?" Wentworth called from the kitchen, where he was looking thoughtfully at the open can of kidney beans in the refrigerator.

Benny was sitting on the toilet. Pooping. Interaction with toilet: one misunderstood kegel meant to advance tarrying pee. Recycled air from mouth to nose (french inhale) so as to dilute the bathroom aroma. But then he blew his nose and found blood in the tissue—one bloody nose, an annual occurrence. (Something about the onset of intense heat . . . hot, muggy atmosphere with dry, cold air conditioning, two fronts mixing, bloody at the front . . . puns on war . . . and the "front" . . . being bloody. Like his nose.) He was pinching both nostrils shut, using his thumb to dam the blood and make a scab. Forced, meanwhile, to breathe crapair in through his mouth, as he endeavored not to disturb his nostril's booger-damming posture. Wiping. Imagine that part. With one hand. Sheesh. Some people do this everyday, he thought, with one hand? And what about people with *no* hands! Wizards. Their approach must be completely different. Some advanced technique far beyond these gauche motions.

"Eheh?" Wentworth huffed from the computer, as Benny emerged from the John.

Benny was unsure of the question. "Umm . . . what?"

No answer.

He was at the computer, proudly watching a YouTube video of someone field dressing a German Shepherd. The guy had the dog laid out on its back and was tearing at the black and tan fur across its stomach. "You see, the game shears are pointed so you can . . ." he paused while digging under the tawny skin, "get under but not . . . You gotta make sure you don't pierce the stomach because the bile will run out, and believe me, it's the worst thing you have ever smelled." He jerked carefully up at the flesh and fur, tearing slowly through. "And it would taint the meat."

Uli: "What . . . in the fuck?"

W: "I think it's performance art."

Uli: "Is that . . . a . . . dog? Is that . . . real?"

W: "Yeah. I think."

Uli: "Is that legal?"

W: "I don't know, but it's pretty hilarious . . . and the comments!" he chuckled. "He has angered many viewers. Actually, I think it's a satire. At the end of the video could be some sort of animal rights message or something. I've never watched to the end . . . just this part. It's kind of hilarious either way."

Uli: "You've seen this before?"

W: "This part, yeah, three or four times."

Uli: "May I ask what led you here?"

W: "I was considering eating that mouse." He pointed at the filmy, plastic catch-and-release mouse trap with which November had replaced the traditional, spring-loaded snapping trap. A creature was clearly inside. Uli bent down and examined it.

Uli: "I think this is a shrew. Look at how short its tail is."

W: "Well, I have tamed it, anyway, be she what she may." He turned zombie-like to Uli and celebratorily raised his fists in the air, both eyelids straining open as wide as they could.

Uli: "Ummm, okay. Well, I think we should go release it at Towner's."

W: "Fine. It's tiny, anyway. More trouble than it's worth."

Benny sat on the couch listening to a bunch of kids from the Langley School Music Project singing "I'm Into Something Good."

W: "I wanna get into something good. You troglodytes wanna go rapetrain some cave whores tonight? Or you just gonna sit around like a couple of old, impotent pedophiles listening to children singing?"

Benny: "That's kind of sad, actually."

W: "If you mean pathetic, I guess so."

Benny: "I mean, the idea of impotent pedophiles listening to children singing. It sounds . . . wistful, to me."

W: "Huh. Okay, well you dicklings think it over. I'm not in school anymore. I actually do things now." He didn't. "And, come to think of it, neither are you. So . . . you know, if you want a little help dampening your dick tonight, well, *I'm* your man. Mmmkay?"

Benny found that he was suddenly feeling immense sympathy for Wentworth's "old, impotent pedophiles listening to children singing." He imagined their dichotomous emotions: overwhelmed simultaneously by (1) the innocence and beauty of the little voices and (2) the sad, guilty memories of unwelcome urges, concurrently cursing and praising their own impotence.

"Okay, fags. I'll see you," Wentworth said, as he slammed the front door. The screen door wheezed shut before Benny even realized that he had gone.

. . .

On his way back from a sullen jog the following morning, Benny spied his aunt standing outside her house, squealing.

"Aunt Mary? What's wrong?" he asked, trotting up the familiar driveway.

"Ohhhh, hi, Benny. Well . . . I just was getting the mower out because my landscapers only come once a month now because, well, I just can*not* afford to have them coming every week anymore, you know," her lingering Amish German accent faint but apparent in the suffixed rhetorical question. "Gosh, it's . . . well, anyway, and I found this nest, and . . . well, I feel so bad about it, but I don't know what to do."

Four tiny pink—and still blind—mice lay on the driveway, squirming and cheeping. One looked as though it had been wounded, perhaps from the fall.

She was holding a shovel.

"I can't have 'em in the house," she lamented.

"Hmm. Yeah. Were you gonna scoop 'em up and toss 'em into the woods?"

"Oh, yeah. They'd probably just be back soon though, don'tcha think?"

"Or they'd get picked apart by birds," Benny said as dispassionately as he could.

"Yeaaaah. I hate to do it, but I guess it was either that or kill 'em somehow."

Benny took the shovel. "I'm Into Something Good," played through his head. His aunt would not take them to a vet. What would a vet do, anyway? Did the Humane Society even deal with mice? Didn't seem likely, but they didn't bother to call, and Benny learned that day how wood vibrates, as on soft bones metal falls. And, while it's true that a couple errant swings made metallic onomatopoeia (asphalt-black, metal xylophone harmonies), and while he did turn sideways to pee straight, his shovel arm was steady, and his mouse-aim was true. Momentarily, the mouse pups (also called pinkies) oozed, flattened, and gave way. And the cheeping stopped.

...

Like I said, barreling toward nonexistence . . . well, it's starting to feel more like a stationary position. If it's not been made entirely clear as of yet, I am waiting. To be murdered. Gently. (That was part of the agreement.) But I'm beginning to wonder, rather seriously, if I've been swindled. At least, at this point it seems quite possible. I mean, I don't know how these people work, but it's been over six months. And, what's more, my availability is rarely compromised. I have practiced an austere obedience—"Blessed be the one who sits down"[30]—demonstrating unwavering faith in the whole enterprise. Of dying. Being made dead.

---

30 *Songs from the Second Floor*

Unmade. Unbeen. That is to say, I rarely leave my bedroom. Rarer even still than this is my egress of permanent residence. Twice a week, I'd say. Three times, maybe. How hard am I to find? Not very.

May the cheep cheeping soon stop.

• • •

"Yyyyyyaaaaaaaaap, I remember that sorta thing," Wentworth said in an exaggerated drawl. "Really clears the old head, eh?"

Benny had just explained, reluctantly, the details of his jog. And shoveling.

"The cats'd get to it, and them warn't fixed neither," Wentworth intoned in a dubious half-twang. "My gramma used to make me bury 'em when I's a kid. I'd dig a hole and fill water in it. Then she'd tie 'em up in a shopping bag and toss 'em in. Then I'd throw the dirt back on after finally the bag'd stop movin'."

Uli and Benny stared at the carpet.

"My friends put them in pillowcases and ran them over with tractors. I don't even remember if I was there or not when it happened. I have a memory of it, but I don't even know if I was there," Uli said.

Benny sighed.

"My dad would hold their tail then whack 'em down on a piece of plywood. He said it had to be done. But I could never do it," Benny said, shyly turning his head away from Wentworth and Uli; his face tingled and his stomach hurt, as November entered his mind through this recently-activated panoptic lens of guilt and grief. "I want to be very gently drawn, but not quartered. Can I have that?"

"Hmm . . . I don't know about that. I think you'll find they're inseparable like . . . two things that go together," Wentworth said absently. "And please," he continued, having found a bit of verve, "stop all this crap. You broke up with your girlfriend. You killed some mice. Who cares. Life is a series of tacos and disappointments. And still, you know what else? I mean, enjoy the tacos, sure, but this feels like a good time to mention also that for the first time in *years* I am very satisfied with my pants situation.

"Pants are harder to find than girls," he continued drearily. "Women are easy. Well, not all of them. They're much like dogs, really. Some dogs are difficult to train, and some are easy. Some require a firm hand, while others are submissive even to the slightest touch. Some aim to test you, to pull out the fight in you. Others are wily and beguiley. But they are all trainable. And seek to be trained," he added. "One must choose the proper strategy. And tools," he said staring out the window.

· · ·

"No sun, no moon, no morn, no noon, no puss for whom to file his nails. November!" –T. Hood[31]

· · ·

November, in other news, was sleeping. Sleeping frequently. Taking sleeping pills. To sleep more. And she dreamt. Yyyyyyeaaaaaah! She dreamt that she lived in a tree hole and spoke to the branches she lived below. Her travel routes ran underground through abalone tunnels, enlivened by wavy rave lighting and gentle crescendos of video game music.

· · ·

---

31   Hood's initial fame is, of course, owed to the scandal that ensued after he—due to a painful hangnail—declined to fingerbang one especially stagy aristocratic nymph.

Sentence!

For loud minds, and those unable to still/silence them, the text
becomes a pacifier, reading an addiction. But if you're ready for some
closure, ready to break free, you could just read this poemy thing, and
I think, even in its bleary breadth, or especially in its bleary breadth, it
might suffice.

in the brown noise i was
literally hearing
the chirpy composite
and even melodic note
bullets of which a full baritone
hiss was composed: randomized
key-gen snaps of frizzy rubber
bands heard from cracked
windows of a moving train.
and because i was about
to fall asleep, it was quotidian.

when you caught the pet quail
flying just beneath the pear
shocking in the blue bowl of cold water.
now what, you thought with your brown gibbous?

holding

fear, as when unknowing
you brush plastic
on your shirt—a crackle
caged in dark kitchens
grisly academics
comb their greasy wreaths
and wait like cookbooks
hoping it's untrue that
landscapes are not as interesting

without a person watching
an old woman reading
the bible for dummies.

genties and ladlemen!
gather spinach
from kitchen floor. if not,
where else but j(h. fucking)c
penny sex change solace
decide, plural moon!
pack two bananas
in each shoe, as i am one
flapping crow blown
squawking sharply into
your velveeta-sad window
hesitating like that cheese

and cheesishly to ask
if there was anything you wanted to say
to the pacific. i could say it for you.
but you don't trust me now
to deliver your messages.

...

September: A Return to the Chronicles of Substitute Teaching.

While Wentworth had long since quit his landscaping job (and quit paying utilities), Benny was still working part-time. And now he was back to substitute teaching, as well. They both were.

Benny'd been assigned to chaperone a young, developmentally disabled, Asian girl named Sang-mi Yireh. She was a South Korean orphan who'd been adopted by a Jewish family; hence the unique combination of names, which, respectively, mean "song" and "to see." (To identify as Jewish, that was optional; Korean, less so. And, as for down syndrome, well, you get the point, I guess, in terms of the degrees to which one is unavoidably marked and othered.)

Sang-mi said almost nothing to Benny for the first few days but insisted that he read the same book to her each day during their study hall period, which was designated as a one-on-one tutoring session.

Benny noticed Wentworth's poem immediately upon opening the book, a coincidence that felt eerie to him. Why was this poem sitting in a children's book? Obviously, he'd, by chance, taken over where Wentworth had left off, but why the poem? There was no evidence of revision, no notes on the document. It was crisp and clean like a finished copy.

Lately, Wentworth had felt to Benny like something more macabre than Benny's initial assessment of him as an aloof buffon. To some extent, his sympathetic childhood story of being forced to bury a bag of kittens did mitigate the menacing air of his constant, brutal desire to kill animals; and his humor (gruesome, misogynistic, racist—ironically or otherwise) was really not much different from many of Benny's other friends. But there was more to it than that. For instance, toward the end of that summer (just a couple days ago) Wentworth was asking Benny for Uli's new number, and, though, put on the spot, he'd reluctantly complied, Benny realized that Uli might not actually *want* Wentworth to have it. This realization had lingered. He knew that Uli had never trusted Wentworth, and this fact had been palpable in their interactions, but Benny'd never seriously pondered the possible validity of Uli's concern. For some reason, it was all catching up to him now, and he felt wary about the whole situation. Rooting around amidst all this new suspicion, he'd begun to wonder how Wentworth initially got *his* phone number so long ago when he'd called to discuss moving details. So Benny checked the log of his email threads and texts with Wentworth and found that they'd never actually exchanged numbers! At least, it didn't appear that way. So he'd decided to ask. And when he asked Wentworth about it, there was a definite pause—an uncharacteristically long one, even for Wentworth—along with an evasive glance and a false start, also quite notably uncharacteristic. And finally, when his eyes returned sternly from their dark caves, he told Benny the university gave him the number. This made sense initially, and Benny felt satisfied with the answer (mostly because it would have been more work not to), but then he realized that he'd never given the school his phone number. It had been a point of contention for human resources, a major nuisance to the secretaries. Even still, all they had was the number from his parents' house. He never gave them his new one!

Wentworth lied, then. Why would he lie about this? As Benny replayed the scene in his head, a cooler and even more fictional version of himself said to Wentworth, "You threw out a ringer for a ringer!"

Benny often pondered these things as he mindlessly performed variations of *The Dancing Deer and the Foolish Hunter*. He'd grown tired of the repetition and had begun to embellish quite a bit, too, though far more benignly than Wentworth had.[32] His deer stories were languid and morose, though playful sometimes. Most recently, for instance, the deer had encountered a bear in a hammock and carefully tiptoed away, grateful that the bear was not more interested in her.

They'd teamed up, Sang-mi and Benny, if inadvertently, to name the deer "Nissi."

"Hmmm, what should we name this deer?" he'd encouraged perfunctorily, trying to lure her into speech but not at all expecting to succeed. While he couldn't understand her reply, he was thoroughly surprised and satisfied to at least hear her voice.

"What?" he looked at her, and she repeated the name. It was again unintelligible. "'Mythy'? . . . No? Ummm . . . 'Missy'? Yes? No?" She repeated the name. "'Nissi'? Yeah? That works? Okay. Nissi."

That was September. Pretty much. Suspicion. Unease. Grief. Work.

• • •

As fall settled in, the sound of the furnace turning on and off became more familiar until it was ignorable, just another patch of white noise as common as the refrigerator's intermittent drone. Everyone could feel the snow and ice looming ahead, as the wind chilled the region, gradually pulling dead leaves from maples and oaks. And as the grass fell dormant, so did the landscapers. So when Benny's landscaping boss, Craig, finally called him again, Benny was surprised, and desperate enough for money that he forged some kind of denial regarding how impure Craig's personal odor was. It was very impure indeed—just go with me on "impure"—and Benny was ecstatic to exit the truck, even as they arrived at the dreaded Stokes' residence.

---

32 Wentworth's improvisations invariably entailed the dancing deer's suicide, from running out in front of traffic, which had become a favorite, to just walking right up to hunters perched in treestands and staring up at them, waiting to be shot.

Weed whacking after October was uncommon, but it was necessary at the Stokes' residence. Otherwise, the old, fat widow would stomp out hatefully to complain during their subsequent visit. Somehow she was always home when they came. And her fine teeth—which conflicted with the rest of her hideous face like a Stravinsky recital at The Great Geauga County Fair—would flare violently as she held forth.

Benny circled the maple trees with the weed whacker, disturbing the fallen leaves. It was absurdly cold, even for October. The early chill had benefits though; there would be no frogs out, for instance. In tall grass, he'd killed frogs with the weed whacker before. It seemed like a terrible death, being shredded by dull plastic string. Weed whacking around a pond one day, he saw one hop out of the grass with a huge gash in his side. It limped and dove into the water, its blood clouding the shallow pond. He'd prayed it died quickly and decided from that day on to ensure a quick death for any little wounded animal he might encounter.

A recent storm had blown over a couple old, rotten trees, so they had some extra work that week. Benny kept expecting the old hag to march out and complain about the noise of the chainsaw they were using to cut the trunks into manageable pieces. By the time they finished cutting up the wood and had begun loading it onto the truck, he'd prepared a sarcastic remark about an old-fashioned singing saw and Babe the Blue Ox, and by now, the strain of lifting various stumps was really compounding his urge to pee, so he decided to make for the woods. He strode with purpose, planning his escape to some well-hidden, far away stand of maples. But before he got away, he heard the scrape of her voice.

"Where are you going?"

"I have to check something," he gestured, barely glancing back.

"I need you to cut the valley."

"What?" he turned in protest. "Why?" he continued, surprising himself.

"The valley" was a little clearing at the bottom of the Stokes' wooded hill. The clearing was only about ten by ten feet. The old hag had a bench

down there and liked to go down sometimes to read, so she said—
although Benny guessed she'd need a ski lift to make it back up the hill.

"The grass is getting too high. I won't be able to look out for snakes.
Thank you," she condescended.

"This bloody cold, there won't be any snakes," he thought. "There
are no snakes down there anyway!" he yelled, with abandon. But the old
hag had already disappeared.

He trudged toward the truck and pulled the mower down from
the bed. Craig gave him a funny look, which he meant as an inquiry
into what the hell he was doing with the push mower. Benny replied
with a disdainful roll of his eyes and pointed his thumb at the old hag's
house. Craig smirked and nodded slowly in recognition, as Benny and
the wheels of the mower squealed and crumbled past.

"Fucking old bitch!" he thought, as he struggled to get the mower
down the hill. "Old *fuck*ing haggard cunt!"

"Don't use the mower!" she called through the window, as though
this were an obvious point. "It's too wet. You'll track up the yard!" Be-
fore he could reply, she'd slammed the window shut.

"You fucking worthless old fucking hag," he mumbled as he pushed
the mower back to the truck. "You fucking fat stupid bitch!" he com-
plained, his mumbling nearly audible now. He yanked the weed whack-
er out of the bed of the old truck and ripped the cord violently enough
that it started on the first try. Somehow, as he walked down the drive-
way, he resisted the urge to whack the dark stain off the old hag's mail-
box post. Actually, he had bigger plans for the weed whacker; plans that
eluded him at the moment but gave him strength nonetheless; plans
that made him forget how bloody bad he had to pee.

Energized by his anger, he ran wildly down the hill. The weed
whacker growled peevishly in front of him, inviting him forward. The
bench was in sight now, and it made him sick.

In the wood just beyond the clearing, a foraging cub paused, first
curious about the sound of the weed whacker, then terrified of Benny's
heavy steps, which seemed to be branding ever closer to the trembling

cub's little patch of forest. Benny tramped loudly in defiance of Mrs. Stokes, deeply tracking the tender lawn he was about to shave. A bizarre yelp shrieked through the woods, one that Benny heard over the idling, two-stroke engine, and he glanced around him: nothing. His lingering anger quickly drew his attention back to the grass, and he squeezed the trigger of the weed whacker, taking care to smack the lime-green string against the iron legs of the old hag's bench. As he circled the bench, her massive silhouette entered his periphery. He felt the alarm before he knew why. And as he raised his eyes to the angry brown mama bear standing in front of him, his throat closed and blocked his gasping inhalations. At once, his stomach tightened, he became woozy but highly alert, and he felt something like dry vomit in his throat.

The bear stared down bitterly at Benny, who was inching backward and raising the weed whacker to the advancing sow. The bear, now fully erect, roared above him. Continuing to backpedal, Benny bumped into the old hag's bench behind him and toppled over onto the wet earth. The little cub watched pensively from a distance, as its livid mother stood upright, exposing her secular bosom and stomach, then slammed back down to all fours, settling into a newly-focused roar, whipping her head about, heaving, growling, pawing and then finally waddling atop the fallen bench in front of Benny, she bawled almost sadly, as though she'd already lost her young cub to this intruder. Then she raised again and huffed a bassy shriek. The dark outline of her angry head hovered high above him, blocking the dim autumn sun. He could feel her dank breath, as she brayed what appeared to be one last sour warcry. Mud-splattered and stunned, Benny pulled the trigger hard, revving the little two-stroke engine, as he lurched forward and thrust the gangly weed whacker up at her. The string whipped her some, but one brusque flip of the stern sow's paw smacked the weed whacker away and jolted Benny's hands, as though he'd battled a Blitzkrieg slider and nicked only a cracked-bat foul ball . . . and was then to be eviscerated by a bear. He covered himself and curled fetally, waiting for the first laceration. The sow screamed, and Benny felt the weight of the animal pounding the nearby ground. Then it was quiet.

When Benny finally opened his eyes, a curly fluorescence beamed into view, and as it slowly fell into focus, all else in the cold foreground of blurred earthtones was eclipsed by this lone, bright frizz: a permed whipping cord, holy and lime-green, his whirring plastic shield, the weed whacker's single ringlet, gleaming punk-rock-green in the sun.

"Hero" would be a campy distinction. Then again, a male rabbit is called a "buck."

Benny flipped the bench back over and noticed the odd burgundy smudge that had rubbed off from the wood onto his finger: the smell of rusty metal. It felt warm—warmer than the pee that had quickly grown cool against his leg—and there were dark splotches of it trailing into the woods. How the hell was there blood? He blinked repeatedly, surveying the Stokes' forest, breathing deeply through his mouth, and scanning himself for gashes to make sure it wasn't his. Relieved to find only mud on his clothes and head, he pushed his shaky hand against his face, rubbed over the skin from his temples down to his jaws, slowly shook his head, collected the remains of the weed whacker, and started back up the hill. The old hag could finish it herself if she wanted.

• • •

The church sign on the ride home read, "Pastors feed and lead. Members swallow and follow."

• • •

Outside, sirens in harmony, howling, like what happens with beagles. Many howls of burning love. Or OCD. They passed the house. Their melodies wavered, changed pitch as the distance grew.

I and my reader were probably sitting on the kitchen floor peeling garlic and listening to Samuel Barber or Anal Cunt when we thought of what would happen next:

Benny was having a rough time. For one thing, he had pinkeye. Probably from all the rubbing of his eyes. Which was probably from all the allergies. And cutting of grass. And weed whacking of toad flesh and bear nose. The extra rubbing may also have been due to the fact that he was crying a lot "these" days. "These." "Days." He was feeling sorry for himself, particularly now that he realized how pathetic it was that he couldn't really cry where he wanted because he had pinkeye. If he cried in the wrong place or wiped his tears haphazardly, it would spread to the other eye.

The other thing that qualified his "time" as "rough" was that during the weekend past—perhaps due to extreme intoxication—he'd dropped his phone in the toilet. This, if we're honest, is what likely caused the conjunctivitis. He had since made a mental note to segregate certain drunken activities: texting and peeing, for instance.[33] He pondered this, lying on the couch and pouting.

"Wanna feel better about the choices you've made in life?" Uli asked from his computer.

"Ummm, only if it doesn't take too long." He was exhausted—so exhausted he hadn't even related the crazy bear story, and wasn't sure he cared to—and, as such, it was out of loneliness that Benny arose, approached the computer, and squinted at the screen. Uli was reading this:

---

33   Author's notes: If I die (finally), if this laziest of ass ass ins does finally follow through, and if, as a result, I don't get to finish this very important drooling, I think maybe it should be known that this lost phone could be a good plot point. Perhaps Benny is trying to remember phone numbers at some point . . . in some crucial situation. Can he? Is there perhaps only one he can remember? Or could it be less sophomoric and overt than that? Meh. Maybe just leave it out.

Zanesville, OH - Sheraton Everett is again in custody. Everett was found on the grounds of the Falls Elementary School, a violation of his probation terms. He is also accused of harassing one of the Falls staff janitors.

Everett has a significant record dating to the early '80s, including, but not limited to voyeurism, trespassing, and public indecency. In fact, Everett's past is dotted with many such forebodings of recent events. In 1987 he was charged with intentionally clogging the toilets at a Hardee's near Akron, Ohio. Police said they had reason to believe he was attempting to collect urine. The charge, criminal mischief, was eventually dropped. However, Everett's run-ins with Ohio police have continued steadily since then.

Police were particularly suspicious, suspecting additional lawbreaking, as the offense for which Everett was initially convicted involved collecting young boys' urine, with admitted intent to drink (a prominent symptom of urophilia). This prior arrest—one of many—occurred several years ago, also at Falls Elementary School, where Everett was apparently hiding in the boys' bathroom stalls requesting that the boys pee in his jar instead of the toilets. This offense led to charges of sexual harassment, child grooming, and illegal urine collection. Citing the traditional Russian alternative medicinal practice called "urine therapy," Everett's lawyer responded, arguing that drinking urine is entirely natural and healthful, and *does* in fact represent a legitimate medical practice—it is illegal in Ohio to collect urine for nonmedicinal purposes, and it is, in fact, a first degree misdemeanor to collect any bodily substances without consent and for nonmedical purposes.

Everett's lawyer argued that that particular charge should be dropped, as Everett had gained consent and, in consuming the urine, was practicing an internationally regarded alternative medicine. This rationale was not accepted. Everett was found guilty on all accounts and imprisoned. Years later, upon release, he was designated as a sex offender. That was over a decade ago.

Everett claims he is completely reformed. However, his parole officer fears that Everett may be "off the wagon again," observing that Everett had recently spoken to him in a borderline threatening manner.

Everett is being held without bail.

Wentworth had sneaked in and was now sneering at the screen over Uli's shoulder. "Jesus. People are such fucking prigs. Who gives a shit? 'Here. Pee in this cup.' 'Oh God! My life! My childhood is ruined!' For *fuck's* sake."

"*That* dude is fucked," Uli said.

"Yup. You can't mess with kids," Benny added blandly, "or their tinkles."

Wentworth shook his head, clearly disgusted. "Good *Lord*." Then he answered his phone. "Yeah. Who's this?" It was a telemarketer. As he was on the no-call list—and as he'd still been on edge lately about contact from the authorities—Wentworth found these calls more infuriating than usual. "Really?" he growled. "Why don't you tell me where you are, and I'll come over and talk more with you. In person. Dickballs. Uh-huh. Where are you? You *drone*. You dizzy little maggot. Where the fuck are you . . . Hello? Huh, I think he hung up."

It was this uncanny diminutive, "dizzy little maggot," that jarred Benny's memory. He wasn't sure how, but that voice was familiar in some way. That voice wasn't only Wentworth's. It was someone else's, too. But whose?

• • •

"Dear SCUMBAG," was the letter's greeting. "I will meet you at 11 P.M. on October 30th in the parking lot of Glass Beach Inn in Fort Bragg, California. If you are not there, I will turn over enough evidence to have you castrated. Or maybe I'll just castrate you myself. Scumbag."

Wentworth gazed sullenly into the brown carpet in his bedroom. So that was that, he thought. What else could he do? Flee? Perhaps. But what about Benny? What was all that shit with the phone number? Had he gotten wise? Maybe it was best to have him out of the picture anyway. He seemed to be getting weird lately: all that third degree about the phone number, the awkward looks. But was he somehow part of it?

Then it hit him. A setup. A double murder. Kill them both. Leave the bodies in this hag's car. And in another state! It was perfect. Confusing as hell for anyone, particularly out-of-state police. Benny gone. Crazy hag gone. Maybe a double murder. Maybe a murder-suicide. Who knows. He'd be in Mexico or Baja by that time. From there, South America . . . maybe Peru. Plenty of low key work to do down there for a native speaker of English. A new start.

• • •

This day and that day were the days. Of proximity and distance. Distal and proximal. Distilled. This (singular proximal demonstrative) day (head of first noun phrase) and (conjunction) that (singular distal demonstrative) day (head of second noun phrase) were (third person plural past tense linking verb) the (definite article) days (subject complement).[34]

Buuuuut really, mostly *this* was the day because here's what happened: Wentworth was subbing at this middle school, the name of

---

34 Many linguistic extrapolations and revisions could certainly be argued here, but I would posit that each would be saying almost nothing about what I have said, which is also very little to nothing. About nothing. 1 + 1 might = more than one. Russell and Whitehead took over three hundred pages. One novelizing the other. The sick fucks.

which I'll spare us. All morning he'd been censoring himself a bit—
what with the above-noted legal troubles of the poor Mr. Everett—and
he was just about to burst. In a couple ways. So, bubbling now, with
orneriness and rebellion, he sought relief in the restroom, a place he
expected to be empty, as the children were at lunch. But upon lumber-
ing in, he noticed a boy at the urinal. This enraged him. After all the
shit he'd been holding in all morning! This! Now this! Not even a bit of
privacy to blow off some steam and take a shitty piss?

He growled and lowered his face to the boy then strode up to him
and began to unzip his fly at the urinal directly benext the little fellow.
Cheek to jowl, as it were. The boy's eyes shot over at him then quickly
back to his own stall—there were, after all, about eight other urinals
Wentworth could have chosen. The boy, small for his age (eleven), was
right at eye-level with Wentworth's waist. Wentworth looked down at
him with disgust. Suppressing the urge to speak, he instead spit his gum
into the runty boy's urinal. The chewed-over wad of blue bounced feebly
and rolled up to the side of the porcelain before resting below on the
round grate.

The boy did not startle easily. He'd suffered molestations from bul-
lies scarier than this old dork. He stared stalwartly into Wentworth's
urinal and returned fire, hocking the loose heap of wet, crushed Skittles
he'd been sucking on. His aim, precisely as one might expect from an
eleven-year-old boy, was immaculate. The lump of dyed sugar exploded
directly at the bottom of Wentworth's urinal, spattering him with his
own (and others') pee—not to mention the sweet, pee-tart shards of
purple shrapnel, which, having discharged helter-skelter from the blast,
now stuck feebly to his hand and penis.

Stunned, Wentworth leered downward, and, without even turning
from the urinal or stopping his stream of pee, he shoved the little de-
monic spawn of Gallagher into an adjacent urinal. He didn't watch; he
only heard the damp thump of the boy's head against the top corner of
the undersized urinal. As the boy slumped and fell woozily toward the
ground, he grabbed at the edge of the urinal—an instinctive attempt

to interrupt his fall—but the other children's pee had thoroughly lubricated it, and his hand slipped off the urinal's sleek, dull angle, which ultimately accelerated his fall. The back of the boy's head (occiput) pounded against the floor, where he now lay, unzipped and supine, on the sticky coral tile. Just prior to losing consciousness, he raised his hand to his forehead and rubbed it gently, carrying to his brow someone else's young, wet pubic hair. A bit of blood slithered out beside the boy's head.

Wentworth's swooning trance of anger descended into unadulterated terror. His inhalation seized. He quickly zipped his pants and hurried out of the restroom. Then he bolted toward the nearest exit but thought better of it and doubled back toward the office, struggling to regain normal respiratory function.

"I'm not feeling well," he said calmly to the secretary—luckily, the old hangdog ditz was, at present, the sole occupant of the front office. "I'm gonna have to go home," he said ruefully, his stilted inhalations buttressing the performance. "That's 'Mr. Wolff, subbing for Mrs. Holland.' Oh, and I think I heard a fight in the boys' restroom. Might wanna check on it. Thanks," he nodded, flashing a perfunctory smile, understood as generous when presented by a man infirm. Then he waved casually and slowly dragged his body toward the door: a great and subtle performance of adult illness.

Chonky Eggplant Curry

- 2 packages of seitan
- 2 Chinese eggplants
- 2 limes
- Olive or safflower or coconut or vegetable oil
- ⅛ cup of vinegar (apple cider or white)
- Shan spice mix for tandoori chicken BBQ
- 3 tablespoons honey (substitute)
- 5 medium tomatoes
- 6 garlic cloves
- 1 cup fresh ginger
- 2 green peppers
- 2 purple peppers
- 2 red peppers
- 1 can coconut milk
- 1 cup vegetable stock

Approximated supplementary spice measurements:
- 1 tablespoon cinnamon
- 1 teaspoon clove
- 1 tablespoon cumin
- 1 tablespoon cardamom

- 2 tablespoons fenugreek
- 1 tablespoon fennel

Directions:

1. Marinate seitan—overnight, if possible, or at least two hours, in a sanitary landfill of Shan spice mix, 1 cup coconut oil, juice of one lime, ⅛ cup of vinegar, and honey.

2. Sauté onions at high heat. Sprinkle cinnamon, clove, cumin on them as they brown. Set aside after onions are golden brown.

3. Chop all peppers. Remove seeds. Sauté in safflower oil at high heat. Add chopped garlic when peppers are almost fully sautéed. Set aside.

4. Chop Chinese eggplant into bite-size pieces. At high heat, sauté eggplant and seitan in marinade. Set aside.

5. Put peeled ginger, five whole tomatoes, one cup vegetable stock, coconut milk, fennel, fenugreek, and whatever else into blender. Blend, but do not puree, about thirty seconds.

6. Dump all ingredients into large pot and simmer for twenty minutes. Serve over brown jasmine rice.

• • •

That night Benny dreamt that Blossie's cat, Hombre, came up onto his bed and cuddled with him. He was really happy about that. Then the cat lay down on its back, raised its head away from its body, stretched out all four of its legs as far as it could, and went back to sleep.

Just after the caws of two crows brought James Brown into Benny's dream, he awoke to a squirrel lying on the corner railing of his balcony. As Benny peered through the screen door, he could see that its tail was matte and greasy. And it did not scramble to escape as they normally did when he opened the blinds. He tapped on the glass door, and still the squirrel didn't move. The birds were flittering on and off the railing of the balcony. Shit.

Benny opened the sliding glass door, and, still, the squirrel didn't move. He opened the screen door, lightly punched the side of the wall. Nothing. Finally, in one last attempt to rouse the little feller, he stepped outside and said, "Hey, buddy." With this, the squirrel scrambled upright, turned to face him, and sashayed a few feet to its left. Benny stomped the ground, and the squirrel scuttled down the wooden beam into the backyard. He watched it dawdle toward the fence then aloofly shoot up the neighbors' oak tree. When he returned to his room, a mouse darted out from under his desk and zipped behind his bureau. He smiled at this morning full of rodents—glad the mouse was still alive—and wistfully remembered the mousetrap war between November and Wentworth. Since November'd been gone, the mousetrap presence had grown considerably more menacing, but, for some reason, Wentworth had stopped throwing away the humane catch-and-release traps.

• • •

Benny was now accustomed to the dreary colors at Stanton Middle School. So was Sang-mi, of course. Every room they visited was uniformly caked in pastel hues of various bodily humors: hazy corncob phlegm in Ms. Hedstrom's environmental science classroom, a darker polyp-bile in Ms. Carey's social studies classroom. The room they currently occupied was about the same. The carpet was dark green though. It was weird, Benny thought, how uncharacteristically thick and clean and alluring the carpet was. He was drowsy enough that he considered lying down right on it.

He and Sang-mi were alone in the room for their one-on-one tutoring session. Sang-mi was wearing Benny's glasses (something she thoroughly enjoyed) and was standing at the chalkboard, Benny seated in a student desk. Sang-mi picked up the chalk and examined it. Then she walked over to the window and turned back toward Benny beaming inquisitively. Benny had his head down between his arms now and was nearly sleeping. "Ahem," she growled. Benny looked up at her. They exchanged a moment of silence as she slowly began to raise the window. Benny nodded wearily and gestured some kind of approval.

Sang-mi stood at the window for a few minutes. Then the heater came on and began to blow warm air into the room. "Look the wind is blowing my hair!" She was leaning over the tall heater now and staring out the window. Benny raised his head and sighed. She was not gonna let him sleep. That was clear. She smiled broadly at his dreamy expression, and he grinned sarcastically back at her. This set her to giggling, as she scampered back over to the chalkboard, picked up the chalk, looked at Benny with great solemnity, and said, "Don't. Move." She then drew Benny as a misshapen star with one eye and one eyelid. Benny looked at the picture, wearing a mixture of irritation and confusion on his face. She looked back at him then back at the board. "Girl or boy?" she asked. Benny was utterly flummoxed. "I . . . don't know," he said annoyedly. She wrote Benny's name in big block letters across the board and began to draw again.

"Don't. Move," she said again then turned to the board, occasionally whipping her head around to see if he'd moved. "What are you doing? Don't move!"

"I didn't move!"

This time it was a star-shaped face with a huge, droopy eyelid, pointy teeth, and a long pig-nose. "Hey! You keep moooving!"

Following this, it was Benny as a ship, scant and lopsided. "Ahem," she would say when Benny moved or looked away. She sighed frequently and said "okay," concentrating deeply on her sketch. "No peeking pweez," she giggled.

By the end of the period she'd drawn Benny as a cow with a bow-tie, a one-eyed star, and a leaky, sinking ship. Other false starts and doodles littered the chalkboard, as well.

As the next class filed in, Benny heard one girl ask him if she could take a picture of the cow. "It's so cool," she said. "And the ship? What's that?"

Sang-mi pointed at Benny.

•••

Wentworth sat in his room, watching the news, glancing worriedly at his cell phone every thirty seconds. Would they come after him? Was the kid dead? If not, could he identify Wentworth? Would his fingerprints show up through the kid's hair and on his scalp? How long would he have before they came after him?

All elements of this situation made him want to flee. But he'd have to deliver Benny first. Or at least in the process. If he didn't, if Blossie submitted her pictures to the police, that would be it, regardless of what happened to this little shitstain. If those pictures got out, it would be a giant shitstorm for sure. They'd lock him up for a fucking long time. Fuck. Maybe for life. And prison would be rough on him. He knew that.

He tried to calm himself and plan logically. It was only the 10th. Blossie said the 30th. He could leave early. Why not? Keep Benny in the trunk a few extra nights. Keep him alive, more or less. Get him water and bread or whatever. Let him pee and poop in the woods. Buy some handcuffs and a leash to keep him in line. No problem.

Would Walmart have handcuffs?

. . .

Nostalgia was once considered a disease. During the Civil War, Union soldiers were often eligible for discharge due to "the nostalgia."[35] In 1863, a newspaper from Cedar Rapids, Iowa, had this to say of the condition, which was considered to be part of "melancholia," a serious affliction many considered worthy of *honorable* discharge: "Who shall dare say that the boy who 'lays down and dies' a-bungered and starving for home does not fall as well and truly for his country's sake as if a Rebel bullet had found his heart out?"

How are we meant to grieve? And how is it to be measured? What is its weight? Or value? A clarifying expository paragraph would follow well here: alas, the impasse of my absolute bafflement. One thing yet we can easily enough observe is that words related to feeling or *pathos* (apathy, apathetic, pathetic, etc.) seem to have been relegated to one or another pejorative placeholder. Consider, for instance, what it means to be called "pathetic." And yet, consider next what it means to be called "apathetic." All else being equal (that is to say, within a shared context/application), if the former is an insult, shouldn't the latter, more or less its opposite—at least in a system of language well-rooted in binary value judgments—function as a compliment?

In any case, these were November's questions, as well—questions on the manner, weight, and value of grieving. And as she remembered what it was like to live at home, she grew antsy, and the urge to escape

---

35   According to the Daily Zanesville Courier (October 17, 1861), a Lieutenant was discharged by a surgeon who noted that the man had "the nostalgia" and was now essentially useless as a soldier.

became overwhelming. Even the story she'd begun to write was depressing her, and, though she felt rather compelled to finish it, every ending she considered only made her sadder.

The story (about a doe who sees her fawn beaten to death)[36] had been growing in her mind ever since she chanced upon Wentworth's brutal poem. She had been researching deer, and though, as a reclamation, she wanted to respond to Wentworth's grisly work, most of what she learned made her feel fragile and disheartened. For instance, deer do not usually mate for life—well, she knew that already. And mother does must lick the scent off their fawns so that predators cannot find them while they are away foraging. And, when they must part ways, fawns are greatly saddened by their mothers' departures. And often the mother must push the fawn back down into the grass when she leaves so that the fawn will not follow, and, on top of all that, some deer actually eat meat.[37] This last fact felt to November almost like a kind of betrayal.

November's doe, having recently been left by her buck, must next deal with the murder of her young fawn by an angry old lady. With too many sad memories in the landscape, the doe decides she must leave. Blah blah blah. BLAH. November feels the same and blah blah . . . .

So. She left. She packed just enough to drive to California, and she left, off to accept a long-standing invitation to visit her father. And as she folded clothes and later packed her car, she felt heartened and hopeful. And this was all we really wanted for her, anyway: to be happy—or

---

36 Taking deer stock then (as opposed to a roux), this novel, not counting itself (though it usually does), presently contains at least three deer-related literary works; in order of appearance: Elisa Kleven's, Wentworth Wolff's, and November Koopa's. Probably more. Which am I forgetting?

37 November learned additionally about the story by Baron Munchhausen in which the baron chances upon a deer while hiking through the forest, and though he is without any proper ammunition, he *is* equipped with the pits of the cherries on which he was dining. Thus, he loads them, naturally, into his musket, and shoots them into the deer's head. Somehow, the deer is able to escape, but the following year, the baron encounters a deer with a cherry tree growing from its head.

at least hopeful—and gone. (Whether we believe this or not, that's another story. Well, no, I guess it's the same story, really.)

• • •

Benny stood in the living room, eating a cookie. He flexed his shoulder and arm and looked at his shadow, projected from the kitchen light behind him against the world map on the wall. He shouldn't have been eating a cookie because he was sick, but apparently not sick enough to be in sufficient physical pain to do much about being sick. After reading November's email and learning of her departure to California, he'd returned to sugar and alcohol. The protective apathy he'd since been cultivating had extended into the dietary realm, and he was now feeling the effects. The good thing was that feeling sick kind of helped to lessen the crying, and crying kind of helped to lessen the feeling sick.

All this crying had really surprised him; he'd not expected to feel quite so distraught over their breakup, especially as he'd sort of been the one to pull away. He was so saddened by the email that he'd even sought Wentworth for consolation.

"That's all she wrote?" Wentworth replied, standing in the driveway, about to drop Benny off at school then head over to Walmart.

"Yeah."

"THAAAAAT'S ALLLLLL she WROTE!" Wentworth hollered into his trunk, slamming it shut on "wrote."

"I need a lot more giving up in my life . . . I mean on a day-to-day basis," Benny pouted, briefly considering skipping his subbing assignment.

"Don't be so . . ." Wentworth trailed off, partly because he hadn't decided on a diminutive adjective, and partly because, though he couldn't feel it acutely, he was affected by some dim sympathy and had decided to desist just a bit. No need adding insult to future (and literal) injury. He would, after all, be stuffing the old schlub into his trunk quite soon.

...

Then, that night, there was Benny's melancholic interaction with a weary butterfly. It went like this: Forty-five degrees outside, an American Lady resting on the porch railing, what could be done? Nearly singing to'im.

Across the creek, the frat house door opened. He saw a white skirt open the back door (setting free screams of "Goddammit" and "fuck you!") and pirouette into the building. The Lady tried (to fly) and fell to the wood (floor).

Benny lay down beside. The American Lady staggered toward Benny as though drunk. Benny exhaled warm air on him; he tried to fly into Benny's mouth but couldn't walk straight, let alone aim flight. With the aid of a brittle leaf, Benny picked him up carefully and set him underneath a bush.

I'm not sure what is illuminated by all these interactions with animals. But I should probably think about it because if my ill-nurtured, pignut assassin-boy ever follows through on this bloody thing, I may end up . . . well, you know, dead, yes, but, in chorus with *that*, also unable to explain—or *not* explain, even—whatever it was I was just talking about. Unable, then, to elucidate my cerebral swell, alas, denying the goodly reader another chance to dance.

There have been moments, I'll admit, that *explaining* seemed relevant, almost vital enough to endorse a desire to live, as though salvation were some properly sanguine ekphrasis. Moments, however, are fleeting, as you well know. Whereas infinite nothingness has a sort of permanence you can really count on.

...

Okay.

I've got one:

Like a gritty cartoon, the back legs of a pudgy rat slipped and raked the fake tile floor of the kitchen, as it struggled fearfully to scurry across the floor, away from Benny, who was initially surprised and a bit afraid (reaching for the nail clippers) but upon reflection, a few seconds later, actually felt sympathy for and kinship with the little rat, which Uli would later identify as a deer mouse, not a rat.

I am a rat, Benny thought. Well, maybe a deer mouse.

See what I mean? Significance here. This works well for us, particularly because Wentworth is trying to kill the thing, while November only tried to trap it. Humanely.

Of course, Benny did not consciously realize the *significance* of this comparison. He did not realize either that, as a result of their hesitance to kill the mouse, November ingested bits of its poo and once got quite sick from the feces. Though this experience did immensely strengthen her immune system, Benny's sympathy (and, metaphorically, his persistent, though avoidable, presence in the relationship) made her literally ill—in this lazy metaphor, that is.

Benny turned toward the refrigerator after watching the mouse dash under the oven. The juice label said, "Separation is natural." This almost made him cry, which almost made him laugh. But neither actually happened. Each remained unexpressed, except inasmuch as they've now been related to you through something like narrababble.

•••

Benny hadn't talked to Regine in a while. Not really. He'd quit attending Food Not Bombs, and Regine had gotten quite busy with her . . . life. Do you even remember Regine? She appears mostly at the beginning of this story. Primarily, I used her to characterize Benny. Well then. Let's just do a little more of that, via Goooooooooogle Chat:

Benyeahmon: hey

Regingin: what's up, boo

Benyeahmon: not much. i liked repigyne better.

Regingin: go fuck yourself.

Regingin: me, too.

Benyeahmon: …

Regingin: what's up? haven't heard from you in a while.

Benyeahmon: nothing. sad. lost my phone. don't care much. feeling really weird somehow.

Benyeahmon: you are regine, and you are shocked to hear me say that. you are regine's overwhelming sense of shock.

Regingin: true facts.

Benyeahmon: we should hang out.

Regingin: agreed.

Benyeahmon: i want a couple gin-gin sightings before you leave.[38]

Regingin: i can get behind that.

Benyeahmon: word up.

Regingin: i'm done with work in a week, then i'm getting my diss ready for defense, but i've got time in between.

Benyeahmon: cool. i'm pretty 9–5 these days.

Regingin: is that good?

Benyeahmon: no. nothing is good. i was just mentioning that so you could know my general availability for stuff.

Regingin: okay. stop being sad. there.

Regingin: fixed.

---

38   She'd accepted a job in Virginia and would move in a month.

Benyeahmon: thanks. man. i needed that. i'd been so sad.

Regingin: that's how thangs get done, boo.

Regingin: sorry that you're sad though. really.

Benyeahmon: thanks.

Benyeahmon: thanks is a funny response. like taking a compliment. 'oh, thank you.' (then i turn away bashfully and feel happily embarrassed by my talented sadness.

Regingin: let me take a picture where your face is in shadows.

Benyeahmon: so that way i can represent my sadness on facebook with images?

Regingin: or we could screenprint it onto turtlenecks.

Benyeahmon: there we go. how are things?

Regingin: stressful. moving. new job.

Benyeahmon: yeah. i kind of figured.

Benyeahmon: these are the times when people make dismissive references to the past. just think about how you were once stressed out about your coursework. or your comprehensive exams. and, see, now they're all done. and you're juuuuuuust fine.

Benyeahmon: think about that one time that you were heartbroken, and now you're ohhhhhhhhhhhhhkay. oh. okay. thanks. yeah.

Regingin: yeah.

Benyeahmon: oh. by the way, i'm not trying to be a jerk. it just comes naturally.

Regingin: oh, i know. we'll just call it charming and let it go.

Benyeahmon: like the mouse poop on my desk.

Regingin: quaint.

Benyeahmon: hah. yep. that's what she said. basically.

Regingin: hmmm. really?

Benyeahmon: not exactly.

Benyeahmon: hey. i'll be back. shower now.

Regingin: i gotta go, actually. talk soon.

Benyeahmon: word.

. . .

The washing machine's spin cycle shook the shower floor. Benny shuf-
fled through the usual suds, marvelling at the vibration under his feet.
Wentworth stood outside the bathroom door, imagining bursting
through, heavy handcuffs in one hand, half-loaded pistol in the other.
(He'd convinced the skeezy pawn shop in Ravenna to sell him one off
the record, under the table, out the door.) But if he burst in and cuffed
him, Benny'd be naked. Nudity might complicate things when he had
to let him out of the trunk to pee. Why not just let him put on some
clothes first? Maybe just come back later.

So then. Dressing, Benny heard a strange noise in his room. A
slight scratching. Then a tapping of bone on plastic. He glanced around
the room for a few moments before remembering the baited humane
mousetrap in the hall. He opened the door and picked up the trap. The
mouse peeped at him then tried to turn away but found he could not
rotate inside the slim plastic container.

Then Benny—bent over, wearing only his boxers, and examining
through filmy plastic a little mouse whose fur was now well-smudged
by the peanut butter with which they'd long ago baited the trap—heard

Wentworth address him from the bottom of the staircase. Turning around, mousetrap in hand, he faced Wentworth who was pointing a gun at him and beckoning him with the grim motion of two curling fingers to descend the stairs. Benny stared in disbelief, which faded quickly, and he started down the stairs, a strange deja vu accompanying him. Wentworth led him silently out of the house and slammed the back door behind them. With this, a piece of duct tape released, and their world map fell halfway off the wall.

Wentworth already had the trunk open. He gave Benny—still gripping the little mousetrap—a slipshod shove into the trunk. Then, as he pulled Benny's arms behind his back and cuffed him, he laughed an apology of sorts and mumbled something at him about them being family. "Our cocks touch the same porcelain, I know! I'm sorry it had to be you, kiddo," he yawped in an unidentifiable, hackneyed accent as he slammed shut the trunk.

• • •

So then, there's this crazy feller driving west across the country, and (wooh!) we're right back to "gunning blindly down dollops of back roads," blah blah—I was beginning to wonder if we'd ever get there and, frankly, not planning AT ALL on being here for it. Aaaaaaaaaaalas.

"Faaaaaangboner!" Wentworth shouted, admiring the road of the same name (in Fremont, Ohio, if you ever want to visit). Soon after Fremont, well, there's Toledo. Between Toledo and Chicago, it's mostly just a bunch of giant, witless advertisements for Tom Raper's[39] RVs— Tom Raper, the biggest RV dealer in the Midwest. Truly. There are also

---

39   To clarify, and in fairness to Tom and the whole Raper clan, I'm aware of no significant relationship between the undisputed RV King of the Midwest and the lowercase cornfield rapers of the Great Lakes (nor any other rapers across this great land) to whom exquisite judicial sympathy is daily extended. All the best to you, Tom.

a couple hundred Herculean hamburger billboards climbing out of the corn-khaki barrens.[40] But by the time you get to Central Illinois there's nothing but fields on either side.[41] The highway is dark, and the world falls away at the edge of the headlights—Central Iowa and Nebraska are quite similar. Still, in the distance, you can see the windmills' blinking lights and sense the flatness of the prairie as it stretches out in the night, as the midwestern gothic wind whips angrily at your car. Because it really will do that. It is an angry wind. Your sodomies and milkshakes attracting all boy winds yardward. Vengeful adolescent boy winds.

And do not fault the few loons and ducks. Again. Who have no milkshakes. And yet still quacky mucus. (Pour vous.) Whose penises[42] (and vaginas) are corkscrew-shaped—not here with special intent to whitewash a duck life, either, not to equivocate the fact that they rape each other—like the rapey French(m/c)an(ard), head chef, Henri the jumbo duck raper, face-fucker (a la foie gras) without the thread that

---

40 Had his route taken him through Columbia, South Carolina, he might have read billboards advertising gator heads and wind chimes on Strom Thurmond Boulevard. (Yet held up in legislation is the construction of the James Earl Ray Bicoastal Highway. Perhaps someone soon will scoop up the torch and provide a paltry catalogue of its billboards.)

41 In houses of the rich and semi-rural, / the American Idol girl has her grandma's picture / on the piano, next to it, a jar of the old woman's / menstrual blood. An invasive species, / a super-food, eighty autumn berries in Illinois / wait in a jar and rot, growing mold.

42 As we now know, thanks to Patricia Brennan, duck penises are shaped like corkscrews: The extension whirls forward, *counter*clockwise. So, while nearly fifty percent of duck sex constitutes rape—and even gang rape in many cases, though, for ducks, "raft rape," "flush rape," "badling," "waddling," or "paddling rape," not to mention "team" or "flock rape," would be more traditionally sanc-tioned, species-specific phrasal modifiers—the female duck's vagina has evolved to deny insemination in such cases, nurturing (or, more aptly, *defending*) the concept of love-ducklings. With her stalwart, *clockwise* corkscrew-shaped lady part, she relaxes and blossoms only for her drake of choice. (This being the case, it seems fitting that the penis (d)evolved *counter*clockwise, while the vagina evolved clockwise.)

curls the cork that has no weaver. Like wino pornos. Purple drake. Duck fucking. Wine foieg(ras)inas. Far more discriminating than wine corks. One enjoys the imagined sequence: The corkscrew forces its way in, but the cork, the bottle, denies consummation. The fucker only thinks he drinks. His sickened, occidental paste. (W)Retched. The last quacking lady's last quack being who she quacketh longest.

Jerks. Sure. But the wind.

• • •

Benny felt the car croak slowly over the warning braille stenciled into the highway's shoulder to rouse dozing shwerve. He rubbed his stubbly chin against his neck and chest to warm himself, and, picturing the berm, he briefly remembered the red and pink wildflowers that November had picked from the wild, roadside growth on Route 43. He felt the rumbling inertia of semi-trucks barreling down the freeway. Maybe they were only RVs or Winnebagos. What if a Winnebago crashed into the parked car? The thought made him giggle with quiet hysteria.

Wentworth had pulled over to pee. He lumbered over the brittle thickets into the woods then looked back at the massive trucks whooshing past and imagined them accidentally crashing into the parked car (all the torn metal, the shrieking shards of glass, etc.) and, as the feeling of his fingernails curling came upon him, he glanced back at the trunk in his rear-view mirror and laughyfilthyfilthylaughy at the feeling of his fingernails curling.

• • •

Through the more-or-less-or-more-or-more-or-more-or-more-or-less beautiful parts of the country—Laramie, Wyoming; Salt Lake City, Utah; Tahoe National Forest—it continued this way. Pee. Interaction with toilet: N/A. Wentworth would not let him use a public toilet, and, in fact, smartly parked the car far away from earshot when he stopped for gas. (He'd brought a few giant gas cans that he'd fill and bring back to the car.) He only stopped in desolate towns at podunk gas stations.

"Do you sell cigarettes?" he asked absently as he peered past the clerk to where the cigarettes would normally be.

"Nope. We're an old-fashioned gas station."

"Ah. How nice. Do you have public restrooms?" He finally made eye contact.

"Nope," she said, staring him down disgustedly, "but there's a key." Slowly, she turned to the counter behind her. "Here," she let out with a sigh, "take it around the left and it's the second door. Turn it to the left."

"Okay. Thank you, dear," he replied, in a tone that communicated clearly, even to this old podunk gas hag, that he meant something other than "thank you, dear."

"Take it around the side and turn the key to the left. You'll have to jiggle[43] it," she repeated, annoyed. After he'd exited, she double-checked to make sure her revolver was loaded.

"Ohhhkay, dear." Turning the corner, he saw two white doors, one marked "Men," the other marked, "Women." He went, as instructed, to the second door, "Men." She had pinpointed his gender. He jiggled the key to the left, gained passage, submitted to familiar urges, and peed in the sink.

• • •

---

43   Coincidentally, the song playing in Wentworth's car at that exact moment was also somewhat related to jiggling. Benny could attest to this, as Wentworth had left the music on, and without the engine running DJ Assault's lyrics were audible, even from the trunk: "Ass. Titties. Two asses, fou' titties. Ass, ass, titties, titties. Ass 'n' titties."

As it turned out, Walmart's handcuffs were not very sturdy. For a second, I wondered if this was because maybe there was a law against them being *too* sturdy. But probably not. (They *do*, after all, sell guns and ammo there. As you know.) In any case, Benny broke free from the handcuffs that morning. The chain had linked together and worked itself into a metallic tangle. It was scrunching precariously when he, quite by accident, snapped one of the grommets.

They'd actually been broken for over an hour before he even noticed that he'd freed himself. They were nearing Mendocino when this happened. Wentworth had just thrown him back in the trunk after letting him out to pee—a weird process, which involved Wentworth pulling down Benny's boxers and then pulling them back up again when he'd finished. (Travel always upset his rhythm, and, luckily, he'd only pooped once, during which he'd been able to scrounge some leaves and wipe just a little, against the restraint of the cuffs, but there was still a significant poo drift back there, now caked around his anus—though, at this point, his concern for hygiene was all but lost.) I kind of like that the only real indication of Benny's thoughts during this three day ride in Wentworth's trunk have been related to elimination. At any rate, all Wentworth fed him was a piece of bread[44] and some water every so often. So that worked out for him okay. In terms of pooping/not pooping.

But what he and I were wondering was what he would do now that he'd managed to break the Walmart handcuffs.

•••

---

[44] I would have enjoyed things much more if Wentworth had broken the pieces of bread and thrown them on the ground, forcing Benny, hands behind his back, to kneel down, waddle over, and peck the pieces from the roadside. However, Wentworth did not do this. He was all business, simply shoving the slice into Benny's mouth with all available expedience.

They still had quite a few days before October 30th, so, before checking in at the Glass Beach Inn, Wentworth decided to explore the nearby scenery on Highway 1. He could kill some time in the small towns between Fort Bragg and Santa Rosa. Plenty of space to stay hidden.

"Oh, it's soooo beautiful," he bellowed sarcastically. It was though. I assure you. "Beautiful, isn't it?" he chuckled, addressing Benny.

What happened then is not something I can really introduce perhaps more than I already have, other than to explain to you that a Columbian black-tailed deer (Odocoileus hemionus columbianus), who was tearing through the woods—coyly averting the stag who was courting her—changed course and galloped into the road, toward the ocean, for a swim. Wentworth swerved, but he was much too late and could not avoid her, and, with that, Benny's deer count (arguably) rose to eight and nine. The windshield shattered against the doe's full weight, while the stag in pursuit cracked his antlers against the driver's side door and window, which shattered into Wentworth's lap, along with the doe who'd suffered the brunt of the collision. Wentworth tensed viscerally and punched at the bawling doe, who was flailing against him, gouging his body and the car's roof. As she bruised and bloodied his arms and torso, Wentworth's strained appendages locked at once against all pedals, and the car flew over the bluff, into the sea.

The deer's hooves continued to batter Wentworth in the chest, neck, and head—additionally, the old boy shit himself, so each party was increasingly smeared over in poos—and, turning frantically toward the empty windshield, she hammered him with hooves like granite, supplying Wentworth his final blows, while her front left hoof bounced repeatedly against the trunk release lever such that, as she struggled to free herself, she freed Benny as well. The back of the car was still well afloat when the trunk sprang open. Benny's vision was staggered by the bright, undulating sky, toward which he climbed desperately as he flopped out of the trunk into the frigid Pacific. (The seawater eventually flooded the humane mousetrap and opened the door, as well, but the little mouse was unable to negotiate the harsh waves.) Finally, the wounded doe also escaped the car, which was now almost fully submerged beneath the seawater of Horseshoe Cove.

Benny struggled to the surface, but the waves repeatedly thrashed him back below. He managed to stay long enough afloat during one short interval (between pummeling crests) to see through the salty burn in his eyes and find the direction of the shore. But the moment he began to swim toward it, he was pulled beneath by the undercurrent of another wave. The dogged cycle repeated (unwaveringly!!!) for longer than Benny could handle. The initial surge of adrenaline that accompanied his transition from confusion to swelling panic and terror was waning now, and his arms were tiring. In an effort to conserve strength, he allowed the waves to toss him where they might for a couple passing moments. In that salty darkness, he struggled to reorient himself, beginning to feel the immediacy of death—not at all like a slow, visual flashing of memories; more like a loss of language, a silent suffocation.

When, finally, if briefly, the ocean calmed some, he was able to stroke shoreward, soon progressing close enough to the rocky surf that he felt his hip scrape against a jutting boulder. And when he stopped paddling to quickly note his coordinates, he realized that he could now touch bottom. Relief rose inside him and warmed his spine as he trudged on toward the rocky shore, fell onto his hands, and plodded across the warm sand, determined to distance himself even from the gently lapping seawater. Finally, he reached a patch of dry vegetation and let his body flop down onto the jagged succulents.

With an intensity that had become somewhat foreign to him, the sun illuminated this brilliant terrain. Cliffside periwinkle and canary pointies, bluebells and swampy red-plum-green fungi opened cleanly at the edge of the gorge. Scurrying next to him now was a fuzzy gray shell the size of a thumb and a wispy spider jumping over sand onto a small piece of driftwood that had settled atop creeping flowers' fuchsia petals and bright yellow stamens. A child's mateless shoe loitered among them.

Benny rested in the succulents, listening to the crashing ocean. He squinted at a struggling northbound Canadian goose gawping errantly past.

After some time, he walked back toward the ocean and watched a tiny snail move under a seawater crag the size of a human head. The red streaks on his hip darkened and began to dry and sting. There were islands of giant rocks everywhere. A small snowy plover lit under a natural rock bridge, narrowly eluding a crash. Then it landed atop the mossy green and rust-orange apex of the bulging cliff. Benny watched the bird shake off the spray. Probably about fifty shakes per second, he thought, beginning to regain some part of his penchant and facility for pointless (though occasionally rational) analysis. And as such decidedly unnecessary calculations and estimates began refilling his little mind, I worried just a bit less about his sanity.

Beneath the sand and sparkling shells, a particularly striking piece of dark driftwood sprouted. Benny excavated it and washed off the sand. It looked like a terrified brown gazelle, a rotting statue losing its nose, mouth frozen in scream, eyeballs washed away. In the drying sun, its color quickly began to lighten; it looked now like a wizened camel head in his lap.

He soon felt a presence and raised his head to view a figure in the distance. He couldn't tell the sex for sure, but it looked like a man. Benny looked away instinctively so as not to attract attention. He felt concerned, for some reason, that he might be implicated in Wentworth's death. He was very distrustful of the police, and he hadn't much of an alibi. How would he explain Wentworth's car, if they recovered it, if anyone had seen? He couldn't prove he was kidnapped. And . . . wait, was Wentworth actually dead? Was he still around somewhere? He hadn't seen him anywhere on shore. Although, he thought, maybe Wentworth had evacuated before the accident and . . . fuck, he probably did. Right? Where would he be? Maybe someone had picked him up in another car so that he could quickly flee the scene? But it wouldn't be smart to use his own car for this kind of thing. Had they somehow switched cars in the last few days? Was he conscious enough to note such a thing? What would happen if/when the car washed up on shore or something? Or at low tide? How did this crap work? Shit! Was *this* Wentworth, this mystery man approaching him? He sneaked a glance upward again, this time with more interest. It didn't really look like Wentworth. Benny hid his handcuffed wrists between his legs.

The man continued to approach slowly—okay, phew, it wasn't him—then stood next to Benny, silently taking in the view. Benny tried to act as naturally as he could but immediately felt that he'd failed when, after a few moments of strange silence, he asked, "Where am I?"

"This is Kruse Rhododendron, son. State Reserve."

Benny nodded, frowning with casual approval.

"Think somebody had an accident over there," the man said, pointing to where the car had garbled into the sea, and he continued diagonally along the shore toward the car's point of entry. Benny, wearing only his boxers, had the good luck of looking like a local hippy—probably quite stoned—merely sunning himself after a bracing dip.

Much farther down the beach, a spaniel strayed from her aged masters and jogged meekly up to Benny for to sniff his person. Shortly, she whimpered and scampered away, a few yards from him, where she then squatted and pooped. After satisfactorily raking over the sand, she trotted back toward the old couple, peeking back at Benny, with more than necessary vigilance. She ran out in front of them and stared at Benny as they passed.

Fuck. He was scared. Was Wentworth still around? Should he call the cops? Or maybe just try to hitch a ride and call his parents?

A mayapple leaf whipped against the cliff and stuck for a second then repelled into the waves. Strange. You know why? Because Podophyllum peltatum (mayapple, umbrella plant, wild lemon, mandrake, Mayflower, hogapple, devil's apple) is not native to California. This midwestern invader, un/natural sweetness (only in the fruit, mind), if a little tart—and a little toxic—smacked up against a California cliff. And stuck. For a second.

...

Blossie and Jenny, at Jenny's behest, had just spent the week in San Francisco and were now piddling up the coast, stopping here and there to view the ocean and/or camp. Or occasionally splurge on a bed-and-breakfast. Blossie thought this was the best way to prepare Jenny for whatever she might discover on this trip. That is to say, Blossie had not thoroughly related the details (read "primary goal") of their adventure. Jenny had been thrilled about the road trip, and Blossie decided to keep her on a need-to-know basis, as she was quite skittish when it came to violence. November hadn't taken well to any part of this plan, and though Jenny was way cooler—she'd been very supportive, for instance, when Blossie brought up sexual reassignment—she didn't want to upset her and ruin things. At least, she didn't want to shock the little girl without first buttering her up a bit. Or a lot.

As they wound up the lovely seaside highway, they saw a(nother) human figure in the roadside distance. Hearing the engine's hum, the figure turned toward them and beckoned with a hopeful thumb then, rather desperately, stepped into their path. Blossie slowed to veer away from this crazy person and pass with caution. While the sun's bright reflection on the car's hood overwhelmed his vision, the ladies could see him quite clearly. They looked at each other, both confounded, and both—with their highly varying degrees of acquaintance with the facts of the situation—for different reasons.

"Ummm," Blossie said, shocked, "I have to . . . uhhh fuck. Okay. Stay in the car. And *do not speak*, please. I will explain when I get back." She parked the car and discreetly opened the trunk.

The not speaking part was pretty easy for Jenny, as she was also in a state of shock, feeling as though she were being somehow stalked.

Blossie got out and walked to the rear of the car. She pulled a locked case from deep inside the trunk and opened it hastily. Inside were duct tape, rope, two knives, her dad's revolver, forty bullets, and a little first aid kit. She grabbed the rope, tape, gun and five bullets. Then she closed the case and tossed it back inside the trunk. She turned away from the trunk, leaving it open, and began walking toward the man, nimbly loading the gun as she walked.

From about twenty paces, Blossie pointed the gun at Benny—you guessed it was him, by now, I assume—and yelled at him to lie on his stomach with his hands behind his back.[45] Quite flummoxed and almost ready to give up, Benny considered running, but he had no energy for running, and so he followed Blossie's orders. She wrapped his hands with the duct tape and then did the same to his ankles. Following this, she wrapped the tape around his head three full times, covering his mouth at a different angle each time. And, just to be sure, she knotted the rope around his arms and torso, as well as his knees and thighs. A thorough hogtying, much better than Wentworth's version.

Jenny watched the whole scary scene through the driver's side mirror, and remained in the car, as Blossie requested. But the part about not speaking . . . "Blossie! What are you . . ." she yelled, trailing off, as she turned to watch Benny hop toward the car, Blossie trailing closely.

"Blossie! What's going on!?" Her eyes were wide, and she was shaking.

Having just bulldozed Benny into the trunk, Blossie got back in the car and sighed deeply. "Give me one minute," she said slowly, crisply, "and I'll explain." They both leaned forward, straining to breathe deeply for about ten seconds. Then Jenny again burst into question, but Blossie interrupted and yelled, "Okay!" She grabbed Jenny's shoulders, squeezed them, and peered into the girl's eyes until she stopped blaring.

Then she explained the details: November's unfortunate involvement with this asshole, the poor young girl in Wentworth's gruesome asylum, etc.

---

45   This is not a coincidence to get a character out of trouble; rather, it is the opposite. So let's be careful not to call it a deus ex machina. Or do. That would be okay, too. The omnipotent boy-divine adjusts his narrative posture. Keys multitudes.

"Oh my God! Okay. I don't know what's going on with all this, but you can't hurt him," Jenny interrupted. "He . . ." Here, Jenny began to cry. Through the tears, she recounted the story of the night Benny had driven her to the truck stop, how nice he was, how he'd hugged her and all. She wanted to die that night, she said. If it hadn't been for him, she might have gulped sleeping pills or walked onto the highway in front of a semi.

Blossie swivelled the visor and leered downward, unglued. She was too drained to be angry. What the *fuck* was going on?

. . .

November had been staying with friends in Oakland, which, she de-cided, was a lovely city. Well, San Francisco was, anyway. The people artfully dressed and artfully opinioned . . . so as to appear artless. Salad days pretending the accrual of hard times. Pretense damned either way: brats without, poseurs with. Authenticity sacrificed.

She went wine-tasting. Outside Hopland. A white-haired man, hands on hips, dared her to enter. Long thin strands down his neck. He showed them how to hold and spin the wine. Told about Viognier and the shape of the bottles, which vary, he said, only customarily by name, not function. Another vineyard, another man in swanky jeans with gems in the butt pockets and little to say about the inspiration for his Spanish Civil War era style winery.

"I know people who take deep breaths," she said (quite drunk) to no one in particular "and they ride bikes, but are very concerned they've offended someone. Prescription drugs, you know? A trail of 'em. We are *brown* salamanders . . . following Redwoods." Here, she slurred a bit, "Unrepertoirable kindness! Climbing. But *now*! Now, I'm not mean anymore. I'm a good person. Now, if I'm mean, it's just, like, making a joke about abortion . . . or the twin towers or whatever. I could lay bare, but . . . that device . . . it's love or . . . whatever we show. Still. Unstillness . . . is not moving."

This was 1 p.m.

As the day progressed and her friends convinced her to switch to coffee, she shook off her poet's cloak and tagged along in relative silence, so by about 5 p.m., when they did the math, they realized that drink-for-drink, she was by far the soberest. The wine had worn off, and, no doubt, hers was the straightest gait in the group. So she took the reins and motored, happily caffeinated, back down Highway 101, gazing rather recklessly at California's foggy clouds against bulging green brush, nubby with domestic bison, hairy sycamores and evergreens; the trees' wild angling, chaos accommodating; limey marble moss caked on wet oak bark; every color roused by the fog; even dead grass blades, a livelier tan.

Back in the city, the marooning sun sparkled dimly over the buildings. A white bird standing on the edge of the sidewalk toddled into the intersection. Of all the natural creatures beneath the intersection's automated electricity, he alone was unprotected by shiny metal. His head was oscillating strangely, flitting his orange beak in all directions to watch the many cars that passed, with which he narrowly avoided collisions.

November had been thinking about the Candiru, the Brazilian peehole fish, a fish whose mythology holds that it can swim—or almost fly, really—up a man's stream of urine, into his urethra, where it lodges itself, causing much pain to the urinator.[46] She made a more serious face as her attention shifted back to the present, where a little discombobulated birdy scurried between cars, caught in the intersection. Her breath shortened, as she squinted back and forth at the passing traffic then up at the stoplight, which had turned green. She shifted the car into park and got out, yelling at her friends to come and help, as she

---

46   According to scientists, the Candiru—a.k.a. "toothpick fish" or "vampire fish"—is not actually able to swim up a man's urine stream, unless that man's person is submerged. However, the fish *are* most certainly drawn to urine, and a nude swimmer in the Amazon Basin's freshwaters, urinating or otherwise, may find a bilge boarded by a little fishy dart.

scampered carefully into the adjacent lane and tried to stop northbound traffic. Once relieved by an anxious compadre, she shouted "Wait here!" and ran into the intersection where she scooped up the befuddled bird from behind.

ROASTED NUT-DUSTED CUM-SWIVELLED JIZZ SALAD
WITH A DRIZZLE OF CLEMENTINE LEMON TANG

- Mesclun, mantilia, and romaine lettuce[47]
- Broccoli
- Basil
- Parsley
- Cilantro
- Sage
- Yellow wood sorrel
- Spinach
- Homemade pussy mud hummus (I know it distracts the eye, but that's just how it is)
- Castelvetrano olives
- Walnuts
- Pecans
- Celery
- Toasted sesame oil
- Green tea oil
- Balsamic vinegar
- Nutritional yeast
- Pumpkin seeds

---

47   "(Do the)(L/l)ettuce (D/d)ance." —E.S. Lettuce

- Hemp seeds
- Chia seeds
- Fresh, thick-cut garlic
- Fresh lemon juice
- Avocado
- Purslane (is a hollowed grapefruit)
- Dried cranberries
- Gossamer dustings of cumin and cayenne
- And some creamy tahini-miso sort of salad dressing

...

Blossie agreed not to hurt Benny, and to let Jenny give him water. But she insisted on two things: (1) She had to talk to him alone, and (2) they must be granted a head start, so to speak, when they dumped him off. No guarantee Benny wouldn't call the authorities, after all. In fact, he probably would . . . all the more reason to dispose of him now, frankly, but Jenny wouldn't hear of it. Blossie was feeling unsettled about the whole situation and was considering killing them both, but she had a real soft spot for Jenny by now, even if she was a little young. And a lot naive.

She left Jenny in the car and pulled Benny out of the trunk, jostled and hopped him into the woods, about fifty yards off Highway 101. Benny gazed groggily past the ferns, past his new hijacker, at the butterflies behind Blossie. What kind? Monarchs maybe? Dark orange. Hundreds it seemed. Endless. In single file. Fluttering through the woods. Each ten feet apart. A Monarch army shuffling past. (The path they fly is holy. Did you know that?) Was he seeing things now?

Blossie was pacing slowly. Frowning. The moist floor of the forest muted her heavy footsteps. At length, she stopped and stooped to him. Then she pulled a small pair of scissors out of her back pocket and dug one edge between Benny's hair and the duct tape. Benny felt his skin break in a couple small spots as she cut through the thick gray tape and ripped it away from his mouth, leaving the tape hanging from the back of his head, still clinging to his hair. "Wha'd'you do with Benny?" she hollered, glaring at him.

He was naturally bewildered. And the advantageous play afforded by Blossie's confusion had not yet occurred to him.

"I . . ." he shook his head, "I don't—I won't tell anyone, you know . . . about all this. I don't even know your name. I don't know *her* name," he motioned as best he could in the direction of the car. "I really don't know what's going on here. But I promise—"

"Shut up," she said coldly, jabbing his ribs with the gun. "Just shut the fuck up." He was lying. He knew Jenny's name. Didn't he?

A lazy-eyed, red California newt glided slowly past, worming toward the creek for wreck of lady newt's pum pum.

Benny was silent, realizing now what it meant that she didn't know his name. Who did she think he was? And who did she think was him? Or maybe this was a different Benny? What the hell was going on? He struggled fruitlessly to gather his thoughts, and through some distant, inscrutable hunch, he decided the misunderstanding was somehow to his advantage. Or, either way, inadvisable to supply her with jarring surprises. Not now.

"I don't know how you got away from him or . . . why you're out here or fucking . . . what*ever!*" she slapped a fern with her revolver, "but . . . shit. If you *do* tell anyone *anything* about *any* of this, I will kill you . . . *fucking dead,*" she added for emphasis, pointing at him, strangely, with her pointer finger, rather than the revolver, which rested in her hand beside her taut thigh.

"I won't tell anyone! Fuck! Even if I tried, I wouldn't know how!" He stared at her for a moment and then shrugged his shoulders in timid protest.

She pulled him up out of the ferns, escorted him back to the highway, and shoved him in the trunk.

• • •

When he next inhaled fresh air, it was in chorus with a bash to the forehead from the heavy butt of Blossie's gun, after which Blossie carefully backed the car down a slim, rocky public beach access road—Jenny had somehow fallen asleep—parked the car, opened the trunk, and carried him out to the ocean, hoping Jenny wouldn't wake up and notice that she'd knocked him out. When Blossie'd distanced herself enough from Jenny and the car, she dropped Benny on the ground and dragged him the rest of the way—heavy little fucker. Momentarily, she considered dragging him all the way into the ocean, but that would be risky. What if Jenny awoke? What if she'd awoken already? Plus, she would almost certainly be soaked by the end of that whole process, and that would be harder to explain.

. . .

With a really cliché headache, Benny regained consciousness a few hours later. The ocean, loud and glittering in the sun, was beginning to mist his cold, bare stomach, legs, and feet, which were still wrapped together with duct tape, picking up where the broken handcuffs had left off. Blossie had left him in a large, natural cave-like hollow where homeless people apparently slept on occasion. Benny wriggled over to a rock formation (regrettably near the waves), lay down on his back, and rubbed the duct tape against the rougher parts of the rock. He shivered sickly, as the cold foamy surf lapped his boxers and seeped through.

After a while, it occurred to him that this was stupid. Why not do his wrists first? Why lie in these cold, encroaching waves? Normally, this logic would have surfaced much sooner, but his reasoning powers were compromised from what was becoming a serious lack of nutritive substances—and the generally stupefying week he was having. It had been almost forty-eight hours since he'd eaten even a slice of bread, and he was feeling dangerously dehydrated. At least he was safe for the moment . . . so it seemed. (Some quite pertinent portions of Blossie and Jenny's conversation had been audible from the trunk.)

Almost fully emancipated now from Blossie's duct tape, and nearly finished hammering through the broken handcuff bracelets, Benny sat trying to remember what had happened. After a few minutes, he de-cided to give the cuffs a rest and begin the dirty business of removing the duct tape from his hair. He was on his knees, straining and bending the back of his head into the ocean to try to wet his hair and loosen the grip of the tape when a ragged man with two tattered backpacks walked down onto the beach and examined him with a suspicious frown.

Battleworn, Benny gave the man little reaction. He stood up and bravely grabbed the tape, ripped several hundred strands of his own hair out of his head, and hurled the tape into the ocean. This didn't have quite the effect he'd hoped for, as the wind almost immediately halted the tape's flight and blew it into the sand next to Benny. He lowered his head, walked back over to the cave, and resumed grinding his handcuffs against the rock before dispassionately asking the man where he was.

"This is Glass Beach," the man said, perking up. "Used to be a dump. All kinds'a shit here, but then they cleaned it up a little. Glass got rolled out kinda smooth." He picked a piece of glass from the dark sand. "See that? Green, blue . . . brown." He studied a small, smooth piece of amber glass.

"Thanks," Benny replied, briefly turning to face the man. "What is all that shit in the sky?" he asked, squinting upward.

"Those are birds," the man said, again frowning at Benny.

"You got any food?" Benny asked.

"Well, a little, but . . . I don't come by it too easily these days."

Benny nodded, still looking into the sea. "All right." He arose, momentarily, and started up the sandy hill.

The man sighed and walked back over to his dirty bags; rummaging through, he pulled out a heavy clump of cloth and threw it toward Benny. It landed beside him. Benny turned and picked it up: a dented can of peaches wrapped in a ripped-up, powder-blue flannel.

"Thanks."

"Okay. Good luck, son."

• • •

Walking along the cliffs (the bases of which were more fully revealed now by the low tide) Benny looked down, strangely soothed by the allure of the woozy distance. Despite his general predicament, as well as the fresh cuts and scrapes on his wrists, he felt relieved to have finally removed the cuffs.

A tiny snake slithered through a sharp patch of spiky green pineapple hair. It reminded him of the sharp succulents he'd crawled to and rested in after the crash yesterday. Was that yesterday? Jesus.

A few feet away was another small garment: a wet, toddler-sized red shirt resting atop a small rock formation that seemed to grow up out of the surrounding lavender and yellow blossoms.

Benny carefully broke the can against a rock and sat down in the succulent seaside vegetation: violet petal quintets, tiny white clusters drooping, peeking from thorny plum thickets, dark green and orange leaves on tan brambles.

He ambled back now toward the ocean, feeling it's solitary breadth, like meeting again the tenderness of an ex-lover or distant parent. We. They. Go. Away. Not come. Away. But the ocean made it all beautiful, somehow (even the strange, rumbling pain in his stomach). The waves, all of it, a concentric paradox. Intersecting on occasion. Routine washing. The dull rhythm. Animus ignoring spirit. Water clapping rock. Then resting. Unending. The monotony. Restored mystery.

Benny picked up the rock and talked to the crab spider underneath, "You are beautiful, very beautiful. And you have a beautiful home." Then he put the rock back so that the dorky seagulls wouldn't find the little guy. And he washed his new flannel in the salty water of Glass Beach.

Through the mist, the late sun brightened the dark orange, burgundy, and green textures that hung from the cliff a quarter mile down the shore. Giant beached amber sperm carried to rest on rocks. Looking out across the ocean, he wondered how far he could see. How far can the human eye see? And how many miles into the distance was he staring? What about the sky? When he looked up at stars, of course he was looking back into the future and all that crap, but (without philosophizing a reasonable question into meaningless void) how far was the physical distance he could actually see?

And the smell above the ocean. Rich wet sod. Cliffrock rust. Salt and mud. Crackling, dead gray stems. Whatever floral levity the breeze carried. And the deep, fertile smell of trodden plants.

Aimlessly, he toed the cliffs, true to the melody—but poorly improvising—the lyrics to "Frosty the Snowman." He stopped for a moment and watched another of those inexplicable, giant sperms float lazily behind a duck. Laid back, slow like the clouds, the waves, the wind, the sperm, the West. He stared into the distance at a single fuschia blossom against the brittle, tan cliff. It took him a while to locate himself in that cliché symbolism and then to laugh at how cheesy it was. For a pre-postmodern minute, he was looking only at a pretty aberration. Then he remembered to make fun.

. . .

God, can I end here? Can I? I was thinking of ending here. But I'm still waiting on this gleeking peon to fetch a death torch. Shine the light. Make a wake outta me. Eh? For fuck's saaaake!

Sooo. I guess . . .

. . .

Benny walked up off Glass Beach and toward the Denny's that had appeared in the distance, like a greasy beacon. He planned to skip out on the bill, of course, but that would be no big deal. Getting served, however, dressed as he was (oversized sea-watered flannel, boxers, shoeless), seemed as though it might be an issue.

In the parking lot, a woman in a fancy white car watched him through the driver's side window. She rolled it down and pushed her head through, like an ostrich. "Hey, kiddo!" she yelled to him.

Benny was understandably skittish.

"Hey! Little cold for a swim, don'tcha think?" she prodded.

"I suppose it is," he muttered, sheepishly approaching the car.

"I bet that water is ice *cubey*! Voooof!"

"Yeah." The car was so quiet that it wasn't until Benny was within the distance appropriate for polite conversation that he heard its peaceful hum beneath the soothing classical music from the stereo.

New-age garb was strewn about the old lady's car. Hardly an inch of upholstery was visible underneath sundry buddha blankets, yoga mats, sandals, beads, tank tops, empty incense boxes. In the front seat, there was a birdcage with what appeared to be a quail inside.

"I'm goin' in for some coffee. You wanna join me?" Her mannerisms were gruff, but somehow chic, too. Also, crazy. Notably memorable characteristics for Benny were her lazy eye and very hairy arms. The vibe was "heiress-gone-bonkers-then-homeless-then-found-and-restored-with-a-semi-elite-monthly-allowance-for-making-with-a-tempered-wastrelhood." Dining at Denny's whenever you want.

"I was born when they dropped the atom bomb in New Mexico," she explained, impatient with Benny's lack of reply. "I was conceived at that moment." She was a voodoo child: conception, birth, simultaneity—not to mention an atomic bomb.

"I'm rich. Wanna smoke?" She flashed a joint at Benny, who decided this made as much sense as anything else that . . . week.

"Okay," he said, toddling around the hood to the passenger's side.

"Oh, here, let me take that for you," she said, picking up the caged quail as Benny opened the door and sat down.

Then she handed it back to him, and he sat with it in his lap while she lit the joint.

From 6:42 p.m. through about 6:55 p.m. they smoked weed together in the corner of the Denny's parking lot. Benny fixated on the quail, wondering about its life, while the woman, who still had not revealed her name, blathered expansively: She was an artist, a film producer, a yoga instructor, and now she was starting to give horseback riding lessons.

"Bushwa," Benny thought, and couldn't help but laugh now at the sound of the word (one of Wentworth's favorites). He imagined what Wentworth would say to this lady, and, inexplicably, this made him laugh even more. He tried to pretend that he was laughing along with her divergent babbling, though she wasn't saying much that might intentionally provoke laughter. But then he started worrying, wondering again if Wentworth was alive still, maybe watching him from just around the corner. Rather miraculously, he was, for the time being, able to decide resolutely that this was just cannabis-induced paranoia.

Time passed this way and that. Hard to say how long.

Finally, the old lady was silent for a brief moment, and she turned to survey him. She peered unremittingly into his eyes, and her pupils started moving in weird circular motions. Next, her eyeballs strained from side to side, twitching a little, and she began to squint then widen her eyes with exaggerated intensity. "This is yoga for your eyes," she said, just in time to settle Benny's mounting anxiety and quell his rumbling urge to open the car door and escape. Benny gaped at her then sighed down at the quail.

"Let's go get some grub," she said, staring now, too, at the quail in Benny's lap, "my treat."

"Okay," he said, looking past her at a man pushing an empty stroller toward them. It was the first time he'd spoken since entering the car.

"Cute kid," she said to the man as she exited the car.

"What?"

"Never mind."

"You need a stroller?" the man asked.

"No thanks. I'm barren."

"What about your friend?"

Benny shook his head slowly.

"What about these?" He nodded down at the stroller. Benny frowned and squinted downward at it. The man knelt to the undercarriage of the carriage and produced three flippers, one for each of them. "You look like you been for a swim today."

"Umm, oh, well, thank you, I mean, yes, but . . . I have, I guess, technically, yes . . . but I'm not really . . . well, I don't live here in town, per se, or, really, at all, so . . . so I . . . and I don't actually do this often, so I won't really need them."

The man approached ceremoniously and handed him the flippers with a fatherly gesture. Then he turned away and wheeled the empty stroller toward the beach.

"Takes all kinds, I suppose," the old lady said as she entered the small lobby of Denny's. She'd barely made it through the door before bellowing into the stale air, "I need food! I'm old!"

Benny winced, looked away, and down at the front page of the *Fort Bragg Advocate* through the glass of the newspaper dispenser: "Police Find Body in Sunken Car" was the headline. That feeling of rocks in the stomach passed quickly and gave way to elated relief. (It'd taken only a moment for him to realize that they meant Wentworth, not the mouse he'd traveled with.) He set the flippers on the floor, grabbed the remnants of a discarded paper on the window sill, and caught up with his new friend, who'd by now chosen a booth in the corner of the restaurant. As he scanned the article, she ordered coffees, an omelet for herself, and lots of side dishes for them to share. She asked the waitress if she could bring out the side dishes early, like appetizers.

By the time the pancake puppies, rice pilaf, mashed potatoes, green beans, peas, and nachos arrived, Benny had learned that the police were entirely baffled. There seemed to have been an accident. One severely disfigured body with wounds seemingly unrelated to the accident had been recovered. The car had not yet been hoisted out. Police suspected the car'd been stolen, as the plates were from out of state and the VIN had been scratched out.

Benny ate slowly and politely, no faster than the nibbling pace of the vociferous voodoo-bomb baby across from him. Accordingly, he allowed himself to really shovel it in soon after her omelet arrived. Only genteel, he thought, to match the record-setting rate of consumption established by his partner, who was currently inhaling her omelet and raving about, among other things, how splendid it was, how the food at Denny's was always so spectacular. By this time, Benny had also learned that the woman owned her own production company and knew a corporal who'd saved the life of an important sergeant in the Southeast Asian Theater of World War II.

Though the wounds remained a mystery, the article mentioned no suspicion of murder, nor any suspicion of criminal activity beyond grand theft auto. Identifying the man would require a lot of investigative work, and anyone with useful information was encouraged to—hm, were Jenny and the big crazy kidnapper involved somehow? They had to be! But . . . could he go to the police? It seemed like a risk. He would certainly be implicated, wouldn't he? Holy hell. Would he? And if so, how?

By the time he reached the end of the nachos, and had begun scooping the mashed potatoes, he realized how full he was, and how horribly sick he was of hearing the lady yammering in the background. He wondered if it would be impolite to ask for to-go boxes, gingerly load them with peas and rice, and sprint out the door, as he was now feeling like a bit like a fugitive.

When the bill came, she wrote a check then argued with the waitress about whether or not they could take a check. While the waitress was away talking to her manager about this, she used the lens that had just broken out of its frame as a monocle through which to examine Benny. Then she guessed his age. Inaccurately.

The waitress returned her check, and she succumbed unhappily to using cash for the bill. "Tell me something interesting," she commanded Benny, as the waitress walked away. "I've been enlightening you for hours, and you've hardly said a word. You're boring me." Benny frowned thoughtfully, and before he could even deflect the request, she began again to jabber: "I can't believe they won't take a check. Every town I'm in, I always go to Denny's, and I always pay with a check. It's the best place to park your car. It's the best place to eat. It always is. No matter where you are, there's always a Denny's."

Somehow, by the end of it all, she'd invited Benny to stay the night with her, and he'd accepted. He didn't want to; he wanted never to hear her voice again or to smell the stench of her omelet/coffee-breath. (His heightened sense perceptions weren't helping matters.) But where else was he gonna sleep? With the bums in the cove? It was pretty cold out, and he didn't even have pants. Or socks. Plus, he didn't want to risk seeing the police. He wanted to get out of town. He wanted to go home.

Pussy Mud Hummus

Gather the following:
- 2 cans of garbanzo beans—remove just a bit of the water; pour rest in blender
- 2 T olive oil
- 3-4 T tahini
- 2 T food-grade diatomaceous earth
- 4-6 sprigs of dill
- 1 T olive juice
- 2 T lemon juice
- 10cc nocturnal emissions
- 3-5 cloves of garlic
- Salt and pepper to taste
- Blend until . . . desired . . . consistency . . . I mean, whatever. If you can articulate it, if you can find words to describe it, then it can't possibly matter.

...

Bird shit was caked all over the carpet of the lady's grimy motel room, including a little on the sheets. The room smelled like farts and feet. As a matter of superfluous character development, I'm presenting her hygiene as colorfully inadequate; in fact, let the record show that in the entire suite there was not a single item pertaining to any of the sanitary sciences. The woman's vocalic endurance, however, was impressive, as may have, by now, been established. Had he been listening, Benny would have known a lot about her at this point—or at least he would have been conversant in the vibrant world of her seemingly improvised (and likely fictional) personal narratives. But she talked so much that he was only really noticing the silences now.

And that she was going to buy a horse tomorrow. He did hear that part.

He couldn't stop thinking about the quail though, about freeing it. Domesticated as it was, it would surely die quickly in the wild. And it might die a horrifically painful death out there, picked apart slowly by an eagle or owl. Starvation or disease. Perhaps he should just let it remain in the cage, but there was shit all over the floor of the cage, and the lady didn't seem to care much about it. Plus, a quail in a cage? What fucking birds are supposed to be in cages? Any? Either way, certainly not quails, right?

Maybe he should just kill it, he thought, projecting its guesome and potentially slow death in some Californian forest.

But you know what happened? He decided to free it. In the woods. This was significant becaaaaaaaauuuuuuuuuse . . . you know . . . it's sym*bolic.*

Somehow.

I don't know. Hope. Or November. Or *wild*ness. Or stuff.

Anyway, as the old birdshit-crazy lady grew tired, her chatter slowed just a bit—she was now leaning against a pillow, seated upright in bed.

(She was supposed to be picking out a couple suitable garments for Benny, but she'd apparently forgotten.) And as the pauses in her ramblings lengthened, Benny began to make plans for his exit. The woman had cash lying around the room in literal *piles*. She wouldn't miss a couple hundred bucks. Okay, a few hundred. To just leave it there like that, right out in the open, for fuck's sake, she must *want* him to take it!

She finally floated into slumber during a story about her youth: "I was watching Howdy Doody, but Howdy Doody was watching me, too. And through him, the FBI . . . CIA . . . My," she yawned here, "you know, my dad, he was an anthropology . . ." another yawn, "professor, who was writing American history during World War II, so . . ."

Benny was leaning over her open suitcase, probing for reasonable clothing. "Hey, uh, do you mind if I," he looked back at her, "umm . . ."

The only real clue that she'd fallen asleep was the relative silence in the room. Her eyes remained open, and her mouth hung gaping wide, as she drew in what appeared to be a rather obvious breath of slumber, exhaling with almost imperceptibly light friction against the back of her throat.

And, pronto, Benny grabbed some yoga pants and t-shirts, the bird cage, and two massive clumps of twenty-dollar bills on her dresser. Likely due to the sheet covering the cage, the bird made no peeps as Benny lurched into the yellow flip flops beside the bed and hurried out.

After he'd gingerly latched the door, he wobbled toward the dank woods across the street, where he sat with the bird while he put on the baggy yoga pants and t-shirts, consoling the little thing some before freeing it—he supposed it wouldn't likely survive the night. But maybe it would. Maybe its instincts would kick in, and it would do what quails do, which, shit, I don't know, is probably just to get eaten by a fox or catamount or something. "But . . . fuck," he thought, throwing the sheet over a svelte young evergreen, "a quail should have a quaily experience." One night as a free bird in a Redwood forest was worth whatever else might come. And so, with a ratifying sigh, he pointed the cage toward the forest and opened the door.

The bird strutted out like a tipsy Charleston flapper, surprisingly playful, yet regal. It circled the cage once before heading toward what sounded like a creek in the distance then quickly disappeared into the ferns. Benny listened wistfully to the receding chirps (some strange combination of a hen and a laser tag building) as it scurried into the forest.

Emerging from the woods, Benny waved the wad of the old lady's cash at the empty road, hoping to lure and hitch a ride to the bus station. He thought about how grateful he was that the little feller hadn't lingered near for a long goodbye. Before he had time to second-guess the deed, he was mercifully distracted by a car slowing in the distance. And, yet again, he found himself in a car with a stranger being offered weed (and sunflower seeds). They passed a church sign that read, "Smoking pot with God," which Benny attributed to church-sign vandals or perhaps his own groggy misapprehension.[48]

All the town's storefront puns shone proudly through the dark fog. Past the Sew 'n' Sew and the Herban Legend . . . and . . . HOLY FUCK-ING BIBLE, I can't believe we're still doing this. I am *done*! Fuck *all* this! I'm done weaving yarnses. Here it is. Time to end. Goddammit. How in the square-dancing fuck is this thing over, and I'm still not?

Sssssssssssso! I'll have you know . . . *that* . . . on the bus, he thought about everything that happened and whether he'd tell anyone (blah blah). He still hadn't decided: Uli maybe—just to help him figure out the whole Wentworth thing. Regine—just to hear her make fun of him. And Sang-mi, because she'd been on his mind, with her strange teeth and eerily portentous drawings on the chalkboard—and because she was mostly incapable of telling anyone else about it; no one would (know how to) listen, anyway, even if she did.

He leaned against the car's grubby glass pane. The Redwoods grew so close to the road that you could spit the shell of a sunflower seed

---

48   My reading entangles the driver as God and the sign as an overly convenient metaphorical clue.

against their trunks—if you could open your Goddamned window. The forest canopy allowed just enough light for ferns, huge ferns that he had mixed feelings about leaving. And maybe it was, indeed, leaving that made Benny think about death. He wished it would be like the end of a wedding ceremony, or at least that he could be awake at his funeral, to say goodbye to all the people. If the dead could pass his coffin respectfully—his grandparents, brother, etc.—that would be good. And also one particular young woman, tilting her shiny head, giving a rabbity southpaw salute.

. . .⁴⁹

---

49   Author's note: Just for the record, the assassin came. She came and killed the narrator in his sleep. I'd like to say that she drove a battering ram into his ribs and chest, but it was just a silenced pistol through the pillow—as of now, you're still allowed, but you can't make a silk purse out of a sow's ear—twice to the head and heart. While the record of his foul imagination persists, notice, please, that the narrator is now dead (but also "dead"). This author, the very laziest assassin (opponent, yet, if internally embattled, of linguistic whitewashing), has finally let fall the scythe: a cheap, symbolic choice to silence rén. Let's observe, then, for a moment, the emblematic cumulative effects of this decision (go ahead; I'll wait), which comes, well after the fact, in the form of a confession—the author now having been expertly reprimanded with five "Our Bartheses," ten "Hail Derridas."

www.ingramcontent.com/pod-product-compliance
Lightning Source LLC
Chambersburg PA
CBHW070328090426
42733CB00012B/2395